PROVIDING PUBLIC SPACE IN A CONTEMPORARY METROPOLIS

Urban Policy, Planning and the Built Environment

Series Editors: **Pierre Filion**, University of Waterloo, **Nicole Gurran**, University of Sydney and **Nick Gallent**, University College London

---

This series examines the interdisciplinary dimensions of urbanism and the built environment – extending from urban policy and governance to urban planning, management, housing, transport, infrastructure, landscape, heritage and design. It provides critical analyses of the challenges confronting cities at the intersection between markets, public policy and the built environment, as well as the responses emerging from these challenges.

Scan the code below to discover new and forthcoming titles in the series, or visit:

policy.bristoluniversitypress.co.uk/
urban-policy-planning-and-the-built-environment

PROVIDING PUBLIC SPACE IN A CONTEMPORARY METROPOLIS
Dilemmas and Lessons from London and Hong Kong

Claudio De Magalhães and Louie Sieh

First published in Great Britain in 2026 by

Policy Press, an imprint of
Bristol University Press
University of Bristol
1–9 Old Park Hill
Bristol
BS2 8BB
UK
t: +44 (0)117 374 6645
e: bup-info@bristol.ac.uk

Details of international sales and distribution partners are available at
policy.bristoluniversitypress.co.uk

© Bristol University Press 2026

British Library Cataloguing in Publication Data
A catalogue record for this book is available from the British Library

ISBN 978-1-4473-5885-5 hardcover
ISBN 978-1-4473-5886-2 paperback
ISBN 978-1-4473-5887-9 ePub
ISBN 978-1-4473-5888-6 ePdf

The right of Claudio De Magalhães and Louie Sieh to be identified as authors of this work has been asserted by them in accordance with the Copyright, Designs and Patents Act 1988.

All rights reserved: no part of this publication may be reproduced, stored in a retrieval system, or transmitted in any form or by any means, electronic, mechanical, photocopying, recording, or otherwise without the prior permission of Bristol University Press.

Every reasonable effort has been made to obtain permission to reproduce copyrighted material. If, however, anyone knows of an oversight, please contact the publisher.

The statements and opinions contained within this publication are solely those of the authors and not of the University of Bristol or Bristol University Press. The University of Bristol and Bristol University Press disclaim responsibility for any injury to persons or property resulting from any material published in this publication.

Bristol University Press and Policy Press work to counter discrimination on
grounds of gender, race, disability, age and sexuality.

Cover design: Andrew Corbett
Front cover image: East Coast Park, Victoria Harbour, Hong Kong Island by Louie Sieh

Bristol University Press' authorised representative in the European Union is:
Easy Access System Europe, Mustamäe tee 50, 10621 Tallinn, Estonia,
Email: gpsr.requests@easproject.com

Contents

List of figures and tables		vi
List of abbreviations		viii
Acknowledgements		ix
1	Introduction	1
2	Conceptualising public space for governance: a complex shared common good	13
3	The nature of publicness	32
4	The governance and management of public space	50
5	Public space management in London and Hong Kong	70
6	The quantitative challenges of public space provision and management	111
7	The qualitative challenges of public space provision and management: quality and responsiveness	147
8	Conclusions and the sketch of a practical theory of public space governance	172
References		195
Index		207

List of figures and tables

Figures

5.1	Shepherd's Bush Green, formerly village common land	72
5.2	Trafalgar Square, a 19th-century urban square, seen at the end of that century	72
5.3	Exchange Square in Broadgate, among the first privately provided public spaces in commercial developments	74
5.4	London and its 33 local authorities	75
5.5	Hyde Park, one of the Royal Parks now managed by a private charity	77
5.6	A complex topography leads to a densely built-up area with fierce competition for land for infrastructure, buildings and public space	88
5.7	Statue Square today	90
5.8	Hong Kong's spatial complexity includes public escalators and lifts and underground and above-ground passageways at various levels	92
5.9	Public open spaces in Tsuen Wan, a New Town	93
5.10	Victoria Park	93
5.11	VeryHK Yuen Long Festival: an NGO-conceived public space with furniture and activities in an otherwise non-descript setting	95
5.12	Hong Kong's 18 administrative districts	97
5.13	A POSPD in the Lee Tung Avenue development	104
5.14	Waste pickers and cardboard recyclers play an essential role in Hong Kong's waste management, and the street is their workplace	106
6.1	Kwun Tong Road landscaped garden around the International Trade Tower, now called 'Manulife Place'	118
6.2	Kingston International Centre POSPD	118
6.3	Landmark East Development signage indicating the physical integration of public and private space under the mechanism of providing PFPDs	119
6.4	Pacific Place, part of its PFPD passageways	120
6.5	The IFC POSPD	121
6.6	The Sha Tin New Town Plaza landscaped roof decks, which are PFPDs	122
6.7	The Avenue of Stars, an example of public space delivered via a PPP	124
6.8	The HSBC atrium, a public space delivered through a deed of dedication for public passage	125

6.9	Times Square, open public space secured through deed of dedication, with a history of controversy	126
6.10	Recreational area in podium of private residential complex in Ap Lei Chau	127
6.11	Cabot Square, one of the many private public spaces in the Canary Wharf estate	130
6.12	Granary Square, privately provided and managed within the King's Cross estate	131
6.13	Privately provided public spaces around the Westfield London shopping centre	132
6.14	The 10,000 m² main park in the Elephant Park development in South London still under construction	134
6.15	Potters Fields Park, trust-managed space on public land	136
6.16	Waterloo Millennium Green, community trust-managed park on public land	138
6.17	Jubilee Gardens, trust-managed public space with strong private sector input	139
6.18	Resident-led 'Right to Manage' public space in the Leathermarket neighbourhood	141
7.1	The now closed Instagram Pier, a spontaneous public space	152
7.2	The Central and Western District Promenade, the official alternative to the Instagram Pier	153
7.3	Foreign domestic helpers meeting and socialising on Sundays in the HSBC atrium	156
7.4	Informal resting space created through chairs on the pavement	157
7.5	Nullahplace in the densely populated Prince Edward area of Kowloon, new temporary public space created by university staff and students in collaboration with a number of local NGOs	158
7.6	Marchmont Community Garden, a small community garden in Central London	161
7.7	Sawley Road gardens: community management of public green areas	162
7.8	Rules and regulations for users of the Jubilee Gardens	163

Tables

5.1	Fragmentation of public space management in England in the early 21st century	80
5.2	Selected examples of Hong Kong ordinances for the four management actions of public space	99
6.1	Mechanisms for indirect private sector provision of public space in Hong Kong	114

List of abbreviations

BD	Buildings Department
BID	Business Improvement District
BOST	Bankside Open Spaces Trust
CBD	central business district
CEDD	Civil Engineering and Development Department
DEVB	Development Bureau
FEHD	Food and Environmental Hygiene Department
GFA	gross floor area
HAB	Home Affairs Bureau
HAD	Home Affairs Department
HK	Hong Kong
HKPSI	Hong Kong Public Space Initiative
HKSAR	Hong Kong Special Administrative Region of the People's Republic of China
HyD	Highways Department
LandsD	Lands Department
LCSD	Leisure and Cultural Services Department
MTR	Mass Transit Railway
NGO	non-governmental organization
NPM	New Public Management
OZP	Outline Zoning Plan
PFI	private finance initiative
PFPD	public facilities in private developments
PlanD	Planning Department
POPS	Privately Owned Public Spaces
POSPDs	Public Open Spaces in Private Developments
PPP	public–private partnership
SAR	Special Administrative Region of the People's Republic of China
TD	Transport Department
TPB	Town Planning Board
WKCD	West Kowloon Cultural District
WKCDA	West Kowloon Cultural District Authority

Acknowledgements

We would like to thank firstly all the many interviewees and all the people that contributed with their time, ideas, wisdom and narratives and without whom this book would not have been possible. This amounts to quite a few people and it would be impossible to thank them all individually.

We would also like to thank the Bartlett School of Planning at University College London for making it possible for one of the authors to take paid sabbatical leave to advance the research for the book; City University of Hong Kong for providing a visiting professorship to one of us; and the research institutions that provided grants that funded part of the research upon which the book is built. In particular, we would like to thank the Royal Institution of Chartered Surveyors (RICS) in London through RICS Research, City University of Hong Kong startup grant (Grant no: 7200590) and the Hong Kong Research Grants Council (Grant CityU 21604520).

Finally, we would like to thank Ayau Abaikhanova, Noella Kwok, Guangda Li, Steven Siu, Leo Tam and Charaine Wong for their help with the illustrations, data checking and formatting the manuscript.

It goes without saying that any mistakes, errors or omissions in this book are the exclusive responsibility of the authors.

1

Introduction

The context

Over the last two decades, a lot has been written about public space. Beyond a specialist concern with the quality, distribution and character of parks and squares in the fields of planning, urban design and landscape architecture, public space now features prominently in the agendas of a wide range of academic and professional groups and is increasingly present in the concerns of the citizenry at large. The COVID-19 pandemic of 2020 comes immediately to mind, as it brought forth with urgency the discussion around the health implications of access to public space and of the unequal distribution of that access in society, adding impetus to a discussion about the public health functions of public space that has been growing in the aftermath of the pandemic. Similarly, the importance of public space as catalyst and container of social protest worldwide became evident after the financial crisis of 2008 and the Occupy movement with episodes in both London and Hong Kong, and again the use of public space as a stage and facilitator for mass protests in Hong Kong in 2014 and in 2019. At a less dramatic level, there is the growing centrality of public space in the thinking about placemaking, a key concept in contemporary urban regeneration and planning.

However, regardless of the variations in the understanding of its role, public space has always been essential for the life of urban societies, even if only for its most basic role of allowing movement and providing a locus for all sorts of transactions. Throughout history urban polities of the most diverse kind have been concerned with ways of providing, managing and maintaining public space as part of the infrastructure that kept those societies going. Cities have always grappled with the issue of how they manage their physical public realm, how public spaces are provided and who looks after them and makes sure they are fit for the purposes for which they are intended. The way this was done might have taken the form of customary practices, laws and decrees, voluntary cooperation resulting from collective action, self-interested activities of people or groups of people and, in more recent times, the institutional and operating machinery of modern states, and especially local government.

This issue is vastly more complex in contemporary large cities, given the pressures on developable land and the competition from other land uses, the complexity of connectivity and mobility issues with conflicts between vehicular and pedestrian traffic and congestion; the diversity of population in all aspects with a variety of often conflicting needs and demands in relation to the built environment and a larger degree of spatial inequality, replicated in a larger degree of imbalance of power and agency capacity; and the quantity and complexity of the resources and governance arrangements necessary to provide and maintain a plethora of public services including a functional public realm with a minimum degree of quality.

Adding to all this, the last few decades have seen the continuous dismantling of the welfare state in many Western countries, with the consequent reduced administrative and budgetary capacity of local governments to perform the duties they had performed for most of the 20th century. The result in many places has been a significant change in the way government works, with a reduction in direct involvement and the increase of enabling forms of intervention which rely on social actors outside government to fulfil duties that once were done by government bodies. A positive take on this process would emphasise the concepts of partnership, co-production and collaboration. A negative take would highlight the dangers of privatisation, exclusion and commodification. In many cities around the world, and especially in large metropolitan areas, we have seen the emergence by design or by necessity of multiple forms of provision and management of public space involving private interests of all kinds, with their attendant impacts on openness and accessibility of public spaces. We are all familiar with the increasing role of private developers and real estate investors in providing new public space as part of development operations, and we are also all familiar with the concept of privately managed public spaces from the POPS (Privately Owned Public Spaces) of New York to their equivalents in London, Hong Kong and elsewhere. We are also familiar with the story of community-run open spaces, either as temporary acts of political significance or as permanent results of citizen activism in the protection of their interests, whether or not these coincide with the wider public interest. As will be familiar to most readers of this book, it is precisely these changes in the way public space is produced and managed that are behind the recent academic interest on the topic.

As we argue in this book, in their effort to provide public space through a variety of means, cities face two parallel and interrelated challenges. One is to secure that public space, however produced and managed, can still retain its public character, and the difficulties, or for some the unwillingness of a neoliberal polity to do that. This underpins the view that privatisation and commodification are now rampant. The other is how to relate to, incorporate and respond to the frequently conflictive demands around public space provision and public space management from increasingly varied local publics in societies that are ever more fragmented and complex. The difficulties in doing that with the monolithic machineries of local government are behind the efforts from groups of public space users to take control over public spaces they have strong a stake in, and thus ensure that their demands are acted upon. These might be community groups, interest groups, surrounding businesses or residents, or groups of neighbouring property owners. In each of these cases, the motivation for securing some control over a public space will be different, as will be the pressures to maintain publicness.

These are all discussions that have been around in the relevant literature for a while and to which the authors have contributed over the years. Therefore, they are not new, and in themselves would not justify yet another book on public space. However, most of the literature adopts what we could call a pessimistic view of public space, based on the assumption of a public space golden age that is now in the past, destroyed by ever-increasing privatisation and commodification brought about by an ever-expanding globalised neoliberal capitalism. Any improvement in the fate of a declining and diminishing physical public realm would only really come about as a result of structural changes in society. Some authors have seen activist takeovers of public space such as those associated with the Occupy movement as embryonic forms of a new social order in which the nature of neoliberal public space would be challenged and replaced. Whereas the pressures of privatisation and commodification of the physical public realm, and of many other aspects of social life, are indeed a reality in contemporary capitalism, public spaces in most places continue to meet the demands of most of their users and are indeed thriving in many of the same cities in which privatisation and commodification are so visible. Some of those spaces will be more accommodating to particular types of uses or particular interests and less to others. Some spaces will be more open, others appropriated by particular groups and less so. Some will be important as civic arenas for a whole city, while others will have exclusively local importance and therefore feel as the property of a particular community. Some public spaces will have one dominant use while others will have a cacophony of different and conflicting uses and activities; all of them are essential to urban life. Privatisation and commodification might be detrimental to some of those spaces but irrelevant to others. Stakeholders and interest groups will exert their agency in protecting what they see as their public spaces, some more successfully and some less, reflecting social power structures, the distribution of social capital, and so forth. We argue that the result of all those simultaneous processes is not necessarily a decline of the physical public realm. Many of the arguments that propose that is so ignore historical and geographical contexts that are essential to the character of public space, ascribing to it a degree of universality that in practice has never existed.

That is where we think we can contribute to the current discussion on public space. We believe that we have three main points to make that have not been made sufficiently strongly in the debate so far. The first is that public space should be regarded as a complex ensemble of multiple types of spaces with different attributes, embedded in a diversity of contexts, responding to different sets of conflictive interests and resulting in varying degrees and modes of publicness, rather than as a homogeneous entity whose qualities can be measured along a simple and uniform scale. The second to some extent follows from the first, and it is that given the diversity of public spaces and of their publics, the attributes that make those spaces public, that is, their publicness, have meaning only if defined in relation to context and to the needs and demands of the relevant stakeholders. Accordingly, the book adopts an understanding of publicness as a function of the bundles of rights different stakeholders – from local users to residents, surrounding businesses, property owners to the general public – might have on the attributes they value of a public space. The third point is that to understand the roles public space might play in any city and to understand the challenges and opportunities that are associated with those roles we need to look at the long-term life of public space rather than its initial design. We need to look at how its publicness attributes evolve and change over time, and how this relates to changing and evolving forms of governance and management. Whereas the initial design of a public space might set out a range of possibilities for how that space might be used and appropriated by different users, it is the series of actions and decisions over time deriving from its management and governance that will make those possibilities real, close some and open others.

The book also has a fourth point to make, which is the value of a comparative approach to the understanding of how cities deal with their physical public realm. More on that later, but by focusing on two of the world's metropolises, London and Hong Kong, we try to understand how different institutional, policy and cultural contexts shape forms of public space provision and management and therefore notions and realities of publicness and the physical public realm. Through examples in those two cities, we try to give a concrete and contextualised form to the more abstract notions about the meaning of publicness that underpin the book's main arguments.

Conceptual background for the book

In this book we develop ideas and reflections on public space accumulated by both authors over the years through several research projects and published in the form of research reports, academic papers and books.

In previous research, we have addressed the issue of public space management and grappled with the concept of public space governance, seeking to define what that entails, how it relates to long-term management, what activities it comprises and how the roles it involves are distributed among different social actors (Carmona, De Magalhães and Hammond

2008). The main concern, then, given ongoing changes in how public spaces have been provided, was with understanding how public space governance is constituted in a context in which many of the activities that make it up might have been transferred to players outside the public sector. We have examined changes in the way public space governance takes place and is translated in management regimes, focusing on contractualised arrangements for the various functions that make it up. In that work we proposed a framework to analyse contracted-out public space governance and its potential implications for the attributes of publicness (De Magalhães 2010), which we revisit in this book.

That framework was later applied to a number of cases of publicly owned but third-party managed public spaces in London to understand how transferred management shapes the attributes of publicness. For that, we had to find a definition of publicness that could relate the various attributes that concept encompasses, to the rights over them as allocated by different management regimes and to the various social actors involved in that process. We concluded that there were variations in the forms taken by publicness, characterised by how different stakeholders on public space access and deploy some basic rights associated with that concept (De Magalhães and Freire Trigo 2017a). This understanding of publicness was further developed through a study of public spaces in London that explored the simultaneous empowerment and disempowerment of different stakeholders in public space governance. We have sought inspiration from some of Elinor Ostrom's ideas on the management of common pool resources to examine the distribution of rights over public space management and to suggest the emergence of a landscape of different types of public spaces, characterised by different entitlements to the basic dimensions of publicness, with both positive and negative consequences (De Magalhães and Freire Trigo 2017b). This notion of different publics and various context-dependent forms of publicness adding up to a complex public realm informs the discussion of how London and Hong Kong deal with their public space challenges.

In parallel, we have also looked at public realm management from the perspective of public service design. Whether or not managing the public realm is done principally by the public sector, the existence of a functional public realm is a part of the common goods binding society together and therefore a public service in the broader sense of the concept. We argue that the concept of 'value' in its most general formulation – that which we want more of – should underpin practical actions if we are to manage public space strategically as a complex macroscopic whole; the role of public space governance is thus to better distribute the values that can emerge in or through public space (Chiaradia et al 2017; Sieh et al 2021). This service design perspective extends the analysis of publicness into the everyday technicalities of public space governance and how benefits of publicness are received. This approach informs the latter part of the book.

This book is therefore the result of an effort to bring together all these strands of research on public space, from discussions around publicness, to public space management and governance, to the role of social actors and the idea of the public realm as a public service and to apply the conceptual framework they provide to the understanding of public space provision and management challenges in London and Hong Kong.

Why London and Hong Kong

Most of the literature in English about public space, public space management and publicness takes as its point of reference concepts and practices that originate and find their full meaning in specific parts of the world. The discussion about key public space issues, such as privatisation, the roles of different stakeholders or the nature of publicness is dominated by arguments that refer to the specific context of the United States and, slightly less so, the UK. It is not just that the empirical cases and the policy processes and policy debates examined come from those countries, but that the very concepts informing them are the particular products of those social, political and cultural environments, and therefore not necessarily universal or context free. As this book will suggest, context is essential if we want to understand the challenges in public space provision and management faced by cities.

An opportunity for one of the authors to have a research sabbatical in Hong Kong in the first half of 2019, together with the active involvement of the other author in public space research in that city created the material condition for a comparative study on public space provision and management in London and Hong Kong. As most large urban agglomerations across the world, both cities face the challenges of providing enough public space to their populations and of making sure that their public space is managed in ways that ensure it is fit for purpose and addresses the needs and demands of their users. Because of historical links, albeit unequal, both cities have some common elements in their institutional and legal structures relevant to public space provision and management. Both cities have a history of private involvement in the production of common goods such as public space, which has played an important part in how they have met the challenges referred to earlier. Both are port cities and commercial cities, notwithstanding the obvious difference in London's history as the former capital city of an empire with global commercial and cultural reach and Hong Kong's history as a colonial outpost of that empire and more recently as a semi-autonomous commercial and financial centre within the much larger polity of the People's Republic of China.

However, these are also places of profound differences in their physical settings and morphology, in their culture, their attitudes to public space and, most importantly, in the way the state, public space users and other public space stakeholders relate to each other, express their demands and negotiate them, and in what rights they have and how these are allocated.

It is precisely this often jarring and uncomfortable combination of similarities and differences that makes London and Hong Kong an interesting pair of cities to look at. It forces us to confront the effects of different conceptions of what is to be 'public', different governance structures and different ways of acting superimposed onto an apparently similar institutional background. Doing that allows us to arrive at findings and lessons of wider applicability which can go well beyond the two cases.

The structure of the book

To explore the issues already outlined, this book is structured largely in two parts: the first develops the theoretical framework in relation to public space, publicness and public space governance in three successive conceptual chapters. We then apply that framework to the cases of London and Hong Kong, with three chapters exploring the challenges both cities face in providing public spaces in the quantities and qualities required, the ways demand for public space is incorporated into policy and action and, finally, how all this shapes public space governance and publicness in both cases.

The first of the conceptual chapters seeks to define public space as a resource that is the object of policy and therefore the subject of urban governance. The chapter introduces public space primarily as a shared resource, a common good with a variety of attributes that are shared in many degrees through rights allocated to members of society not necessarily and not always in the same way, as this allocation will reflect historical customs, power relations, local circumstances, and so forth. As its name suggests, public space as a shared resource is defined by predominantly public characteristics, namely openness and accessibility, related to its inherent and necessarily public spatial function as the connective spatial tissue between private realms in the city. However, the variety and complexity of those attributes and forms of sharing makes public space a difficult object to define. The chapter discusses the difficulties encountered in the literature around precise definition of public space and examines the archetype that emerged in the academic literature of the late 20th century and, subsequently, in popular political discourse, of an idealised public space, owned and managed by the state for the use of an undifferentiated public. We try to circumvent some of the limitations to this decontextualised idea of public space with considerations about the nature of public space as a common good, the nature of common goods provision in cities in the 20th and early 21st centuries and how it has changed from a mainly (but never exclusively) public sector duty to a more complex arrangement in which their defining attributes are not secured purely by public sector ownership. The chapter also touches on the implications of a decade of austerity economic policies in most Western countries and their impact on public space provision and management, the changing relationship between the public sector, especially local governments, the private and the community and voluntary sectors and the provision and management practices that have evolved from that.

However, no matter how public space is defined, publicness is a defining characteristic that needs some conceptual precision. It qualifies public space as a common good and sets out the challenges for provision and governance. But what is it? Chapter 2 discussed the archetypal conceptualisation of public space as open for all, accessible by all and provided by the state. The discussion in the literature tends to take that conceptualisation as its basis and take a prescriptive stance towards publicness, framing it in terms of absolute values to which any public space should aspire. The main problem with this approach is that it often fails to recognise context: the enormous variety of public spaces and the functions they perform to different kinds of citizens, which cannot be understood just with reference to an undifferentiated standard. Taking this discussion at its heart, Chapter 3 proposes a concept of publicness that better relates to context and can inform the operations and operational design of public space management and provision. We start with a critical review of what have been described as the essence of publicness in the literature, including openness, inclusivity, conductivity to encounters and so forth. We argue that these attributes may constitute high-level goals or principles but are often formulated in an abstract and decontextualised way. The complexity of public space and the attributes that are valued within it mean it is not a unitary common good and each public space possesses a different bundle of attributes. No matter how we may define publicness, it needs to reflect how that wide variety of attributes is contained, sustained, enabled or afforded so that they can be enjoyed as a complex bundle, in different ways by different people. To use a categorisation coming from economics, some elements of that bundle will be enjoyed as public goods whereas others will be enjoyed as common pool or club/toll goods, or even private goods. Therefore, in Chapter 3 we discuss what the concept of publicness means if it needs to be understood in the specific context of individual public spaces. We argue that such a publicness is space- and time-specific and needs to be specific to the space it qualifies. The chapter suggests a conceptualisation of publicness in which its form, type and degree result from the way rights are allocated to, or appropriated by, those with stakes in any particular space, and presents it as a system of rights that is interpretable in its context of application. The chapter concludes with the outline of the analytical framework that will be applied to public spaces in both London and Hong Kong in later chapters, based on the idea that publicness can be defined dynamically as a system of rights over the operational dimensions of access and use, and the collective choice elements that define agency in relation to a public space.

A context-based definition of publicness is essential for a critical discussion of public space governance arrangements. Who has the power to regulate rules of use and access to a public space, who determines how the space is maintained, what is preserved and what is not, how a space is resourced and how any capital investment is deployed, and who coordinates how all this takes place ultimately determines who and how benefits from a space and its attributes, and hence the kind of publicness that characterises that space. Chapter 4 expands the discussion around publicness to put forward a conceptualisation of public space governance. In this chapter we elaborate on a conceptual framework that examines the mechanisms governing the allocation and exercise of rights to the attributes of public space that define publicness. This includes the right to manage, the right to exclude, the right to arbitrate disputes and conflicts between different and conflictive interests. The chapter draws on arguments put forward by Elinor Ostrom and others around collective action and the role of property rights in the management of common pool resources to translate the understanding of publicness discussed in the previous chapter into management and governance actions shaping the life cycle of public spaces. Public space governance is presented as the constant rearrangement of allocated rights over the attributes of public space responding to pressures from different stakeholders and shaped by sets of rules that regulate that rearrangement. We make the point that the way public spaces are governed, that is, how the rights over publicness attributes are allocated and managed, and the conflicts that emerge from that process are negotiated, is itself an important constituent of publicness. This is especially so if publicness is not seen as static but the dynamic result of the interplay between the interests of different stakeholders and their relative power to transform them into rights.

Those three chapters on public space, publicness and public space governance provide the conceptual framework with which to approach the two cities which are the object of this book. However, before we can discuss the challenges to the provision and management of public space in London and Hong Kong, a contextual chapter on both cities provides an expanded overview of the recent history of governance and management of the public realm in general and open public spaces in particular. Chapter 5 also provides a rationale for their selection as objects of study, elaborating on their long-standing history of non-traditional forms of public space governance, which has acquired a new impetus with recent changes in urban governance worldwide. The emphasis is on how public spaces in these two cities have been produced and managed over time; the systems and institutional arrangements put in place to produce new spaces and to ensure that many of their publicness attributes fulfil their functions in the long run; the governance systems that represent the different interests with a stake in public spaces; how all these have evolved and the reasons for any significant changes. As befits a comparative study, the chapter is divided into two parts, one dealing with London, the other with Hong Kong, both structured along similar lines, describing and discussing public space provision, management and governance and concluding with the challenges both cities face. As the chapter suggests, both cities face quantitative and qualitative challenges in the provision and management of public space, the former referring to the need to provide and maintain an increasing amount of spaces for public use, the second relating to the incorporation of the evolving needs and aspirations of all the relevant stakeholders into provision and management. Furthermore, as both cities address those two challenges, they have to put in place forms of public space governance that can cope with the complex nature of public spaces and multiple forms of publicness associated with them. This is the third challenge.

The following two chapters apply the analytical frameworks discussed earlier to those sets of challenges. Chapter 6 discusses the first set of challenges to the provision and management of public spaces in London and Hong Kong, through an analysis of empirical cases in both cities. In the previous chapter we termed them quantitative challenges, as they refer to the challenges of providing the required amount of public spaces of appropriate quality in the neighbourhoods where they are needed and, consequently, of finding enough resources to maintain those spaces over the long term to standards that will not compromise their viability and usefulness. The chapter looks first at the issue of provision in Hong Kong, and the ways capital investment in new or refurbished public spaces has been sought outside public sector investment budgets and primarily from private property development operations, often associated with investment in transport infrastructure. The chapter looks at the production of public facilities in private developments or on privately leased land, including public passageways and public open spaces and the land leasing and deeds of dedication mechanisms that make these possible. In London, the chapter discusses the use of planning obligations to obtain new public space as a planning gain from development operations of different types and the mechanisms used for it. This is followed by a section that examines the challenge London faces of maintaining existing and new spaces. The chapter discusses negotiations between local authorities and property investors to secure long-term management of public spaces, the transfer of management rights to public space stakeholders of various sorts and various forms of outsourcing management responsibilities to private and voluntary bodies. The chapter concludes with a discussion of how both cities' responses to the quantitative challenges can potentially affect the more immediate operational rights associated with publicness, the rights of access and use.

We then move on to the qualitative challenges associated with the provision and management of public spaces. The first of these qualitative challenges is adapting public spaces to local needs, that is, having the capacity to diversify provision and management mechanisms so that public spaces, existing and new, respond to local contexts and to the particular needs and aspirations of those more likely to use them. This is directly related to another two related challenges, those of engaging users and stakeholders in public space provision and management so that the space does meet local needs and is therefore well used, and of establishing the accountability and mechanisms that allow for meaningful user input into those processes. Those two challenges express therefore the ability of those cities to understand and accept localised public space needs and demands from their population and to translate those needs and demands into a diversified portfolio of public spaces that addresses them. Facing those challenges requires some form of permeability to bottom-up input so that demands from public space users can shape public space management. Chapter 7 discusses both cities' responses to those challenges by looking at the mechanisms they have to reshape public spaces to adapt them to the needs of their users and, in turn, how this affects the allocation of those rights that make up publicness. These are mechanisms through which users and, more generally, all those with a stake in a public space can engage with public space providers and managers to make their aspirations heard and through which multiple and occasionally conflicting demands are brought together and compromises produced. Whereas the previous chapter addressed issues that had a direct impact on the operational rights that make up publicness, responses from both cities to the qualitative challenges narrated in this chapter have a direct impact on agency rights, the collective choice rights that are at the root of what it is to be 'public'. The chapter concludes with a typology of how these qualitative challenges have been addressed in both London and Hong Kong and what this says about the public realm in both cities.

Finally, in Chapter 8 we go full circle in our attempt to first define public space provision and management, then look at how London and Hong Kong face key public space governance challenges, and lastly reconceptualise public space governance in a way that can address those challenges. In order to do the latter, the chapter draws together the conceptual discussions and empirical evidence from London and Hong Kong to propose a practical theory of public space governance. The purpose of the practical theory is to bridge scholarly, especially theoretical, work and the challenges of practically governing and managing actual public space in cities around the world. In order to put together the sketch of such a theory, we bring together the key arguments presented earlier in the book of public space as a common good, a contiguous spatial field between private realms, an essential but complex resource whose public value lies in the benefits that it brings to its users and stakeholders, and the city as whole. For these benefits to be effectively and fairly realised, public space's publicness, defined by rights to access, of use and of agency has to be established and maintained, with the challenges discussed in the previous chapters addressed. Using insights from the empirical evidence from London and Hong Kong, we elaborate on a practical theory of public space governance based around the common good nature of public space and its socially constructed character and its role as a resource for wider urban governance. Public space has to fulfil a number of basic functions, from circulation to providing an environment for meeting, well-being, place identity and so forth, and in doing that maximises public value. This is highly contextual, and the allocation of publicness rights is simultaneously the tool and the basic condition for the production of public value. The chapter puts together the basic blocks for this rethinking about public space governance and concludes with a reflection on the dilemmas London, Hong Kong and cities all over the world face as they use their urban governance institutions and instruments to meet needs and demands for public space at citywide and at local level and make sense of an increasingly complex and fragmented physical public realm. As we hope to demonstrate, the conclusion is positive.

2

Conceptualising public space for governance: a complex shared common good

Introduction

This is the first of three conceptual chapters discussing the nature of public space and public space governance. It begins with considerations about the nature of public space as a kind of shared resource or common good, with a variety of shared attributes, and about how these attributes define the public nature of public space. As we shall argue, public space as common parlance would have it today, as a good or service both provided by the state and available to everyone, is a 20th-century concept, a somehow simplistic view of a complex common good whose precise definition often eludes us. Despite this, there emerged in the academic literature of the late 20th century, and subsequently in popular political discourse, an idealised archetypal public space, owned and managed by the state for the use of an undifferentiated public, although such an ideal has rarely existed in the history of shared urban space. To address these issues, the chapter develops considerations about public space as a common good, and how the shared character of many of its attributes defines the public nature of public spaces. To anchor the discussion in its historical, geographical and cultural contexts, the chapter introduces the nature of common goods provision in cities in the 20th and early 21st centuries in the West – when these goods became synonymous with public sector-provided goods – and how it has changed from a mainly public sector duty to a more complex arrangement in which their defining attributes are not secured purely by public sector ownership. The chapter also touches on the implications of a decade of austerity economic policies in most Western countries and its impact on public space provision and management, the changing relationship between the public sector, especially local governments, the private and the community and voluntary sectors and the provision and management practices that have evolved from that.

The challenge of defining public space

As a vast literature on public space testifies, defining that concept is not a straightforward matter. Definitions encompass a variety of notions, with emphasis variously on the functions public spaces perform in society, the proprietary regimes under which public spaces are held, the physical characteristics of those spaces, the uses and activities they should accommodate, the nature and variety of their users; and are often shaped by the type of public space problem that is being discussed (see, for example, Benn and Gaus 1983, Taylor 1995, Ellin 1996, Oldenburg 1999, Banerjee 2001, Low and Smith 2006, Mitchell and Staeheli 2006, Watson 2006, Németh and Schmidt 2011, Varna 2014). Public space can have a very broad meaning and include all communal and non-private arenas of social life, which do not necessarily imply physical space and include the media and the virtual spaces of the internet (see, for example, Taylor 1995, Ellin 1996, Watson 2006). In this latter broad sense, it conflates with the notion of the public realm as the arena in which most forms of collective social life and politics take place. In the urban planning literature, the concept refers usually to all those physical spaces that are not strictly private in the sense of not being normally accessible to the general public. This could include not only the publicly owned and openly accessible areas of the city but also all those physical spaces with relatively unrestricted access in which social and civic functions with a public character might be performed, regardless of ownership or intended function (Ellin 1996). This definition would include all the parks, squares, and also public streets, as well as railway station concourses, public libraries and other accessible areas in publicly accessible buildings. An extension of this understanding as used in the urban sociology literature would also include what have been termed the liminal or 'third' spaces of cafes, bars, bookstores and so forth, privately owned but with relatively open access (Oldenburg 1999, Banerjee 2001). Conversely, the definition of public space is also often narrowed down to a stricter legalistic or managerial interpretation, limiting it to those spaces legally defined in a zoning plan as open public spaces, or as those that fall within the remit for local government open public space services: government-owned parks, civic spaces and town squares. The urban design and planning literature often adopts this narrower understanding of public spaces as public parks, public squares and other officially designated open green spaces (Carmona 2015). A very simple explanation for this state of affairs is that different authors are defining public space for a different practical or scholarly purpose, whether it is to explore the design of public space, or to regulate it, or to understand its roles in society. We will return to this point later.

Those definitions differ in the spatial scale they refer to, in the interpretation of the meaning of 'public' and even in the conceptualisation of 'space'. However, what they all have in common is that they are all located along a scale bounded on either end by openness and closeness, or accessibility and inaccessibility, which is expressed in the duality between public and private, and nature of the rights of use and access associated with those two apparent opposites. Madanipour (2003), in his study of public and private spaces, demonstrates the complexity of the transition from public to private, with several overlapping levels of publicness and privateness between them.

The potential for variation in what is public and what is private is considerable. The notions of 'public' and 'private' are themselves complex products of historical evolution, varying through time, from place to place and with different ways of defining boundaries between them. As societies change, activities that once took place in the public realm might acquire a more private character and vice versa, thus changing the public/private character of spaces over time. Public spaces can be the loci for a variety of uses and activities, some of which have a more private or a more public character, whatever the precise definition is chosen for those two terms, and as shown by Guadarrama Sánchez and Pichardo Martínez (2021) this mix of private and public uses will vary in time and space.

The next section explores the evolution of the societally defined concepts of public and private, concepts which qualify and give meaning to shared spaces in the city. Since the qualifying concepts themselves are time- and space-defined, so must be the concept of public space. This account goes some way to explaining why contemporary public space governance arrangements in London and Hong Kong are as they are.

The evolution of the idea of 'public'

The definition of 'public space' is context specific, and this is because the definition of 'public' itself is context specific, as we explore here. The idea of 'public' today as a qualification of goods or services is related to the ideas of people, citizenship and collective control. If we apply to urban space the contemporary understanding of the word 'public', public space means shared space provided by and managed 'in trust', by the state, for 'the people', and to which 'the public' have access. This has not always been the case. How did such an idea of 'public' come to be applied to shared spaces in the city? In the West, the distinction between public and private that would result in the notion of public space came into being with the differentiation between the representative state, civil society and the market after the Middle Ages, and the consolidation of modern notions of private property (Habermas 2001). The word for public itself derives from the Latin word *publicus*, that which belongs to the people, the *populus*, and by extension in ancient Rome qualified those in public office; land, money and slaves owned by the people; and accessible space such as roads (Hylen 2020). Private, in turn, comes from *privatus*, originally denoting a person not acting in an official capacity, and therefore acting on their own as a *privus*, a single individual. In ancient Rome these were complementary terms without the antithetical connotation they would assume in modern times (Wunder 2022).

Arendt (1998) sustains that the boundaries between a private and a public realm held a particular meaning until the late Middle Ages: the former was the domain of individual/family matters, whereas the latter was the arena of political matters. However, the emergence of the concept of 'society' in the modern era put an end to that form of division between both realms. On the one hand, the idea of 'society' gave a new and wider meaning to matters that were once within the exclusive remit of the private realm (the individual/family) – for example, health, education, economy. On the other hand, the operationalisation of the concept of 'society' entailed the assumption that its members had *one* common interest or *one* common opinion. For Arendt, it was precisely because of this *apparent one* common interest that 'society' became understood as the 'public realm', which is in reality a 'hybrid realm' that conflates what were formerly public and private matters (Arendt 1998: 59). This historical process underpins the emergence of the modern concept of 'public interest', which in turn has shaped the way we have come to understand common goods, public goods and public spaces. In the medieval times, the 'common good' was the materialisation of different individual interests over one common thing, which necessarily led to a negotiation between the interested parties over the maintenance and enjoyment of it (Arendt 1998: 59). Accordingly, far from representing an assertion of the public realm, the medieval 'common good' was an assertion of the *private* realm. Drawing on Arendt's work, it could be argued, then, that a discussion of public spaces should at least recognise the inherent tensions embedded in the concept. In so far as they are 'common' in the sense of 'shared-by-negotiated-agreement', the framing of public space should acknowledge the legitimate conflicts between its private nature – the concrete individual interests over a concrete site – and its public nature – the societal concerns about the management of its resources.

The current understanding of 'public' as in public space or public service, with its association with government and the state – the public sector – as the guarantors of the 'common good' – was consolidated in the 19th century and the first half of the 20th century. This close association of the qualification 'public' with ownership, provision and management by the state and its organisations reflects the role of government and the state as the main incarnation of public matters – the *res publica*. In the Western democratic polities that emerged from the end of the 18th century, with the progressive extension of voting rights, the state and governments came to represent – at least in theory – the expression of the will of the citizens, the public interest, and therefore what the state owns and controls, it does so on behalf of its citizens (see, for example, Rose 1994). This build-up of the predominance of governments as representation of society's public interest eroded and did away with other forms of shared ownership and management of collective interests, resulting in the conflation of the idea of public with the idea of state owned and, importantly for our present argument, state provided. Over the course of the 20th century, the view that property regimes such as common property, in which common goods were owned and managed by their users and beneficiaries within a given community, had to disappear as the capitalist economy evolved and they were replaced by more efficient private or public property regimes (which of the two depended on the ideological position of the author in question), to avoid the depletion of those goods and their ultimate destruction, most famously captured by Hardin's (1968) 'tragedy of the commons', became received wisdom. In this context, in most Western societies the provision and management of goods that cannot be adequately supplied through private property regimes (and therefore through private exchanges in the marketplace) has become seen as the responsibility of the state, of government. In the case of public spaces, the conflation of public with government ownership involves mostly local government, which has replaced other forms of provision and management for spaces with similar roles. This 'replacement' was never complete, and in the past two decades a rediscovery of those other forms of management has taken place in the face of the perceived shortcomings of state provision of goods and services, the impacts of privatisation, the inadequacy of a strict public–private classification and, in some places, austerity policies (see, for example, Blomley 2004 or Harvey 2012 for a discussion of the process of *commoning*). Notably, urban public space is a major arena in which revived and new forms of service provision are made visible.

While that modern distinction between public and private has also taken root in cultures outside the West, itself an idea with indistinct scope (see Qian 2014 for a discussion of this scope, which is one that we share), these concepts do not have the same ancient philosophical and hence cultural roots. In the Chinese tradition, which is relevant to Hong Kong, the term most usually translated as 'public' (*gong gong*) historically meant the concept of the princely ruling power, and was not associated with a community of people. The character used now for public (*gong*) derives from a noun meaning an ancestor or an honorific title of a leader. As with the word and character for private (*si*), itself a descriptor of identity and belonging to a low social class, both refer to social class and the position in relation to power – ruling elite or low class respectively (Too 2007). The concept of *gong* came to mean the imperial government as the generic ruler and, by extension, the idea of public as what is official, what belongs to government. The opposition between public and private takes the form of a separation between what is individual/familial/private and what belongs to the ruling system and the state. A similar conflation between public and governmental without the accompanying idea of control by a community of citizens can be found in Japan (see Yoshida 1999), whose ancient culture was closely related to that of China (Radovic 2020). The Japanese characters usually translated as 'public' is *ko kyo* (Radovic 2020), which, the reader will note, are identical to *gong gong* in Chinese. In Japanese, the character *ko*, the usual translation for the word 'public', implies government before it does any notion of a community of people. In both cases the idea is that public affairs (or public space) are matters for the government and not necessarily something that belongs or is of concern to the general public. This is despite the fact that the idea of governing for the people has been a central tenet of communist Mainland China or the dominance of Western-style forms of democratic governance in Japan (Radovic 2020). This meaning of 'public' is clearly recognisable in Hong Kong, where governance by elites is still very much alive. Similar understanding of 'public' is present in other parts of Asia as, for example, in Turkey (Zandi-Sayek 2001), where the development of the state has followed a different trajectory from the West. As we will show later in this book, in the case of Hong Kong the very clearly drawn and strongly enforced 'official' distinction between 'private' and 'public' was and remains a central tenet of the territory's governing philosophy, and infuses many aspects of life in the city, including its public space governance.

A contemporary public space has materially different meanings for its users (and managers) in different localities, but also across time. The government/public sector provision of public space as a dominant form applies to only a particular and relatively short recent period of history. The incorporation of public space into the list of services provided by governments on behalf of citizens became the rule only with the formation of democratic modern municipal government in the West from the middle of the 19th century and its full realisation in the 20th century. This is the institutional setting that has allowed public space to be considered public in the sense that it belongs to and is managed by the state on behalf of the collective interest of the citizenry. The public spaces of antiquity so often cited as models and predecessors for many of the current public spaces (the agora, the market square, the town square, monumental open spaces, the tree-lined avenues and so forth) were 'public' in a very different sense of the word. These would have been provided and managed by very different polities, often representing the interests of a very limited part of the population, or by powerful rulers, religious or military authorities. These were often spaces owned and managed by the ruling elites or powerful groups for their own benefit. Other public spaces were for the most part left in the public domain, with no clear ownership, or were owned and managed under common property regimes, and subject to private appropriation and negotiation between authorised users, as in many European medieval streets or village commons.

All this means that 'public spaces' in all these times and places are actually *different things* from each other. The definition of 'public space' is consequently context specific, because ways how these different societies decided to share it are different across those times and places. This context-specificity of public space constructs also means that a contemporary public space in London might not mean the same for its users as a contemporary public space in Hong Kong, even if they look very similar and perform the same functions. Equally, and more to the point, the public spaces of the ancient agora in the city-states of ancient Greece, the forum in cities in the ancient Roman world (Russell 2016), or the street in the ancient Chinese city (Heng 2007) might seem at first glance as examples of what we understand as public spaces, with the kinds of physical structures we might expect in public spaces and similar types of use, but are fundamentally different in terms of their regimes of provision and management, their rules of access and use and their function in society.

Different functions, relationships between citizens and government or ruled and rulers have also led to the creation of different types of public space. More precisely, spaces whose justifications for existing were new and reflect new perceptions of needs in society: the emergence of public parks in Western cities in the 19th century is directly linked to the rise of public concerns about public health in the wake of the Industrial Revolution. Society's concerns translated into pressure on governments to provide open green areas for the benefit of the general population, in many cases repurposing and opening up old aristocratic estates to the public. In contrast, the same public space typology, the urban public park, appeared in cities in countries such as China only much later, as a product of 20th-century Modernist planning, making accessible to the wider population a good that had until then been the preserve of the elites (Shi 1998).

It should be clear from this discussion that, at least in the wide range of ways that scholars have so far set out, 'public space', its essence and its role has not been defined in a way that is universal everywhere and across history. Yet, until recently, most debates on public space tend to ignore the historical evolution of the 'public space' concept, and instead hold aloft as a 'natural' condition of 'publicness' what is in fact a very time-and-place-specific constructed relationship between shared-use urban space and state provision/ownership. That has often been treated as the 'gold standard' of public space, referenced in so many academic and public discourse debates about public space. Consequently, the emphasis of much of North American and European debates on public space has focused on the link between the aspirations and rights of the public and the forms of ownership and management of this particular asset, and how the reduction of the role of the state through forms of privatisation might compromise that link and reduce the sphere in which the public can manifest their aspirations and constitute itself as public. Elsewhere, however, where the identification between state ownership and the interests of the public is differently configured, the concern may be, for example, with how the interests of citizens can actually be incorporated into the provision and management of 'good public space' by a not-always-responsive state with its own interests which do not necessarily coincide with many of the localised aspirations of the people. This description certainly fits with many aspects of historic public space governance everywhere, including in London and in Hong Kong. It also fits with many aspects of contemporary public space governance around the world. This book seeks to demonstrate that the 'archetype' of public space being provided by the state on behalf of the people, and for their benefit, as well as being 'open to all', *needs rethinking* if public space governance ideas are to be applicable to changing contexts, in time, and in different places and cultures.

The archetype of state-provided public space: the ideal and reality

There is by now a long-standing archetype of public space as a common good that should be provided by the state, which itself would guarantee that it will be open and accessible to anyone. This archetype of public space as state owned and managed is a product of the evolution of the modern democratic welfare state and the increase in the list of goods the state should provide to secure the welfare of citizens, an idea that had its genesis earlier in the 20th century but was really put into practice very widely in Western countries after the Second World War. While state provision of public space has become the norm, other forms of provision have become the exception. The stereotypical public space owned and managed by a public body, provided to the general public as part of the duties of governments to see to the well-being of their citizens, with nominally free and open access and use as long as these happen within the framework of rules and norms of behaviour accepted in that society, is seen as clearly different from its polar opposite, private space. Private space is owned by individuals or groups with their own interests, and therefore not there to serve the public interest. Even if these private spaces are open and accessible, this is conditional to those private interests and therefore out of public control. Most public open spaces squares, parks and streets in our towns and cities in most parts of the world are seen in that light: spaces that belong to accountable public bodies, are managed by them and nominally open and accessible by any citizen. However, a close look at the diversity of public spaces suggests that this stereotype only partially reflects reality.

This view of public space as a state-maintained and provided public good has informed how city administrations and many citizens around the world have seen public space for most of the 20th century. It still corresponds to a large number of actual public spaces, even if not to all of them. It also still dominates most of the discussion around public space provision and management, certainly at a municipal level. However, as we suggest in Chapter 4, trying to apply these archetypal qualities to the management of actual public spaces and for delivering on the aspirations of users regarding the public spaces they have a stake in, is often problematic, since so many public spaces do not fit within the archetype. Many of them never did and have always required different conceptualisations so that they can function usefully as public spaces. Moreover, the institutional structures that give rise to the archetype, the service-providing local governments, have also changed considerably since the middle of the 20th century, and with them forms of public service governance, provision and management. On top of that the public's aspirations, including for public spaces, have become less homogeneous (see, for example, Hoppe 2011 on the rise of 'publics' and the clash with Modernity). Varying and often conflictive aspirations for public space have questioned the idea of a uniform and universal archetype and require a much more nuanced and localised approach to the common good public space. As a result, the archetype of 'public for all at all times' alone has become less adequate for understanding and shaping the practical operations of public space provision.

Despite the dominance of the archetype, it should be stressed that *not even in present times do all public spaces correspond to the exclusive public sector provision model sketched in the foregoing*. Many pre-modern forms of public space provision have survived and adapted well, and in the UK alone, many privately owned open spaces (by private persons, private trusts and private institutions) have remained in private ownership but acquired many of the attributes commonly associated with public spaces, such as open access to the general public, relatively unrestricted use and so forth. Historically, many privately developed neighbourhoods in 18th- and early 19th-century London provided squares and other spaces for the use of their residents, some of which have allowed relatively open access. This is true for many of the famous London Georgian squares, some of which were later acquired by local governments, others of which are still in private hands in the form of trusts or otherwise but operate as open public spaces. In Hong Kong the provision of various facilities with public attributes, including Public Open Spaces in Private Developments (POSPDs), is a common practice, established through a range of contractual mechanisms between the government and various property owners. As discussed later in this chapter, private provision and management of public spaces is an increasingly growing phenomenon all over the world. From the POPS in New York, to their equivalent in London, Sydney, Berlin, Hong Kong and other cities, an increasing proportion of new public spaces is provided and managed in ways that deviate from the late 19th- and 20th-century tradition already described. The rest of this book explores the resurgence of a wide range of these approaches, but first, we need to set out concepts that allow us to do so systematically, including establishing a definition of public space that makes it amenable to discourses of governance.

The essence of public space

To be able to study 'public space' — spaces in cities shared by the citizenry — across different social, cultural and political contexts, we need a conceptualisation that helps us make sense of the fundamental roles of public space, and, hence, also of how they are provided.

We have seen in the previous section that the ideas of 'public space' are socially and geographically produced. These have changed along with historical changes in the societies in which they are produced, especially in relation to each society's evolving understanding of 'public' and 'private'. Rather than a discrete object, whose 'publicness' is immutably related to a precise definition based mainly on morphological characteristics (for example, a town square is necessarily and always a public space, a shopping mall is always private) or on the nature of uses it contains or fosters (for example, if one is able to march in protest, this is always a public space; if one is restricted from playing a musical instrument, then this cannot be a public space), public space is a responsive product and a dynamic reflection of what a society understands as the common goods that should be available to its members, how those goods should be provided, who should have access to them and how and under what conditions. Nevertheless, there are some elements in the notion that permeate all the historical and geographically varied cases of public space and can provide us with an operational definition of what public space is, which will be used in the discussion in this book: its shared-ness and its spatiality.

We argued in the previous section that public space is associated with the idea of a 'common' or 'shared' good. A normative view of this idea is that those goods should be available to *all* members of society, regardless of their social, economic or political situation. As such, they should be provided and managed in a way that ensures that they retain their 'common good' character and are accessible to all intended beneficiaries.

What, then, is a 'common good'? There is a tradition in Western philosophy that defines common good as goods (institutions, facilities, cultural norms) that are made available to all members of a civic community as part of the bonds that create and maintain that community (Plato 1968, Locke 1988, Rawls 1999). To the examples discussed earlier, we could add public safety, judicial systems and facilities such as public parks as other examples of goods provided by a society to its members as an essential justification for the pact that keeps society together: the ability to provide for the common interests of its members.

However, the concept of common good is a general and high-level statement of principles, of what sort of reciprocal bonds a society should have and how they may be fostered by these goods. It does not in itself illuminate the processes whereby actual goods are provided and which ultimately determine how individual members of that society can access them. For that, we turn our attention to an established understanding, which comes from economics, of the nature of the different types of goods a society produces and consumes, and how they are allocated to users and consumers.

Forms of provision of goods in contemporary market societies include market mechanisms, planned state action, collective arrangements between suppliers and users, and a hybrid of all those (Ostrom 2003). All these forms of provision involve an allocation of the rights to benefit from scarce and subtractive resources to those who most want or most benefit from them. Accordingly, the main qualities of goods for determining the dominant forms of provision are the ability to restrict those who benefit from that good and the extent to which one person's use subtracts from the ability of others to consume or use that good (Ostrom 2010). Economists trying to understand how markets provide goods for consumption, and why some goods might be over- or undersupplied, have come up with four basic types of goods, based on those qualities (see Ostrom 2010 or Webster and Lai 2003). Purely private goods are those that are excludable (it is possible to exclude those who do not pay for consuming it) and consumption by one person prevents consumption of the same good by another person (consumption is said to be rivalrous or subtractable). Most of the personal goods we consume in our everyday life fall into this category. At the other end, public goods are those for which it is not possible to exclude anyone from consuming it, and consumption by one person does not prevent anyone else from consuming it at the same time (so, non-excludable and non-rivalrous/non-subtractable). The usual examples of public goods are clean air, defence and peace. Common pool goods are those for which beneficiaries are hard to exclude, but each person's use of that good subtracts from the pool of goods available to other users. Fisheries and agricultural irrigation systems are classical examples of this type of good for which it is difficult to exclude anyone from access but for which consumption of the good by one person reduces how much of the good is available to others. Finally, club goods or toll goods (Ostrom and Ostrom 1977) are goods for which exclusion is possible, but consumption of the good by those with access to it does not subtract from the consumption of others with the same access. Toll roads, fee-paying cable TV services and members' clubs are the usual examples.

The logic of this categorisation is actually 'how a good is consumed', rather than how it is supplied, but, as discussed, understanding how the good is consumed is highly relevant to the understanding of provision and what provision mechanisms have emerged to deliver a particular type of good.

Private goods are easily provided through private exchange in markets, as suppliers and consumers can interact and gauge individually how much of a good they should consume or produce. Purely public goods are behind the concept of market failure, as markets will either overproduce or, more commonly underproduce them. The impossibility of excluding anyone from consuming the good prevents suppliers from gauging demand accurately and disincentivises production, as there is no direct way of making users pay for the goods they consume. Market failure has been one of the main justifications for state provision of public goods paid for by overall taxation, and hence the close association of the idea of public goods in this sense of non-subtractable and non-excludable with the idea of public goods as goods provided by government, the public sector. Club/toll goods and common pool goods have been provided variously by groups of suppliers or users, the state and the market.

In reality, this classification is an abstraction, albeit a useful one. Very few if any goods are really exclusively public goods and many goods that are intuitively private are not exclusively so. Goods and their attributes are all in a spectrum varying from being completely excludable and subtractable in their use, to being non-excludable and non-subtractable. Moreover, in real life, goods and their attributes move along the spectrum in time, usually from the public good end towards the private good end as congestion and overuse make use more rivalrous and subtractable, and the users that are most affected by those changes try to secure their rights over a good and its attributes by limiting access to it and reaffirming their own control over the resource. Very often technological progress creates ways whereby a hitherto non-excludable resource becomes excludable, as in the evolution from lighthouses to global positioning systems.

Webster and Lai (2003) give a very good explanation from a property rights perspective of how this happens and why, with goods moving from being non-excludable and non-rivalrous in their use to non-excludable but rivalrous as they get congested by intense use. Pressures in society for reallocation of rights over those goods to overcome the problems of congestion then lead to new forms of exclusion that alleviate congestion, making use of the good excludable but non-rivalrous – a club good in their terminology, and then a private good when further congestion makes consumption rivalrous. Residents' parking schemes are an example of that – as the number of cars on the streets increases, free parking comes under pressure and the right to street parking becomes exclusive to residents, who usually pay for the privilege, and as long as there are enough parking spaces in a neighbourhood to accommodate all residents, consumption is non-rivalrous. As the number of cars increases further, parking becomes a private good, with consumption by one resident preventing consumption by another. The transfer of management of public space to a non-governmental organization (NGO) or residents' group is another: although the public space itself might be physically open to all, the attribute of deciding how it is managed and maintained is transferred to a group with membership rules, making it a club good, normally because the budget of the local authority is congested with demands from many other local services. Many goods can remain in that condition for a long time, although in some cases the club itself becomes congested, use becomes rivalrous and ways are devised to turn that good or attribute into a private good or to substitute it for a private good equivalent. As an example, we can think of a congested public green space being replaced in the urban fabric with condominium-style fenced and communally owned space, subsequently being replaced with private gardens. This actually mirrors the evolution of the typology of open spaces within public housing estates in England: conceived originally as open areas and then fenced off to outsiders and subsequently replaced by private gardens when redevelopment occurs (van Kempen, Dekker, Hall and Tosics 2005).

Ostrom in her work on common pool resources also recognises that goods can evolve and change from one category to another as in a sliding scale, but she contests the inevitability of the move from public to private and the overrun of the forms in between by demonstrating that the nature of goods, their forms of provision and the institutions that sustain them are context dependent (Ostrom and Ostrom 1977, Ostrom 2003, 2010).

In practice, as we will see later, there are many more shades and mechanisms of publicness, as this book will show, especially as many goods are actually composites of many different attributes, all of them goods in themselves and positioned at different points in that sliding scale. However, these basic categories allow us to explore how a second important feature of public space – its spatiality – affects access to its attributes. What we will see in the next section is the nature of the challenge that public space's spatiality presents for its analysis and the operational design of its management.

Is, then, public space any particular type of 'good', as categorised in the foregoing? To answer this, we need a deeper understanding of the possibility of restriction to use/consumption, and the logistics on which it depends. To understand both of these, we need to understand public space's spatiality.

Public space's spatiality

There is a well-known parable told by David Foster Wallace about the fish who do not know what water is. 'Space' is to people what water is to fish, as the social sciences have been rediscovering for the past 30 years or so, as they grapple with the spatial turn (Crang and Thrift 2000). 'Spatiality' is 'the effect of space on actions, interactions, entities, and theories' (Mayhew 2009). 'Spatiality is a social construct, not an exogenously given, absolute coordinate system … but a product of the political economic system' (Sheppard 2004 in Mayhew 2009). 'From the perspective of spatiality, space and society do not gaze at each other but rather are mutually embedded' (Ettlinger and Bosco 2004).

To be able to grasp public space for the purpose of understanding its provision, a provision-suitable definition is required that enables the mastery of the mechanics of its use. Space and society are not just 'mutually embedded', they are also mutually constitutive (Blomley 2013). It should be obvious that they are. Urban space in particular, is designed by societal actors. Thus, an understanding that enables mastery requires an understanding of the processes of mutuality constituting public space's spatiality.

What are the characteristics of this spatiality that influence its constitution as 'public' and its management as a shared resource?

Firstly, we have already suggested and will develop this theme in the following chapters, public spaces can have multiple functions that can be interrelated in complex ways, depending on context. In fact, public space embodies multiple goods, not just a single good, from space of circulation, space for relaxation, contemplation, encounters and socialisation, symbolic events, trade, sports and so forth in all possible permutations depending on where they are, the public they serve, the specificities of the site and location. This means also that public space will offer different combinations of goods to different people.

Secondly, the use of public space is simultaneous for multiple users. Most of the attributes that make up public spaces (the greenery, the open views, the health benefits of the presence of trees, the co-mingling of people and so forth) can be enjoyed simultaneously by many people. Not only that, but simultaneous users also 'produce' the space for each other, as their actions, even just their presence, impact on other users. Thirdly, multiple users imply a diversity of stakeholders and multiple publics. Many different people want to use public space for different purposes. The general understanding of public space has long emphasised the ideal of physical openness as a defining characteristic of public space. However, that 'public' is made of both diverse individuals and different 'publics' (Iveson 2008). Since there are many diverse publics, there are also many and diverse public spaces, and governance actions on public space require decisions about prioritisation of stakeholder needs and preferences. We will explore this issue further in later chapters.

Fourthly, the attributes of public space are not fixed but are co-produced and reproduced dynamically by users. Production takes place when people interact with other people in the space, or about the space, and it also takes place when people interact with physical elements of public space as well. Not only do people who act in a space produce the space for anyone else in the space at the same time, they potentially also produce the space for people who use if afterwards, say, if they litter. Interactions *about* a space might include the negotiations over proposed improvements to a space. All of this means that public space governance needs to take into account not just processes of physical production, but those of social production as well.

Finally, many of the attributes related to public space take the form of externalities, as indirect costs or benefits generated by the location of a public space to those who happen to live or work near it. As public spaces are fixed in their locations, many of their public good attributes will also be captured as private goods by surrounding property owners and occupiers. Commercial property owners and occupiers will capture the accessibility, buzz and vibrancy of popular and accessible city squares or streets, translated into greater footfall and capitalised into higher rents and property values, which naturally exclude those who cannot afford them. Similarly, the amenity value of public parks, green spaces and tree-lined residential streets might be enjoyed as a public good by visitors during their visit, but it is appropriated privately by surrounding residents (and capitalised in property values) who are able to enjoy it at all times as a private or toll/club good.

Therefore, what characterises public space is precisely the idea that it is a shared common good, physically defined as container of specific functions in the urban fabric, and that it presents by definition many of the characteristics of a *public* good as already referred to: open to all without restriction – so non-excludable in principle, and capable of being consumed simultaneously by many without this detracting from anyone's individual consumption of it. From that perspective, the archetypal public space is indeed not just a common good but also a public good: a park, or urban square or street from which it would be difficult and certainly not desirable to exclude anyone from benefitting from it, and if we leave aside the potential for congestion, its use by one person would not detract from the use by another.

Many of the attributes of public space effectively *do* indeed work as public goods, such as the amenity value of a large area of green space, or the positive impacts on air pollution of large concentrations of mature trees, or the potential to see and meet other people, or still the possibility to go from A to B without major impediments. However, not all do it. Others might be public goods only within narrower bounds of use conditions created by the fact that they can quickly become congested, and consequently individual consumption begins to subtract from the consumption by others. In other words, the benefits and costs of public space and the public good character of its attributes are not fixed and given but are produced and reproduced dynamically by users. This is the fourth characteristic of public space. If a children's playground space in a public park gets frequently overcrowded, measures might be put in place to restrict access to, say, children of a particular age group, or to fee-paying users only. Even the use of public thoroughfares by pedestrians can become congested to the point that users with mobility impairments might be effectively barred from access. Consequently, many of the benefits from a public space will not be public goods as defined in the previous paragraphs. They might vary in character as they are used, as for example the sports facilities in a park that might accept bookings from any user, but they might be accessed for a fee and will be either private for the duration of the use (when consumption is rivalrous/subtractable as in, for example a tennis court) or a club/toll good (for example, a non-congested public swimming pool in which consumption is non-subtractable – a congested one will be akin to a common pool good). They might also have permanent exclusion rules and toll/club good character, such as children's playground areas that will not allow adults except accompanied by a child. Moreover, many of the life-giving elements of public space, those that might make them thriving and attractive such as cafés, restaurants, farmers' markets, street sellers will be private in their essential attributes, although those private goods will also produce public goods in some of their amenity benefits (the presence of people and the feelings of safety associated with that, the buzz and vibrancy, and so forth).

Public space is therefore not actually a single good but instead overlapping packages of attributes, of multiple and overlapping constituent public spaces. The multiple publics, and individuals, enjoy multiple benefits, produced by multiple attributes and delivered through multiple institutional arrangements that take the form of public, private, club/toll or common pool goods. Different benefits accruing to different stakeholders may stem from the same attribute, and the same benefit may draw on different attributes, there may be multiple possible institutional arrangements to deliver any benefit, or to exploit any attribute. Unexpected benefits may arise and can be exploited in these processes by users. Public space users themselves, by using space, may create benefits for other users, intentionally or otherwise.

How is this relevant to public space and its management? Multifunctionality, diversity of users and simultaneity of use create all sorts of challenges for public space providers, such as which functions and whose needs to prioritise. Since users are also producers, producing (dis)benefits dynamically in a way that can affect others, the question arises of how providers maintain the quality of user experience for all. The very inter-dimensional richness described here hints at the logistical challenges involved both in providing and even in describing what public space is.

Conclusion

What, then, is public space? From the foregoing discussion, public space is firstly a shared common good, made up of bundles of attributes that will themselves have the characteristics variously of private, public, club/toll or common pool goods, depending on how they are consumed, when and in what circumstances. Public space is therefore a physical embodiment of a common good that provides a series of attributes valued by society and which allow its members to circulate, mingle, relax, improve their health, trade, enjoy the amenity value of green and open areas and so forth. The working definition of public space that underpins this book is therefore not restricted to design or planning typologies that emphasise shape, size or intended use. Naturally, these have a role: small neighbourhood squares are not the same as large parks or civic spaces, local streets are not the same as traffic corridors, designated open spaces in a legally recognised city plan are not the same as undeveloped spaces unofficially appropriated for leisure even if in practice they might be used in a very similar way. This definition is not restricted to normative views of what public spaces should be and which underpin most of the literature on the concept of publicness. We will deal with that concept in Chapter 3. By including the consideration of what sort of good public space is, or more precisely, what sort of goods the various attributes that make up public space are, we can investigate how these goods have been provided and managed, how users and other stakeholders engage in the provision and management of the spaces they care about, and what are the potential and risks posed by current trends in both provision and management in cities like London and Hong Kong for public space as a common good.

Secondly, and as an important part of the conceptualisation, public space as a common good refers to a particular spatiality. In these terms, public space is the contiguous spatial tissue connecting all 'private' realms. This spatially focused definition is general enough to be universal in the sense of not context specific, even if the shape and operation of any specific space to which it applies will be context specific. However, the specific logistical and spatial manifestations of governance of each of these spaces would be a context-specific socio-technical construct, and we will discuss this further in Chapter 4.

In this chapter, the 'situating of ideas' about public space underpin the conceptual framework being presented in the following chapters and which will be used to interrogate the experience of both London and Hong Kong in the second half of the book. We started by discussing the genesis of the idea of public space, where it came from, how it shaped current perceptions of what it should be and therefore what are the challenges books like this should be addressing. We tried to situate the concept and perception of public space in historical and geographical contexts before drilling down into what might be the essential elements that notions of public space try to capture. For that, we have deliberately eschewed the attention on the physical attributes of public spaces or their morphologies and focused on the societal qualities that public spaces present, which coalesce around the idea of common good, a complex and multifaceted common good. However, as we point out, if we want to understand how this particular common good is provided, we need to understand how the attributes that make it complex and multifaceted are themselves provided. We borrowed from the discussion of the nature of goods in property rights and economics and looked at how two dimensions associated with all goods – excludability and subtractability of use – relate to the attributes of the common good public space, as a starting point to the discussion about how these are provided and what the implications of that are.

The arguments presented in this chapter and summarised here serve as the background to the discussion in more depth of two key conceptual elements we need to bring together to examine the provision and management of public spaces in London and Hong Kong. The first is the concept of publicness: what the qualities are that, applied to the attributes of the common good public space, make it or its qualities 'public'. As the provision and management of public spaces requires a formulation that is more complex than the archetype of the local authority-created and run public space, the need arises to understand publicness in a way that can be applied to the multiplicity of guises in which public spaces appear, can allow for qualitative judgements about individual public spaces and can provide more robust parameters for the discussion of policies related to public spaces. The concept of publicness is the subject of the next chapter, in which we build on the insights provided Ostrom (2003, 2010), Webster (2007) and Ostrom and Hess (2010). At a general and overarching level, we will hold on to the idea of public space as a shared common good providing a bundle of attributes valued by society. We will consider what sort of goods public space offers in terms of the benefits they deliver, and to whom, how these goods have been provided and managed and the rights that are allocated in this process, how users themselves and other stakeholders exert those rights to engage in the provision and management of the spaces they care about, and what are the potential and risks posed by current trends in both provision and management in cities like London and Hong Kong for public space as a common good.

The other main conceptual element to be explored is the idea of public space governance, which will be the focus of Chapter 4. As mentioned before, public space as a common good is part of the infrastructure that binds society together, part of the trade-offs between individual and communal rights and aspirations. As such, public spaces are also loci of different and often conflictive views of what those trade-offs should be about, which types of needs and aspirations should prevail and how decisions should be reached about the possible compromises between those views. Provision and management of public space are the result of these decisions and compromises, but also shape them. We explore public space governance as the sphere in which decisions about public space are made, from who has access to it and how, to how the space is maintained, to who takes part in these decisions and how. This conceptualisation of governance will be applied to examining two things. Firstly, the reconfiguration of the institutional arrangements for managing public space in light of the patterns of change in local governance more broadly, in the 20th and 21st centuries. Secondly, in the context of shared urban spaces, the roles of different actors (for example, government, citizens, private sector and voluntary sector providers of space) in reproducing these rights regimes and, thus, 'public space' itself. This sets up the contemporary scene of public space governance in London and Hong Kong, two world cities in which these patterns, while sharing some roots, have played out quite differently.

3

The nature of publicness

Introduction

Publicness is a defining characteristic of public space. But what is publicness? Chapter 2 identified the archetypal conceptualisation of public space as being 'open for all at all times', and mostly provided by the state. The discussion in the literature tends to take that conceptualisation as its basis and take a prescriptive stance towards publicness, framing it in terms of absolute values to which any public space should aspire. This chapter argues that this type of approach might be appropriate to some iconic spaces, the ones that have universal appeal and define the character of a city, but it fails to recognise the enormous variety of public spaces and the functions they perform to different kinds of citizens, which cannot be understood just with reference to an undifferentiated standard.

This chapter proposes a concept of 'publicness' that informs the operations and operational design of public space management and provision. We start with a critical review of the diverse attributes of 'publicness' in public spaces, including 'openness for all', inclusivity, conductivity to encounters and so forth. We argue that these attributes may constitute high-level goals or principles but are abstract and do not relate easily to publicness as applied in a specific place and time.

Public space's complexity means it is not a unitary 'thing' and each public space possesses a variety of different attributes. Instead, 'publicness' of public space is a consequence of how that wide variety of 'goods' are contained, sustained, enabled or afforded so that they can be enjoyed as a complex bundle, simultaneously and dynamically. Some may be enjoyed as a public good as defined in the previous chapters, but others are enjoyed as common pool or club, or even private goods.

We go on to discuss what the concept of 'publicness' means if it needs to be interpreted for application to specific cases. We consolidate ideas around publicness, in which the form, type and degree of publicness result from the way rights are allocated to, or appropriated by, those with stakes in any particular spaces. We argue that such a publicness needs to be specific to the space it qualifies. Publicness is space and time specific.

The chapter concludes with the idea that 'publicness' – if it to be a useful guide to governing public spaces – is not a static state of abstract values, but a system of rights that is dynamically interpretable in its context of application. We propose an outline of the analytical framework that will be applied to public spaces in both London and Hong Kong in later chapters. The framework is based on the idea that publicness is maintained/given by a system of rights over three aspects: access, use, collective choice regarding public space.

Publicness in the literature

As we saw in the previous chapter, 'public space' is not an absolute concept, defining an object that can be easily spotted and separated from other spaces which would be 'non-public' or private. We argue that there are historical and geographical elements in any definition of public space and that, given the multiplicity of roles they perform in human settlements, public space is in fact a collective of spaces with different dynamics and different normatives. However, there is still a key defining character of public space that justifies the existence of the concept, which is its publicness: it having characteristics that are appropriated or used or belong to a collective, a community that goes beyond the individual and his/her closest family group.

The discussion about publicness is often dominated by an archetype-based definition of public space, which frames it in terms of universal, absolute and immutable values to which any public space should aspire. This chapter – in particular, the second section, argues that such prescriptions fail to recognise the enormous variety of public spaces, and both across those, and even in one space, the hugely diverse functions they perform to different kinds of citizens, which cannot be understood just with reference to an undifferentiated standard.

'Publicness' can be bestowed on a particular space by a combination of its position in the urban fabric, its legal status, its history, or related to the activities performed in it or made possible by it. Some conceptualisations of publicness are prescriptive, in the sense that public spaces should present certain universal characteristics to qualify as such. Spaces that do not present those characteristics would not be true public spaces, regardless of their physical characteristics or the uses taking place on them. Others are mostly normative, highlighting a series of rules and norms defining scales of publicness, often with the implicit proposition that it is incumbent upon public space managers to elevate a space along that scale (from less public to more public). Others still are descriptive and take as their starting point existing spaces recognised as public, to identify what makes them accepted as such. As we point out later, different authors draw on one or more of these features to define publicness.

For many, the defining elements of publicness reside in particular physical and legal normative attributes of a space: the extent of openness and accessibility, and the nature of the rules governing its use, as well as the sources of control over entry, accessibility and rules. Low and Smith (2006: 3) emphasise the role of rules of access, the source and nature of control over entry, the nature of sanctioned collective and individual behaviour and the rules of use as the key differentiator between public and private space. Mitchell and Staeheli (2006) see the essence of publicness residing in rights of access and of being there, for all citizens.

Others have defined publicness as a function of those same physical and legal attributes of accessibility (to place, activities, information and resources), ownership and control of the space, but have also included a prescriptive view of the functions public space should perform in order to be considered as such and the nature of those who benefit from them, such as Benn and Gauss (1983) and Akkar (2005). Similarly, Németh and Schmidt (2011) try to operationalise a measurable definition of publicness based on ownership (public or private), management (inclusive and open or exclusive and closed) and the diversity of users and uses.

Another group of authors take further the idea of publicness as related to the provision of particular functions and prescribe the social outcomes those functions should produce. Kohn (2004: 11), for instance, defines public spaces as places owned by the government, accessible to everyone without restrictions and fostering communication and interaction. The emphasis here is on the attributes of (public sector) ownership, accessibility and intersubjectivity. Publicness in this case would be a function of state control – implicitly a democratic state that would express the will of its citizens – open access to all citizens and an inherent ability of spaces that are open to anyone and under the control of democratic governments to generate a particular set of social relationships between users that could foster interaction and communication between them. Worpole and Knox (2007) base their view on the value of public space on the opportunity those spaces create for shared use and activity, meeting and exchange, regardless of ownership. These would be the defining attributes of publicness. In a similar vein, Watson (2006) emphasises public space as essentially a space of protest and for the expression of minority interests. It is the ability to provide the locus for such activities that defines publicness. Varna (2014) in turn defines publicness on the basis of ownership, modes of control, physical configuration and the degrees of animation and civility that public spaces should foster. For some, publicness is related to the creation of spaces for encounters with difference, which according to them are essential to a democratic polity (Watson 2006). Anything that reduces the possibility of such encounters would reduce publicness. The obvious questions arising from this formulation are what happens in a polity that is not fully democratic and what would be the relationship between potential encounters with difference and democracy: do they reinforce each other or does the lack of the latter constrain the former? Or, instead, are they mutually indifferent and do the encounters fostered by publicness have a more functional purpose of allowing society to function and are they only weakly related to the democracy? The corollary of many of these formulations is that any public space should perform particular functions by definition and foster a particular type of social relations as a condition for being called public.

However, the social outcomes of processes such as communication and interaction between strangers in public space might not happen as often or in the manner these authors suggest, even in the spaces most conducive to these interactions. Non-verbal interaction and communication between people co-present in a public space might be very important for the functioning of society (see Ikegami 2000), but the social outcomes of those processes might be complex and contradictory, and not the clear causal link between co-mingling and a more open and inclusive society as sometimes depicted in the literature. There is also plenty of evidence in psychology studies showing that the depth and likelihood of different levels of interpersonal relations depend more on issues of trust than on the qualities of the space where these might happen, and therefore could not be considered as an intrinsic characteristic of a space but are, rather, far more dependent on the social context in which the space is inserted (see, for example, Di Masso 2012). In the same vein, Amin (2008) suggests that some of the 'fostering civility and identity' attributes of public space are increasingly played out in non-spatial parts of the public sphere such as the internet, and, furthermore, for those attributes to be realised in any particular space a set of other social and cultural conditions need to be present that go well beyond the mere existence of a space, no matter what its attributes might be. They are not therefore attributes of the space but of society in its relationship with a space.

The majority of these formulations of publicness also suggest an absolute idea of public space, which would have certain prescribed physical and legal attributes, would function under certain norms, its attributes and benefits would be accessible by everyone, and should foster communication among users and a sense of civility and identity, leading to a more open and tolerant society. The more a public space does that, the more public it is, and the closer it is to an ideal type against which all others should be measured. Publicness, therefore, would be a universal and absolute concept with a measurable dimension, with spaces being more or less public the closer or further they are to the norm. The search for this quantifiable dimension of publicness informs a significant part of the publicness literature (see, for example, Varna 2014, or Németh and Schmidt 2011 and the many subsequent papers which try to apply their method), and its concern with measuring the degree of publicness in different public spaces either to express value judgements about spaces of different kinds or under different regimes, or to inform urban design practice or policy.

However, whereas it might be desirable in some circumstances that all parts of the physical public realm should conform to the same norms and standards as those public spaces considered as exemplars, the fact is that they do not and, given the wide difference in context and purpose among urban public spaces, there is no reason why they should (Carmona 2015). Most people would agree that good public spaces should be fit for purpose and perform their functions well, whatever these might be, but actual public spaces, accepted by everyone as such, do not always do so. Moreover, we cannot reasonably expect an iconic civic space with citywide and even global symbolic significance, such as Trafalgar Square in London or the Piazza Del Campo in Siena or Tiananmen Square in Beijing, will perform the same functions and produce the same social outcomes as a local community playground, a quiet resting space tucked away in a residential neighbourhood or a local commercial street. What may be a strength in one case can be a blight in another.

The point we are making is that, rather than absolute parameters and an ideal end state, actual publicness by necessity involves relative attributes, which might be more or less depending on the particular circumstances of a public space and might vary within the same space as those circumstances dictate.

Let us consider the attribute of openness, the ability of everyone to access a public space as the main criterion of publicness. Even if a space is theoretically accessible to everyone (that is, no paying of fees or entrance restrictions), it does not mean that in practice this is the case. People might not access a space because they live far from it, or transport is not adequate or is costly. There might be other obstacles to access, such as for instance the closure of parks and squares after dusk, with the result that no one can access them at night, as is the case of many of the historic public spaces in London. Some public spaces might be freely and openly accessible, but there might be restrictions on the use of some attributes of those spaces. Streets would be understood by most people as public space, but one might be not allowed to park a car everywhere, as there might be restrictions on the use of this attribute of the space. It might be restricted to residents as in many residential streets in cities all over the world, or it might be subject to payment – and therefore selection and exclusion – as in many urban commercial areas.

Discussing public goods and the idea of complete openness to consumption by everyone (in the sense of unrestricted access and use) that should characterise them, Webster (2002) argues that very few of these goods – public spaces included – are really public if the definition is to be taken to the letter. After all, most of these goods are in reality congestible, exhaustible and, as we will show, excludable too. A person's ability to benefit from many important attributes of public space, as for instance openness of access and use, will depend on several factors, and in many respects those attributes will be consumed as club goods – that is, goods for which there is degree of exclusion – by those not excluded from them by, for example, access costs, property prices. Moreover, what might be perceived as a perfectly acceptable constraint to publicness in a particular context, say the lockdown of a neighbourhood park or square in the evening for management purposes, or the fencing off of a bit of a local park to create a child/parent-only space, will more likely be perceived as a restriction on public access and use if it happens in a large civic space in the centre of a metropolis.

Besides not being amenable to framing in absolute ways and being relative to context, public space attributes might or might not be complementary. The attributes of a public space might be valued differently by their users: some will be looking for a space for relaxation, some for exercise, some for meeting their peers, some will be looking for a place to walk a dog, or the fastest route from A to B, and so forth, and are likely to value those attributes that allow them to better do whatever they are seeking from the space more highly than those that don't. In fact, the attributes that facilitate a particular use of a public space might just make another use more difficult (as, for example, the restriction on ball games in many open spaces to protect the attribute of peacefulness and safety).

All this suggests we should think of publicness as a composite concept, made up of qualities linked to the various attributes of public space, which will not be necessarily complementary and might even be conflictive, and whose presence and intensity will be highly context dependent. Some of the literature already cited does indeed try to capture the variety and difference among publicness attributes when trying to formulate an ideal and universal degree of publicness. Varna (2014), for instance, uses spidergrams with different spokes to measure the intensity of different publicness attributes. Similarly, Németh and Schmidt (2011) apply different scales to measure the degree of quality of the attributes they consider more significant. However, the foregoing arguments raise the issue that these efforts to obtain an ideal and absolute degree of publicness, allowing for quite diverse public spaces to be compared to one another and classified along a scale, might be missing a trick.

The question this chapter raises is whether there is any sense in treating publicness as a universal absolute concept when trying to understand issues affecting real public spaces and the potential actions that can be taken to address those issues. The foregoing argument reinforces the idea that publicness should be seen as a conveyor of a relative set of qualities: for any public space, there will be attributes that are more public or less public, more open and accessible or less open and accessible, depending on the criteria used to define the limits between publicness and privateness, but also on the manner in which those attributes are consumed.

What type of good is public space?

The idea of publicness as a relative concept, shaped by the particular negotiations that take place in each context, is not new and does not in itself represent a negation of the very idea of publicness as something that should be all inclusive and encompass everyone. If we agree with Arendt that plurality is the main condition for political life (Arendt 1998), it could be argued that any attempt at reducing this plurality to a homogeneous abstraction – that is, the people or the society – undermines the political dimension that is part and parcel of the notion of publicness. In this sense, the idea of public space as a space for everyone as an undifferentiated collective would actually be less inclusive than the idea of a space in which individual stakes are recognised and negotiated among concrete individuals. Following this logic, it could be argued that publicness has to do more with the way in which this negotiation process happens – and therefore relative to context – than with a predetermined definition.

In a similar way, this differential appropriation of the space and its attributes would bring us closer to what Lefebvre (1991) calls 'differential space', in which the particularities of the context are recognised and placed at the forefront of the negotiations defining the use of the space and its publicness. Public space as a normative ideal would represent an absolute concept, a totality. That totality would overrule the 'lived space' in which users negotiate and define the rules for the appropriation of the attributes of each individual space, in favour of a 'conceived space' in which those rules are externally fixed and contextless. In this regard, the idea of a public space in which all attributes are in principle always equally accessible to all overlooks the particularities of each space – the particular set of social relations and physical attributes that produce that space. Consequently, the idealised, normative form of public space would be one that masks or supresses the negotiation of rules of appropriation between stakeholders.

With that in mind, how can we approach a conceptualisation of publicness that recognises that public spaces are different, that they have many attributes that are valued differently by users, that there are important contextual variations shaping the interplay between publicness and privateness, openness and exclusion, and that these apply in different and often conflictive ways to the functions that can be performed in any given space? To define and evaluate 'publicness' across the hugely diverse range of specific public spaces requires criteria that are interpreted in each of those context-specific concrete situations.

In the previous chapter we defined public space as a common good (one that society provides to its members to fulfil a relational obligation to care for particular common interests, and in the process allowing society to function as such). Public and publicness in this sense are commonly understood as the opposite of private when discussing the broader set of common goods of which public space is one case. We talk about public housing, public transport, public services and so forth, as opposed to their private equivalents. The differentiation is variously based on the mode of delivery and who does it, the scope and composition of the recipients of the good, the magnitude and intensity of roles of those goods in reinforcing bonds in society, the degree of public accountability to which they are subjected and so forth (see Haque 2001). In this sense, and especially in welfare state societies with a large role of the state and the public sector in the provision of public goods, common goods are generally viewed as goods that are or should be provided by the public sector for all citizens, out of tax revenues, and synonymous with public goods.

We have also made the point that what distinguishes a good that is public from one that is private – and other categories in between – is whether one person or many can benefit from/consume it simultaneously and whether people can be excluded from benefitting from/consuming it, therefore restricting the numbers of beneficiaries/consumers (see Ostrom 2003). In principle, a good that everyone can benefit from fully and which is available to all is a public good, while a good that can be made available to specific individuals, who will be the only people benefitting from it, is a private good.

However, when we talk about public space as a good, we are using this word as a shorthand for a bundle of different attributes, each of them a good in its own terms, some derived from public space as a physical entity, some from the uses that can take place on it because of its morphology, facilities or location, some from the nature of the users and some still from the psychological and social impact the space has on the users and their interactions. Also, these are attributes that will be consumed in different degrees and different forms by different users. Some of these will by their very nature be more public in the sense of not excluding anyone from enjoying them, others will be less so. Some might even require restrictions on other users. Take, for instance those attributes associated with being there in the space, which in an open public space can be enjoyed by anyone with the means to go there without excluding anyone. Never mind that, as we pointed out earlier, one's very being there and occupying space, strictly speaking, privatises that very space, as others are excluded from using it at the same time. Compare those with the attributes associated with vistas over the space or the increasing amenity value the space provides, which will be appropriated privately by property owners to the exclusion of others. While both 'view' and 'space occupation' have privatised something, the latter does so momentarily, the former, more 'permanently' – a greater effort would have to go to change who appropriates the attribute 'view'(for example, selling the property).

Or take the attributes of public space that are affected by congestion, in which the enjoyment of it by one person or a group of people will prevent others from enjoying the same or another attribute, as happens in congested streets or parks. The space of public space is, strictly speaking, a common pool resource, as it is quite easily congestible and exhaustible if overused.

That said, many resources in public space will be consumed as club/toll goods – that is, goods for which there is degree of exclusion but non-rivalrous consumption – by those not excluded from them by mechanisms such as access costs or property prices. However, we will show through other examples in this chapter that momentary, and more permanent club goods are created and consumed all the time in public space, due to the simultaneity of use and the ubiquity of externalities in public space.

While, clearly, any public space, be it a local park, iconic square or residential street, will present a wide array of attributes, valued and used differently by different people, who will also value differently the public or private nature of those attributes, even the same space or same feature can be valued differently by different users. Physical openness, the access to facilities, the symbolic qualities, the capacity to foster a particular use, the amenity value, the health benefits, comfort, safety, aesthetic qualities, functionality and so forth are all attributes valued differently by users and beneficiaries of a public space and with different public/private profiles. A user of a public swimming pool in one of London's lidos might value the swimming facility attribute of the space, rather than its ambience, and also value the ticketing and booking arrangements that prevent congestion and make swimming lanes more private. Similarly, residents around a local park might value tranquillity and visual amenity more than visitors, might view congestion from a different perspective and might welcome surveillance measures, gating and closure arrangements and anything that discourages excessive use by strangers, such as, for example, residents-only parking restrictions that make access by non-residents difficult. The point is that all public spaces, no matter what their physical attributes are, the functions they are supposed to perform in the urban tissue or the activities they should stimulate, or the types of behaviour they should foster, will have attributes that are more or less accessible, more or less open, more or less public and more or less private.

These different and often conflictive valuings of the attributes of public space suggest that public spaces are above all places of conflict as well as of synergy and complementarity, where different expectations come together and need to be made compatible with each other through restrictions, compromises and consensus building – and we discuss this in the next chapter. However synergetic and harmonised these expectations might become, those attributes will still be valued differently and different groups will still seek to maximise their access to those they value.

The implication of the foregoing is that publicness, however defined, might actually mean different things to different people as their ability to benefit/consume attributes of a public space will be different. Ascribing absolute values to publicness, in the sense of fixing the values that define a public space as public means masking the fact that these values will express the way particular groups appropriate/benefit from the various attributes of that space. It could be argued that in a democratic polity, what is publicness in the sense of what attributes public space should have, who should benefit from them and to what extent, is set in a democratic arena – usually to the mediation of elected local governments and their policies. However, this still means that in effect different public spaces situated in different geographical and social contexts even within the same location might have different distributions of the attributes of publicness, as translated by varying combinations of interests and the respective mobilisation ability of the relevant constituencies for each space. The same applies to the proposition that publicness, in the sense of the ability to access and use the attributes of a public space, should always benefit the more disadvantaged sectors of society as a principle (see, for instance, Kohn 2004 or the various essays in Madanipour, Knierbein and Degros 2014). No matter how laudable this position might be, the fact remains that in practice many of the attributes of public space are not in the power of governments to regulate or policy to shape, and the actual context of a space will determine how attributes are used and appropriated. A local green space deep within a wealthy neighbourhood, with parking restrictions around it and away from public transport connections might be theoretically accessible and usable by all members of society, but in practice it will not be. Even in spaces that are accessible by all, attributes that have direct impact on property values such as vistas or amenity effects will not be to the benefit of all.

How can we, therefore, express the concept of publicness with all its relativity and nuances in a way that recognises the contemporary challenges to public space and provides the tools for tackling them through appropriate forms of public space governance?

Outlines of an operable, context-specific concept of publicness

As we saw in the previous chapter, public space is not easily or immutably distinguished from other spaces which would be non-public or private. We saw that the concept of public is not intrinsic to a morphotype but is socially constructed; both what resources or goods are public (in the sense of how they are consumed) and to what extent they are public (in the sense of openness to consumption) are contingent on specific context and on the constraints on their use arising by design or otherwise. In the following paragraphs we summarise three ideas we have sketched earlier that are relevant to this discussion and to the conceptualisation of publicness which we then present in the following section.

The first idea is that publicness is context specific to the space and the attributes of the space it qualifies. Here we discuss publicness as applied to public space and its attributes by reflecting on the implications of those features of public space's spatiality, discussed in Chapter 2, for an operational concept of publicness (that is, a concept that can be applied to a specific space and inform its governance and management): complexity, diversity of stakeholders, simultaneity of use, dynamic production of externalities, co-production of public space attributes. Publicness is also specific to the level of abstraction at which it is applied, whether we are applying it as a general abstract principle or as a specific operationalised dimension. Throughout this chapter we have argued that high-level abstract principles of publicness such as openness to all and unrestricted freedom of action can provide aspirations and ideals but will not easily fit with the constraints present in actual public spaces and will provide poor guidance to their management.

The second idea is that publicness is abstraction-level specific. General and abstract conceptualisations of publicness as set out in the literature in the first section of this chapter do not account for the wide variety of public spaces, their attributes and the hugely diverse functions that public spaces perform for different citizens. We have argued that such values might just be a generic description of the qualities of some iconic spaces with citywide and even global symbolic significance, but, as we said before, they will be ill-suited to understand, assess and manage other kinds of public space such as local public spaces of interest mostly to local residents. The same qualities valued in the iconic spaces taken as abstract values might even be detrimental to the functions and qualities of those local public spaces.

Even in those iconic spaces, the oft-cited universal defining characteristics of public space, such as openness and freedom of use, are only ever applicable as high-level principles. For example, in London's iconic Trafalgar Square, there is a by-law against playing musical instruments without an appropriate licence. This presumably prevents the space from being swamped by buskers or performers, who might conflict with the desire of other users to enjoy the space for a whole lot of other purposes. In Hong Kong, the infamous removal of a pioneer pedestrianised zone in Sai Yeung Choi Street South, bringing back vehicle traffic with its attendant noise and pollution, was deemed the only solution to the inability of the government to manage uncontrolled busking within the existing legal framework.

Both these examples are illustrations of the principle of needing to restrict the actions of some users so as to enable publicness for all. In all public spaces, there are users who, by their actions, produce attributes of the space for others, and some of these actions are subject to restrictions to truly enable the overarching high-level public benefit to be realised for everyone. Openness for all as an abstract and high-level feature of publicness can be delivered only if there is in practice restriction of openness for some activities and persons. Therefore, the operational specification of publicness in specific cases may run counter to those prescribed at the high level in order for them to be ultimately and overarchingly public.

The third idea is that publicness is space and time/historically and geographically context specific. The difference between a principle's abstractness and the specificity of its application means that publicness in the latter configuration is necessarily the outcome of a process of interpretation, as discussed earlier. This interpretation must take into account the nature of the actual public space – its complexity, diversity, use dynamics, co-produced nature and the simultaneity of its use, and its externality-producing nature at a point in time and space – so that an appropriate distribution of benefits between different stakeholders in that space must also be appropriate to the place and time in which 'publicness' is applied. This would mean considering social, economic, political and governance norms of that context, as well as the specific context of application. The implication of this is that operational publicness might actually mean different things to different people in different periods, as their ability to benefit/consume attributes of a public space will be different. Another implication is that this recognition of the varying meaning of publicness through place and time also recognises that the fact that particular groups appropriate/benefit from the various attributes of that space in particular ways, and that changes as the context in which they do so changes. Since public space has diverse stakeholders, including diverse users, and often using the space intensely, delivering publicness at an operational level means a distribution of benefits to stakeholders that is socio-politically acceptable to and, ideally, sufficiently agreed by stakeholders.

These basic ideas about publicness are central to how an operational concept of the term can be constructed. This is what we try to do in the next section.

Publicness as the allocation of rights

We have so far laid the foundation for the key point in this chapter which we present here, which is this: 'publicness' – if it to be a useful concept for the governing of public spaces – is not a static state of abstract values, but the result of a dynamic allocation of rights over public spaces and their attributes, which needs to be interpreted and understood in the actual context (place and time) in which it takes place.

We sustain in this book that the key to understanding publicness is to understand to what extent different groups and individuals can benefit from the various attributes of a public space and how they can do it. Elinor Ostrom bases her work on the nature of the institutions that have emerged to manage common pool resources – resources that are open to all but for which consumption is subtractable, such as fisheries or rural water systems – on the idea that social dilemmas and problems of collective action can be better understood and acted upon through identifying how different rights over the attributes of goods are allocated among their various users. As mentioned in the previous chapter, Webster (2002) and Webster and Lai (2003) take a similar approach in their propositions about how to understand the evolution of cities and manage the collective action problems urban life poses through a property rights approach: how rights over different goods and their attributes evolve, change and are reallocated.

These authors draw on an earlier literature on bundles of rights associated with any particular good or attribute of a good to explore the implications for the management of that good that come from the ways those rights are allocated to different stakeholders. Schlager and Ostrom (1992) talk about rights of access, withdrawal, management, exclusion and alienation over common pool resources as those that result from the rules and institutions that regulate the use and management of a resource. These rights can be de jure and clearly defined in legislation or de facto, resulting from custom and socially accepted practices. Some of these rights are operational rights, that is, they imply an authority to do something (for example, to access a space or to use a facility), whereas others are collective action rights, that is, rights that define future rights to be exercised, such as management or exclusion rights.

As we discussed earlier, public space is in fact a composite good with a multiplicity of attributes that have the characteristics of variously public, private, club/toll and common pool goods. What defines these characteristics is the nature of the rights associated with those attributes and who they are allocated to. This allocation of rights over the attributes of a public space to the many real or potential users would define the publicness of these attributes, its nature and degree.

The corollary of this proposition is that publicness is not primarily about fixed parameters intrinsic to all public spaces, which can be measured in each space and compared against others. Instead, publicness is about rights: operational rights of users of public space to enjoy the attributes they value and collective choice rights to act to protect those attributes, especially when they are threatened by whatever reason, including congestion or other detracting activities. Moreover, in the course of the life of a public space those rights are not fixed but will be redistributed among those with a stake in that space as these stakeholders use their voice and power to reshape the redistribution of rights in their favour. The way rights over public space are defined, recognised and exerted is also part of the story. It constitutes the institutional set-up for publicness, the mechanisms through which society recognises the public character of public spaces, manages potential conflicts between stakeholders exerting their rights with different views and aspirations and sanctions those who transgress them.

Furthermore, what are basic overarching rights associated with the use of any public space as a resource, and how widely these rights are distributed and to whom, and how they are actually exercised, will not be the same for different public spaces. As we discussed earlier, the context in which those rights exist, the nature of the stakeholders involved and the attributes they seek to have rights over might well be different. The nature of the stakeholders and attributes of an iconic urban square will be fundamentally different from those of a very local community playground area. Consequently, rights to use the place as a locus of political and civic expression will be fundamental attributes, frequently exercised, of publicness in Trafalgar Square or similar iconic civic spaces but will not figure prominently or at all in a local green space organised around a children's playground.

Following the foregoing reasoning, this book proposes a view of publicness based on how the attributes of public space are accessed and used by those with an interest in a space – the stakeholders – understanding it as the result of the allocation of rights over those attributes. The outcome of this process can have many forms rather than a single ideal one, depending on the context and the interests at play (see De Magalhães 2010). The distribution of operational rights associated with openness and accessibility to the attributes of a public space are certainly key elements of what we understand as publicness, but this is only partly determined by the design and morphology of the space or by the regime of provision of those attributes, whether by government, private agents or communal organisation: it is also the result of arrangements and negotiations between interests – those of users of different kinds, residents, public bodies, managers and so forth. The publicness of a space or of any of its attributes is an expression of how many and the extent to which different interests in those are contemplated and met. By looking at the distribution of rights and responsibilities over a space, it is possible to conceptualise 'publicness' in a way that takes into account the conflicts and tensions that characterise the sharing of that space as well as the power relations within it. At the same time, it allows for an understanding of how these conflicts and tensions are managed and governed, and on whose behalf.

Conceiving publicness as defined by the nature of the rights over the various attributes of a public space and by their allocation implies that different attributes of the same public space present their own 'publicness' profile of where they are in the public–private continuum. Users of that space will value these attributes differently and will react to, for example, pressures associated with congestion and decline of amenity value of those attributes. The result might be a rearrangement in the respective rights different users will have in relation to different attributes of that space, which might be formally recognised or not. The shape of this new reconfiguration of rights will depend among, other things, on whether those users have their voice heard and the power to renegotiate their rights over an attribute they value, or whether they cannot secure those rights, vote with their feet and move away in search of similar attributes and rights over them elsewhere – the exit option in Hirschman's (1970) exit or voice binary.

This is what is behind the transfer of some rights over public space to particular groups of users as, for example, when a park's friends group manages to obtain some power over the management of that park, possibly to use their own resources to make up for levels of maintenance and investment that are below what they would like to see. Or similarly, when the full management of a public space is transferred to a not-for-profit trust that is capable and willing to raise the necessary resources to renovate a park and takes over the responsibility to manage that public space over the long term. The same reconfiguration of publicness rights is at play when private developers are made to provide new public space as part of their planning obligations, with the legal obligation to keep the space open and accessible but negotiate with the public authorities to retain legal ownership and the right to manage that space because the potential occupiers of the development would want a level of maintenance higher than what public sector budgets can provide. It is the same process again when residents set up a Neighbourhood Watch group and take it upon themselves to keep an eye on the safety of the street, supplying information to the police and exerting the right to decide what constitutes suspicious or threatening behaviour in their streets and, ultimately, who is not welcome to it. Conversely, outmigration from declining urban neighbourhoods by those with the means to do so to gated communities, in search of better level of, and more control over, a better quality of public realm is a clear example of the exit option.

What types of rights should, then, define the publicness of a public space? The attributes people might value in parks, squares, streets and other places we might consider as public spaces are many – from the simple right to be there, the right to use their facilities, to enjoy the health and amenity benefits of open space, to circulate unimpeded, to the right of have some agency on what happens to a public space one cares about, on how it is managed, how its symbolic elements are treated, how exclusion rules might be shaped and so forth. As we have affirmed many times before, they are also context dependent.

For a conceptualisation of publicness that should apply in contexts as different as those in the two cities discussed in this book, we should group those rights in a way that is universal enough to make sense in multiple situations and contexts, while simultaneously retaining the ability to address the specific conditions of individual public spaces. Schlager and Ostrom (1992) list a number of basic rights associated with common pool resources, reflecting the different kinds of generic attributes those involved in the use of those resources will try to acquire, and whose distribution among those people will shape how the resource is governed. As we have seen, these are grouped into operational and collective choice rights. Both are loosely associated with the twin concepts of spatiality and sharedness, discussed in Chapter 2.

For public spaces, we should look at the basic rights associated with any space that is generally perceived as public. The first of these is the right of access, since the general expectation is that a public space should be provided and managed in a way that secures a relative open access to most members of society (the 'openness to all' principle discussed earlier). Rights of access encompass rules and mechanisms that regulate whatever restrictions there might be on how individuals access the attributes they value in a particular public space, be they physical access to the site or the access to a facility or other attribute.

There is also the expectation that people who have physical access to that space would be able to use it and enjoy its attributes (physical, symbolic and so forth) – that is, the right of use – without other restrictions than those dictated by broadly accepted social norms of behaviour and rights of other users. Rights of use refer to the rules and codes of behaviour, and enforcement mechanisms that regulate how individuals that have access to a public space can enjoy its attributes, be they physical attributes or, for example, the confirmation of a symbolic function.

Rights of access and use are basic operational rights generally associated with the idea of public space and its public character. However, the very notion of public is also associated with collective choice rights: the expectation that the users of a public space, the public, would have some say on key decisions regarding its management and future, even if indirectly through some form of representation mechanism, so that they can protect the attributes they value, and that their stake in the space is recognised as a form of ownership. This does not have to mean necessarily ownership of the space *strictu sensu*, but that represented by a degree of agency and power to have a say on what happens to the space. These rights include the right of management (the right to have a say in, and influence what happens to the space, how it is managed, maintained and run); the right of exclusion (the right to have a say in, and influence decisions on what uses should or should not take pace in a space, what behaviours are and are not allowed and, ultimately, which users can access the space and on what terms).

These collective choice rights could be all grouped under the title of rights of agency: the right to have some form of control over a public space. These rights would be expressed in the rules and mechanisms through which the various stakes in a particular public space are recognised and heard in its governance and management, and through which conflicts and disputes between different stakes are addressed.

These rights might be allocated through the legal instruments that allocate rights over common goods in a society to all citizens, or through specific contractual arrangements between public space providers and representatives of the citizenry or of groups within it, or through ad hoc negotiations between public space providers and managers and groups of users, or, as often happens, through a combination of all of those. Users of public space might exert their rights of access and use within the terms set in by-laws and regulations establishing the terms for use and access to public spaces in a locality and have their agency rights determined by the nature of their relationship with local government as citizens. In other circumstances, they might exert those operational rights within the terms set in agreements and contracts between local government and the private provider and manager of a public space, and exert their collective choice rights indirectly through the client role of local government vis-à-vis the private contractor. In other circumstances still, all those rights, including collective choice ones, might be transferred to a group of users who have manage to obtain power to shape them and determine the extent of their allocation to other users.

Therefore, publicness could be defined as a function of the basic rights of access, use and agency over a public space and its attributes, and the nature of the distribution and exercise of those rights. These will be allocated to all those with a stake in a public space through a variety of mechanisms that will necessarily include estate actions (through laws, regulations and contractual agreements), market rules (as in the amenity and other benefits accruing to surrounding property owners) and collective political action, when communities or groups of stakeholders take over state functions and circumvent market mechanisms in pursuit of their own interests. Most of the discussion on commons and commoning that has become part of the discourse around public space and the need to go beyond the dichotomy public–private can be synthesised in a discussion about which rights are allocated to various groups and communities and how this happens (see Foster 2011).

The allocation and exercise of the many rights that make up publicness to a variety of different and occasionally antagonistic groups of stakeholders is a dynamic process which involves mobilisation, negotiation and compromises. The continuous process through which this happens, and publicness rights are defined, bundled up, unbundled and allocated to the various parties defines public space governance. We will explore the concept in the next chapter.

Conclusion

What this chapter strongly suggests is that the analysis and guidance for action around public spaces and their modes of provision in a complex metropolis is not amenable to simplistic formulations about some public spaces being more public than others and ideas about reducing all public spaces to one particular conceptual formulation. More accurately, those formulations of more or less public also need to be understood in relation to whether they are operating at an abstract general level or a concrete, specific one.

The assumption this chapter has made, and which will be explored in the context of London and Hong Kong in the following chapters, is that, as public spaces are diverse, play different roles and attend to different interests and aspirations, so are the actual forms publicness assumed in each of them. Different allocation of publicness rights and forms of allocating those rights might or might not be adequate for what its stakeholders intend and aspire for each of these spaces, and the combination and distribution of these different spaces and different forms of publicness might or might not be desired for a city.

Therefore, the main aim of this chapter has been to present a conceptualisation of publicness which is centred on the rights allocated to the users of the attributes of public spaces or those with a stake in them. As discussed in the chapter, these rights can be summarised as the operational rights of access and use, and a more varied bundle of rights grouped under the collective rights of agency. The argument in the chapter has also been that publicness is contextual and variable, as it relates to the relationship between the users of a public space and the bundle of attributes they value in that space, and this will be different in time and space. That conceptualisation seeks to understand how public spaces of different kinds perform their functions, taking into account the reality that this happens in different contexts, with different sets of stakeholders with varying interests and aspirations and benefitted differently by the allocation of publicness rights. By incorporating this diversity, we hope to provide a finer-grained understanding of public spaces themselves, their role in urban life and, of more relevance to policy and practice, the challenges to public space governance that come with those different arrangements that allocate publicness rights to different stakeholders in different degrees, therefore shaping the way people experience cities.

We will explore these issues in Chapters 6 to 8 in both London and Hong Kong, but before we can do that, we need to understand and conceptualise public space governance, that is, the policy and practice sphere in which the diverse interests on public spaces come together, negotiate and compromise and, as a consequence, rights over public space are allocated and reallocated.

4

The governance and management of public space

Introduction

Publicness is very much dependent on public space governance arrangements. Who has the power to regulate rules of use and access to a public space, who determines how the space is maintained, what is preserved and what is not, how a space is resourced and how any capital investment is deployed, and who coordinates how all this takes place ultimately determines who and how benefits from a space and its attributes, hence its publicness.

This chapter thus expands the argument presented in the previous chapter into a conceptualisation of public space governance. The chapter develops further a conceptual framework of public space governance put forward by the authors in previous work. It examines the mechanisms that govern the allocation and exercise of rights to publicness attributes – including the rights to manage the space, and how disputes and conflicts between different interests are addressed. The chapter develops arguments put forward by Elinor Ostrom and others to develop this conceptual framework in which the definition of publicness as discussed in the previous chapter is translated into governance tasks and made a part of the daily life of public spaces. The chapter presents public space governance as the constant rearrangement of allocated rights over the attributes of those spaces, responding to pressures from different stakeholders and shaped by sets of rules that regulate that rearrangement. It makes the point that the way public spaces are governed, that is, how the rights over publicness attributes are allocated and managed, and the conflicts that emerge from that process are negotiated, is itself an important constituent of publicness. This is especially so if publicness is seen not as static but as the dynamic result of the interplay between the interests of different stakeholders and their relative power to transform them into rights. Both this and the preceding chapter provide the main framework for examining public space issues in London and Hong Kong.

Public space governance and management: what is it and how it relates to publicness

In the previous two chapters we made the point that what defines a public space, well beyond any physical or regulatory typology, is the nature of rights citizens might have in relation to the attributes they value in that space. We suggested which rights over these attributes are more significant in defining publicness and made the point that the allocation of those rights is context dependent, and will vary with the nature of the space, its location in the urban fabric and the nature of those with a stake in a particular space. It will also vary over time, as the character of a location changes and, with it, the relative composition of stakeholders, as forms of local governance change, and as the physical layout of the space adjusts to pressures coming from use and the passage of time.

Public space governance is actions that allocate rights in public space. In public space governance's sphere of action, decisions are taken regarding these rights that might privilege particular interests, aspirations and opportunities instead of others. This 'sphere' involves, then, the ensemble of institutions, mechanisms, rules and modi operandi in which management decisions are made, conflicting interests are brought together, disputes are arbitrated and rights over public space attributes are assigned. The making of strategic choices about provision and management takes place in this sphere, and the definition of how the four processes that make up management are carried out and by whom, which ultimately shapes the distribution of rights and responsibilities over public spaces and their attributes.

Thus, publicness is very much dependent on public space governance arrangements because the management of a space, its physical maintenance and management of all the social process that take place in it, as well as how that space has been designed, are critically important in determining how that space is used, for what and by whom. Publicness is intrinsically linked to the management of that space, which can therefore increase it or decrease it, or do so for some stakeholders and not others. This is the focus of this chapter. Taking forward the idea that publicness is a function of the rights over the attributes of a public space, the chapter now discusses the mechanisms through which those rights over public space attributes are allocated, how they relate to the way a space is governed and managed, how the conflicts of interest between stakeholders are negotiated and how the fabric and the attributes of a public space are maintained.

We should start with a short clarification of the concepts of governance and management, as they might appear occasionally interchangeable. Governance refers to all patterns of rule in pursuit of solving societal problems, but also grasping societal opportunities (Kooiman 2003, Bevir 2009). If we emphasise the 'all' in 'all patterns of rule', this implies that the scope of governance can stretch from determining normative aims and values, including the design of systems to manage public space politics, all the way down the operational minutiae of everyday street cleansing and emptying the bins, where it clearly overlaps with the idea of management. Governance actions are not limited to those by governments and include those that are enacted by private, community or voluntary sector actors and even users, and that contribute towards achieving governance aims. In this sense, the concept of governance is closely linked to the idea of co-production of common goods and services (Goss 2001). Management, on the other hand, tends to be associated with techniques of governing, under pre-established normative parameters. The implication is that 'public space management' would take as given normative values that should govern public space and concerns how those values are translated into objective actions.

If publicness of public space is to be defined by the configuration of rights to access, rights to use and agency rights, then the concept of management might be sufficient to enforce rights already determined, or design implementation of some operational rights, but high-level principles of how societal problems and opportunities involving public space are subject to patterns of rule must surely be addressed by governance. Yet, since the term public space management is in far wider use, both in practice and in academia, we can say that public space management can be defined as the sphere, within public space governance, in which societal demands on and aspirations for public space are articulated and realised. This takes place through the intersection of four sets of processes (Carmona, De Magalhães and Hammond 2008, De Magalhães and Carmona 2009). Here, we set these out briefly before exploring how publicness is affected by alternative arrangements of each process.

The first set of processes relates to investment and resourcing, the process of securing financial and material resources and utilising them in day-to-day management tasks and in capital funding as and when significant redesign and redevelopment are required. In public spaces that are owned and maintained by public bodies, the allocation of resources to them reflects those bodies' spending priorities, which might or might not have been determined through consultation with the main users and stakeholders and would be the result of processes for determining policies and the resources to implement them, with varying degrees of transparency.

The second set of processes involves the definition and deployment of maintenance routines. In order to keep a public space functional and capable of offering the attributes for which it is valued, it needs to be physically maintained. As with any physical good, public spaces and their infrastructure and equipment are subject to wear and tear, decay and the pressures of use and, often, overuse. Part of the process of managing public spaces requires the setting and deploying of procedures and routines that ensure that public spaces are usable, uncluttered, clean and safe, that the surfaces of roads, street furniture, lighting, vegetation and facilities of all sorts are kept to desired standards. Although for the most part this is a managerial and technical set of activities, it is far from being neutral and with no wider significance. Defining maintenance routines, especially in resource-constrained situations, means prioritising uses, levels of quality and attributes of a space, often to the detriment of others, with direct implications for which interests in that space are favoured, which users benefit more and which less. As many examples of poorly maintained public space suggest, maintenance decisions can change the character of a space and compromise its viability.

The third set of processes is the regulation of uses and conflicts between uses: the processes through which rules for using and accessing public spaces are set, the framework for solving conflicts between uses is defined, codes of behaviour in public space are agreed upon and rule enforcement powers are distributed. How this is done and who does it can vary and have varied, as we discuss in more length later in the chapter. This regulation happens through devices such as municipal by-laws, ordinances and sets of rules established by the body responsible for a public space. These rules set out what can and cannot be done in a public space; define conditions for access to the space or its parts, such as opening times, and access limitations to children's play areas; and establish rules of behaviour for those using the space (such as restrictions on the production of noise or alcohol consumption), all in addition to laws and general rules of behaviour that govern social interaction in society as a whole.

The fourth and final set of processes encompasses the practices and activities associated with the coordination of the multitude of interventions in any particular public space implicit in the three previous sets of processes. They are the practices through which the actions of the wide array of people and organisations involved in the previous three processes are brought together and coordinated. In recent history, local authorities and other public bodies have tended to hold the responsibility for coordinating the actions and processes of upkeeping a public space, resourcing it, programming and carrying out major works, and setting out the regulations for its use. Coordinating all these activities would have been an implicit and natural consequence of the fact that many of those spaces would have been owned by those public bodies and maintenance, investment and regulation activities would have been carried out in-house. However, even in those circumstances, it was not unusual that many components of those activities were carried out independently by different departments within the same public body, with very little coordination between them – the 'silo' problem identified in the literature (Richards et al 1999, Bundred 2006). Research from the early 2000s in England showed how many of the activities of public space management were dispersed among several departments of the same local authority, often with little coordination among them (ODPM 2004). Indeed, this lack of coordination has been one among the reasons behind pressures to adopt private sector management practices, contracting-out of maintenance activities and devolution of management responsibilities for parks to stakeholders outside the public sector (De Magalhães and Carmona 2006, De Magalhães 2010).

These four interlinked governance processes of coordination, maintenance, investment and regulation, acting on a particular space with its own locational context and physical characteristics, continuously shape how that space can be accessed and used, and how users and other stakeholders interact with the management body and express to them their interests and intentions with regard to that space, and determine which of those interests are prioritised and how inevitable conflicts between different views and aspirations are addressed.

In the next section we will first introduce a brief history of public space governance, before describing the evolution of some of the themes that have shaped the investment, maintenance, regulation and coordination arrangements of distributing rights to resources.

Public space governance: a brief modern history

From piecemeal provision to bureaucratised municipal provision

In many countries and cities, including in London and Hong Kong, public space governance is still normally associated with the public sector, and more specifically with local government. However, this has not always been the case.

The modern history of cities tells us that quite a lot of what is today's 'public space' was originally privately provided within the legal framework of the day, as is the case with many of London's Georgian and Victorian squares. In England and much of western Europe, other elements of public space also derive, often in piecemeal and non-linear manner, from much vaguer property regimes which left parts of the urban tissue in the public domain until the needs for regulation and improvement in urban infrastructure and welfare, emanating from an emerging urban and industrial society in the 18th and 19th centuries, led to control over them being vested in municipal corporations and subsequently in their successors, democratically elected local governments (Hasluck 1948, Parr 2020). For example, the history of road provision in England in this period, first via parishes (which were local governments, at the time unelected), then later, many via turnpike trusts (organisations founded by Acts of Parliament but acting as private toll organisations), before the beginning of roads being provided directly by the state.

Specifically in the UK, the development of local government as provider of public services is the result of the consolidation of multipurpose, elected local authorities, a process that started in the early 19th century and reached its apex in the post-war years. During the Victorian period, the growing demand for infrastructure, health, education and poverty alleviation produced by rapid industrialisation was met through the piecemeal increase of state intervention, replacing or, more often than not, coexisting with a plethora of voluntary bodies, private companies, charitable organisations and private philanthropy, which had traditionally provided those services (Leach and Percy Smith 2001). This was also the case with public parks provision and the services related to road and waterway infrastructure (Southworth and Ben-Joseph 1997). Simultaneously, local government became gradually more democratic, moving away from business-dominated municipal corporations and coming to embody a wider array of local interests. For public space this has meant service provision through local government's hierarchy of operational structures, responsive to users' needs primarily through the accountability mechanisms of elected government.

This later process is inserted in a gradual codification of the functions of a welfarist state during the 20th century. Provision of public spaces became a public service, along with health, education, social housing and welfare. Vital functions performed by public spaces (linkage between places, traffic corridors, leisure, health improvements, meeting, civic and ceremonial spaces and so forth) became accepted as key to the well-being of modern societies, and thus part of the array of common goods whose adequate provision should be secured by the state and funded through taxation. Therefore, state-provided and maintained public space is itself a historically specific construct linked to a particular type of state, a specific form of governance (which largely equates governance with government institutions) and a form of relationship between state and citizens mediated through the mechanisms of representative democracy on the one hand and a provider–user relationship on the other.

These forms of provision and management of public space and associated institutional framework of governance became dominant throughout cities in the West as the 20th century progressed. They were also spread around other parts of the world, often as part of colonial administrative structures. In colonial administrations in Asia, the purpose was always primarily to further colonial priorities and ensuring that whatever business this entailed was enabled by the physical environment. However, just as private and communitarian modes of provision did not fully disappear in the metropolitan capitals themselves, in many colonies the imposed formal structures of governance of common goods never fully replaced vernacular forms of provision, which coexisted as a mean of providing such goods, including public space (see, for example, Dovey and King 2011).

In British colonial settlements, the formal provision structures were generally implemented based on the prevailing social attitudes of the day in relation to the roles of different population groups and the parts of the cities in which they lived, and were operationalised through the legal apparatus brought from the metropolis, crafted to work with local circumstances of culture, economics, politics and geography. This produced a distinct, though not completely separate, history of public space governance. British colonies in East Asia were characterised by high population density in the urban centre and, correspondingly, intense use of public spaces (see, for example, Edwards 1992, Cheng 2012). This density meant shrinking dwellings via intense subdivision of units, and the spilling out onto the street of what we would today understand as domestic or private activities: eating, washing, working, sleeping, buying and selling (Ho and Lim 1992, Savage 1992, Rimmer and Dick 2009). Street life was lively and chaotic (for example, Savage 1992) and almost entirely un-European. While a lively street culture is often seen as a distinctive 'Asian' trait (Miao 2001), this 'undifferentiated land use' is universal to pre-industrial cities and, we would argue, even early industrial cities (Southworth and Ben-Joseph 2013). If we compare this to contemporary development in England, it will become clear that such vitality in streets was also a characteristic of cities there, especially poorer neighbourhoods.

While the public space governance discourse in England and Western cities unfolded alongside the formalisation of local authorities, being powered by the demand for and concerns about infrastructure, education, poverty alleviation and public health, and the development of democratic rights in general, in the colonial settlements, the public space governance discourse tended to mainly be around 'public health'. This was seen as least threatening to the continued authority of the colonial power, while being critical for ensuring the smooth functioning of the colonial enterprise. In other words, in contrast to Western cities, colonial power relations ensured that there was a focus less on rights and more on benevolence, an echo of which is seen in the governance culture of Hong Kong to this day (Law 2002, Cheng 2012).

While public health was a genuine problem, its corollary of a desire for class-based – or, in the colonial settlements, race-based – spatial segregation and 'cleaning up' has been widely discussed (Cheng 2012). It was indeed the dominant colonial public space discourse. Another thread, hinted at earlier, is that while the formal legal and policy structures framed public space governance of such cities, in British colonies at least, these coexisted with vernacular rights regimes of the majority populations, which were nevertheless subject to the overarching formal governance framework. This policy of 'letting the locals govern their own affairs' via leaders whom the colonial administrations would recognise, was an approach that also allowed minimal government. It also usually resulted in a proliferation of micro-scale economic activities that were regulated by those vernacular rights regimes which also served the needs of the population and, in public space terms, create high-vitality streets. These activities were normalised as better than welfare and were thus tolerated (Cheng 2012).

Bureaucratic management and its problems

Throughout the 20th century, and certainly since the end of the Second World War, activities that make up public space governance and management have been for the most part located within public authority service delivery structures. Given the functional origins of the majority of ordinary streets and squares, management has been designed based on the functions and activities using those spaces, not on the spaces themselves. Public space itself has been viewed merely as the context in which other activities and services take place, rather than the subject of a service itself. As a result, by and large, care for the majority of public spaces has come to constitute an implicit part of the general environmental management responsibility of the government. This has been particularly true in the UK, but also applies elsewhere. Yet the Weberian professionalisation and compartmentalisation of public service delivery structures in general during the 20th century and the lack of a specific focus on public space has meant that public space has been managed by a collection of bodies, often located in separate government departments specialised on narrowly defined services, which happen to take place in public space. In the UK, these departments were, and still are, those of local authorities. In Hong Kong, the Urban Council, the successor of the Sanitation Board, provided public space from 1952 until its abolition in 1999, upon which the Special Administrative Region (SAR) government departments took up the responsibility, advised by the District Councils, of which there are 18 across the SAR. This is notable, because this was a centralising move at the time when there was recognition in the UK of the value of the local (Yu 2013, 2018). We will see in Chapter 5 more of how delivery is structured in London and Hong Kong.

Thus, while publicness in terms of rights of access and use to public space was opened to an ever-wider group of people, in line with democratisation throughout the 20th century, the bureaucratically designed mechanisms put in place to deliver this in the sphere of 'urban public space' created problems of its own. This approach is still the dominant form of public space governance, and it is to a large extent as a response to its perceived or real deficiencies that alternatives outside the public sector have gained ground (De Magalhães and Carmona 2006).

From state bureaucracy to New Public Management

Much has been written about the main ideological thrust of government responses to the crises of the post-war welfare state in the 1970s both in the UK and in the US, its suspicion of the public sector and its reliance on market forces and civil society, and about whether or not the decline of state-centred welfarist regimes was unavoidable. For the purposes of our discussion, it suffices to say that deep transformations in the economy and society in the last quarter of the 20th century (economic globalisation, the move to a service-based economy, increasing affluence, the fragmentation of social life and so forth) and the policy responses to them brought about changes in the relationship between central and local governments in many places, society and government, the economy and government, which challenged hierarchical, 'command and control' forms of government (Kooiman 1993, 2003, Andersen and van Kempen 2001, Hajer and Wagenaar 2003) which had hitherto shaped state action. Much of this was inspired by new approaches to the function of the public sector, which in turn led to the rethinking and reframing of public sector cultures, structures and procedures around the world (Pierre and Peters 2000, Goss 2001, Leach and Percy-Smith 2001). This was manifest in the emergence of a global movement in public administration practice known as the New Public Management (NPM). NPM is a complex body of ideas and approaches, but the most salient for public space management is its importation of private sector practices to 'fix' what it saw as the inefficient, expensive, out of touch and even corrupt public sector (Box et al 2001).

Measures to roll back the public sector were given a boost when budgetary constraints became critical. The financial crisis that started in 2008 gave an extra impetus to cuts in government funding to a whole array of public services and public sector activities. In many countries, policy efforts at national level to reduce the costs and size of government led to a curbing of powers and spending of local government and a redistribution of resources within public services. In the UK, whereas politically sensitive statutory public services such as health and education might have seen occasional increases in resources, others saw a drastic reduction, and some were removed from the state sphere altogether. Public space-related services suffered a steady decline in funding, which was reversed in the early 2000s in line with the acceptance of the need to encourage investment, as already described, but started again after the 2008 financial crisis and the policies of austerity that were adopted to address it (Audit Commission 2002, DTLR 2002, Neal 2013).

Public sector and local government reforms in the UK in the 1980s and early 1990s came to involve a plethora of privatised public sector bodies, utility providers, area-based urban regeneration organisations, local authority departments, semi-public delivery agencies and so forth, all responsible for parts of the space, or for different services, or different operations within the same service. This fits a general pattern followed by other public services which has caused forms of collaboration between different sectors and jurisdictions to become a necessity (Bailey 1995, Sullivan and Skelcher 2002).

As with most public services, public space governance had to move from its former 'predict and provide' nature to an approach that involves contracting out the delivery of services and the transfer of governance responsibilities to third parties. A fundamental part of these changes is that the relationship between those involved in the provision and management of public services has become increasingly defined by contracts (De Magalhães 2010). Particularly in the UK, where these processes have been well developed, the intra-organisational functional relationships between different departments of a local authority in managing a public space or any other public service determined by functional hierarchies have had to coexist with contractual agreements between a service-commissioning local authority and a private or voluntary sector service provider, capable of offering some form of advantage in the provision of those goods/services such as reduced costs, technical expertise, flexibility, sensitivity to localised demands and so on, to overcome perceived or real deficiencies in direct public sector delivery. What is delivered, its quantity and quality, accountability systems and the penalties for non-compliance have to be described and fixed in legally binding contractual dispositions. With services such as refuse collection, grass mowing, street cleaning, grounds maintenance and so forth contracted out to external parties, integration between service design and delivery has often become dependent on contractual or quasi-contractual arrangements between the client commissioning the services and the contractor delivering them.

As has been argued by Peel, Lloyd and Lord (2009), contracts have come to dominate relationships between the state and the recipients of public services in many areas of policy, as part of an effort to reapportion rights and responsibilities for service delivery and influence service user behaviour. This is linked to the increasing complexity of governance arrangements and of the ways found to secure accountability and control under those conditions. This pervasiveness of contractualised relations in policy delivery in the most diverse fields of policy has led some authors to talk of 'contractual governance' as the emerging set of institutional structures and regulatory arrangements between the state and a variety of third parties, based on contractual norms of rights and responsibilities, reciprocity, encouragement and sanctions (Vincent-Jones 2000, Peel, Lloyd and Lord 2009). As a public service, the governance of public spaces has not been an exception, and contracts and contractualised relationships have provided the framework within which responses to failings in the 'traditional' state-led provision of services were sought.

While the effects of these approaches to the public sector and its services were observed globally, how they played out was different in different countries, depending on a government's macroeconomic approaches, the party politics in play, the political system itself and state tradition (Lee and Haque 2006). Hong Kong's experience of NPM's impact on public space governance is different from that of the UK, already described. Certain aspects of NPM and its core approaches are a natural fit for Hong Kong's macroeconomic approach of 'non-interventionism', its pro-market, lean government stance, financial conservatism and anti-welfarism – regarding welfare not as a social right but as charity. These have always been hallmarks of its governance approach since before its handover to China in 1997, and until 2020 remained largely in place. Some actions such as setting up public–private partnerships (PPPs) on large projects such as the West Kowloon Cultural District (WKCD) have borne fruit for public space investment provision, although many years late and over budget (see, for example, Lee and Haque 2006, Shen, Platten and Deng 2006, Hayllar 2010). The lateness is in part due to the perceived lack of public accountability. Less ambitious cooperative working with the private sector, including via agreements to provide public space, has always been a significant feature of public realm provision in Hong Kong. Such practices have been enabled by Hong Kong's history of giving ground to, but also working closely with, business elites, but also fuelled by the limited space supply. This drives spatial sharing arrangements which are both pragmatic and creative.

However, as Lee and Haque (2006) also note, other aspects of NPM were in direct conflict with the political culture in Hong Kong. A key plank in NPM was the transformation of the public organisation's role from that of direct service provision to indirect provision via managing contracts for external providers, be they private or third sector organisations. In the words of Osborne and Gabler (1992), a shift from rowing to steering. This is associated with managerialism, transparent performance reporting and a focus on results. In Hong Kong, politically strong, unionised and traditionally powerful civil service actors, both elites and rank and file, objected to the imposition of managerialism, whose purported function was precisely to break the traditional bureaucratic work practices. At the same time, a weak and non-elected political executive, who did not enjoy strong legitimacy or hold sway over the civil service, was often unable to impose reform (Lee and Haque 2006). Furthermore, the civil service culture of Hong Kong is procedure and rule based, and not performance driven (Lee and Haque 2006). Consequently, in Hong Kong, 'contracting out' and explicit performance management as accountability reporting, at least in the operations of public space management, was only ever partially implemented.

Cultural changes and new functions of public space

The widespread adoption of NPM approaches and financial crises were not alone in challenging 'traditional' bureaucratic public space provision. In the UK and in many other places, as NPM was being rolled out across public sector services, new demands were put on public space by policy makers and users of space, which have had visible impact on public space provision and management. On the one hand, the perceived need for cities to compete to attract the more footloose investment of the globalised economy led to an increasing concern with the vitality and viability of town and city centres and the role in this of public space quality (see, for example, Urban Task Force 1999, DETR 2000, Crouch 2010, Whitney, Hess and Sarmiento Casas 2020). This meant a new emphasis of public space beyond its traditional purposes, and strong new associations with processes of urban redevelopment. In the context mentioned earlier, of withdrawal of the public sector from direct intervention and of a scarcity of resources, such urban redevelopment processes were often privately led, structured around the logic of private real estate operations, for which new or redeveloped public space played a role in enhancing and securing marketability and long-term property values. There are plenty of examples of new public spaces in major cities around the world, produced as part of large real estate developments which are themselves the product of urban regeneration and place-marketing strategies (see, for instance Kohn 2004, Németh 2009). The popularisation of privately owned public spaces associated with new commercial developments, the POPS of the literature, is certainly part of this process of explicit commodification of public space and its explicit use as an instrument of forms of economic development associated with and dependent upon increases in property value.

On the other hand, and at the same time, demographic and cultural changes have put new diversified and often conflicting demands on public spaces from their potential users. Social and spatial fragmentation and the diversification of lifestyles brought about by long-term increases in affluence have meant a larger differentiation in users' aspirations, requiring public space governance systems that were demand sensitive and flexible. For instance, in English town and city centres, the emergence of a young, alcohol-based subculture providing the mainstay of the evening economy and vital for the economic viability of those areas has created a context dominated by sharp conflicts between uses and rights of use across space and time, in this case between night-time and day-time users, or between different age groups (Roberts and Turner 2005). Added to that, the often fragmented, one-dimensional and undifferentiated character of public space governance systems as described earlier has made it very difficult for users to engage with them. As a consequence, many localised public space demands and aspirations have gone unacknowledged, leading to dissatisfaction and a sense of alienation, which in turn have made it more difficult for local authorities to tap into community and private resources of all kinds – finance, expertise and commitment (DTLR 2001, ODPM 2004).

Again, if this general description is accurate enough to describe the particular context of London, we need to contrast these developments to those in Hong Kong. There, global competitiveness is a result of the city's unique position as a global financial services centre, as well as China's preeminent international gateway, and none of this is predicated on the nature of Hong Kong as a place, nor the quality of its public space (Lai 2012). Within the city, the particular dynamics of the relationships between developers, local authority, local residents and businesses have so far not promoted placemaking as a desirable activity. First, from a property development perspective, land cost and, correspondingly, development profits are very large, and any value added by placemaking is judged to be small. Second, at the same time, property as a class of investment product is extremely popular, even as a retail investment product (Haila 2000). The difference made by better-quality place has been judged so far to be unimportant. The relatively small presence of long-term property investors, for whom place quality is important, might explain why the emphasis on placemaking associated with commercial and residential developments is not the same in Hong Kong as it is in London.

As a result, from the Hong Kong SAR government's perspective, we see Weberian bureaucracy alive and well, in the hands of the civil service. The strong culture of rule-following and obeying silo boundaries is in line with this picture, and the public space governance outcomes would appear to epitomise how performance comes a distant second. Thus, the distinctiveness of places – an outcome – is almost always sacrificed for what those in positions of authority think 'fairness' should be, which is that no place should operate to different rules than any other. There are some exceptions, but they are relatively rare, and are usually subtly implemented.

Whatever the local differences, in both cites the cumulative results of these contextual demands on public space and its governance in the context of structural changes in public service delivery have exacerbated the shortcomings of 'traditional' public space government arrangements. These shortcomings are centred on issues of lack of coordination among agencies, the lack of flexibility and fine-tuning ability of monolithic bureaucracies to respond to ever fragmented demands and increasing aspirations, and the constraints on accountability at neighbourhood level by citywide public organisations (ODPM 2004). In London specifically, decline in funding for public spaces has added to those shortcomings. In Hong Kong, where formal governance mechanisms are far less flexible to respond to new demands, a situation made worse by the difficulties in having new rules made, the practical reality of everyday management has posed a different set of challenges. Informal and more flexible street-level arrangements have emerged to 'make the city work' in the face of rigid and obsolete rules that need to be adhered so, at least in appearance (Cheng 2012, Lai and Da Roza 2018).

What the nature of public space as a 'thing to be governed' came to demand in both cities, but also elsewhere, are governance mechanisms that could cut across specialised remits and have some purchase on the cumulative impacts of apparently unconnected activities, acknowledge localised variations in demand and aspirations, be sensitive to differences and flexible to changes, and access resources wherever these might be available (De Magalhães and

Carmona 2009). As with other public services under similar kinds of pressure, responses to the challenges to state-led delivery in public space have also been shaped by a drive towards contractualism, that is, the centrality of contracts or contract-like arrangements as organising mechanisms in social policy and economic management (Vincent-Jones 2000: 318). While this has not either replaced the bureaucratic departmental structures described earlier, nor necessarily fixed all the perceived problems associated with them, it does suggest an operational approach which is quite different. In this light, POPS, Business Improvement Districts (BIDs), PPPs and the outsourcing of key public space management functions to third parties that we can see in many places around the world, in London in particular and in Hong Kong to a considerable extent, emerge as different ways of reconfiguring rights, roles and responsibilities in public space governance, and of using contractual relations to define, articulate and link them to urban policy and broader societal objectives. This is, of course, not a socially neutral process, and for every right or role reaffirmed or expanded in a contract, another might be ignored or constrained.

Evolving forms of public space governance and the allocation of publicness rights through contracts

This chapter makes the point that understanding how evolving forms of public space governance influence and shape publicness means grasping how these forms of governance shape key publicness attributes and set the conditions for their appropriation. As suggested in the previous section, that understanding should start with the premise that contractualism has expanded as a form of managing relationships in governance in general and in the delivery of public goods and services in particular. Whether or not this is desirable is a moot point. The provision of public services and goods in the UK, as in many countries, has become increasingly reliant on contracts between a publicly accountable public sector client and a contractor capable of offering some form of advantage in the provision of those goods/services, such as capital investment, reduced costs, technical expertise, flexibility, sensitivity to localised demands and so forth. Accordingly, contractual relationships have played an increasingly important part in emerging forms of public space provision. Contracts between business occupiers, property owners and local government and other public service providers regulate the operation of BIDs in their public space responsibilities; leasehold agreements with contractual stipulations regulate the transfer of public space ownership to not-for-profit trusts as well as the functioning of those trusts; contracts and service specifications regulate the contracting-out of public space management and maintenance to third parties. In many places, as in both the UK and Hong Kong, planning gain mechanisms and associated contractual agreements are used to obtain new and/or renovated public space from private developers as a condition for planning permission, sometimes in exchange for larger development limits as in the POSPD of Hong Kong, sometimes as part the of the deal to make development possible. Often too, these new or renovated spaces remain in private hands but have to be managed as public spaces as defined in contractual dispositions with legal force. Whereas most of the foregoing are translated into formal contracts, there are also less formal contract-type relationships such as, for example, those between local government and public space friends and users' associations, which secure the role of the latter as consultees in public space management, as well as various kinds of semi-formal partnerships. From a public space governance perspective, the key question is, therefore, whether contracts and contractual mechanisms and sanctions are adequate means of securing the attributes of publicness which are valued in the spaces to which they apply. Can public space governance secured through contractual instruments guarantee relatively open access and ensure that restrictions on access and use are broadly acceptable by most potential users and stakeholders? Are contractual sanctions adequate to discourage what Madanipour (2003) refers to 'small group control'? Are contractual mechanisms capable of securing a say by all relevant stakeholders in how a public space is managed?

For an answer to these questions, we suggest that three interrelated sets of issues need to be considered: they refer to the way contracts recognise rights and obligations and therefore power in public space governance; to the contextual factors influencing which rights and obligations are relevant for any public space; to the substance of contracts in terms of which public space governance responsibilities they refer to and how these are distributed between parties.

'Traditional' public space governance, internalised in the machinery of local government, allocates rights over attributes of public space in the same way that rights over other common goods are allocated: within accepted rules and restrictions for the use of those goods, all citizens have in theory the same rights to use and make decisions about those goods. Those rights are allocated to all citizenry through the unwritten contract that exists between citizens and their governments, which might be more or less transparent, more or less democratic. Citizens pay their taxes and in exchange governments deliver common goods and public services. However, as we discuss in the previous chapter, the actual exercise of those rights over public space is constrained by a variety of factors, including distance, geography, cultural preferences and so forth, or subtracted by congestion. Moreover, interest groups using their voice resources in the sense of Hirschman (1970) exit or voice duality might secure some operational rights associated with maintenance and management, especially if public bodies cannot secure the attributes those stakeholders value. In doing so, they might also be taking over some collective choice rights which will no longer be shared with all other citizens. We can imagine a group of local residents who form an association to improve the state of their local park and take over some of the park maintenance tasks under some sort of informal agreement with their local government. The point being made here is that even in local government-led public space governance, contractual relationships play a role in ascribing rights to public space, but in many of the newer contractual public space governance practices this is much more explicit and relevant.

The emerging, contract-based public space governance practices involve some form of reallocation of rights over some of the attributes that constitute publicness, and specifically an allocation of rights away from the public domain and towards private parties (Peel, Lloyd and Lord 2009). Contractual instruments shape this reallocation of rights by recognising interests. Groups of citizens and organisations in a development trust for managing a publicly owned park will have secured the right to have the attributes they value in that space (aesthetic, amenity and so forth) prioritised in relation to attributes valued by other people, even if, as is often the case, this is moderated by the client power of a local government department. They will have a right to have a say on how the park is used, on how restrictions to access and use are applied and how money is spent in maintenance and upgrade by virtue of living or having their place of work in the vicinity of that park, or of some other recognised stake. In this sense, many of the emerging forms of public space provision and governance seem to accept the 'club- or toll-good' dimension of public space attributes, in the sense of goods and attributes that can be consumed in ways that are non-subtractable or non-rivalrous by members of a group, but with exclusion rules applying to non-members (Ostrom 1990, Webster and Lai 2003). It could be argued, as Webster does, that public space and its attributes have club good properties by definition, as club characteristics of joint appropriation and exclusion in explicit and non-explicit forms (through the friction of distance, through property costs, through other barriers to access) are defining aspects of urban spaces and largely unavoidable. Moreover, as we discuss in the previous chapter, even many of those attributes of public space that might initially present public good characteristics on non-subtractability and non-excludability might over time be affected by congestion. Congestion will affect differently the various attributes of a public space, which in turn will prompt stakeholders who value those attributes to try to secure operational and collective choice rights over them to protect their interests.

The often-implicit justification for recognising club-like interests in public space is that it allows for the relative strengths of claims over its attributes to be taken into account and transformed into a more effective and efficient tool of management. The assumption is that, because the members of such a club have the strongest stake in a particular set of public space attributes, they will manage these more efficiently and to best effect, and this applies to businesses protecting the quality of a commercial district as well as to residents securing the amenity value of a local park. However, by the very nature of public space there will be many divergent and often conflictive claims on it, and therefore a choice needs to be made on which of those will have the upper hand, which will be formally recognised, which will not. Households living around a park will have a claim on the amenity value of that park, which might clash with that of local youths who might use the park as an evening meeting point. Whereas efficient resource allocation in its broadest sense might provide one set of criteria for assessing those claims and allocating rights, it is certainly not the only one possible or desirable (for example, fairness, compensatory justice). Whichever criteria prevail will determine who/which claims get allocated the rights over particular attributes of public space, and this initial distribution of rights will determine to a large extent the outcomes of any future negotiations over those attributes, such as the ability of other interests/claims to gain access to them.

Moreover, some claims which could be regarded as legitimate by society might not be immediately visible, might be too diffuse or manifest themselves only occasionally and therefore are unlikely to make their way into formal contractual arrangements. Research demonstrates that particular social groups are less likely to use public parks and therefore less likely to get involved in their management (DTLR 2002, Thompson et al 2005, Rishbeth, Ganji and Vodicka 2018). These groups will not be in a position to advance their interests in, for example, how a park is managed, even if it is socially desirable that they do so. Therefore, a central question in investigating whether or not publicness would be reduced through contractualised provision would be to understand whether a wide range of stakes in public space can be recognised as rights and transformed into efficient management tools without in the process ignoring others, less visible but equally valid.

The second set of issues that needs to be considered is the role of context-specific variables in determining publicness. Public spaces have particular locational, functional and morphological properties which condition the kinds of publicness attributes these spaces might offer. Publicness attributes in a park or square in a prominent city centre location, an important commercial street or a small suburban residential street are bound to vary, as these spaces will be used and valued differently by different users. In each of those public spaces there will be a different range of stakes, interests and demands, with their own relative power and influence. As a result, the process of negotiation between different stakes around the key elements of publicness is likely to lead to different outcomes, depending on the nature of the space and the interests it creates. We should therefore expect that a BID in a central retail area will desire different goals in regard to the key concerns of openness, accessibility and accountability, and address them differently from a voluntary user group made up of residents taking control of a small local park. Similarly, the negotiations involved in securing a publicly accessible square or leisure space from a private shopping centre development, and the subsequent arrangements for keeping those spaces publicly accessible and open, with public sector oversight, will be different and involve different expectations and compromises from those involving the provision of similar space in a mostly residential area, with the potential transfer of management responsibility to residents once the space is ready.

Moreover, the manner in which those negotiations will be translated into agreements between the main stakeholders will also vary. This suggests the potential for a landscape characterised by several forms of publicness, the outcome of a variety of agreements between different sets of stakeholders, with key publicness attributes assuming different forms in different places. In other words, a landscape made up of many 'clubs', with different rules of membership, access and use. This might not be as radical a departure from the current situation as might appear, and in fact it might largely mean a formalisation and intensification of informal club-like mechanisms already in place. Whichever the case, the key question for an understanding of the publicness implications of locally specific public space governance arrangements is whether the unequal and differentiated sharing of publicness attributes it suggests leads to a consistent reduction in the enjoyment of those attributes in some types of places and for some people rather than others, and what are the implications of this.

Finally, the third set of issues relates to the substance of public space governance contracts. Contracts set roles for the involved parties as client and provider or principal and agent (Vincent-Jones 2000). In a typical contract the client – usually a local government body – has the responsibility to specify and deliver the services associated with public space governance. The contract transfers in whole or in part, some or all of those responsibilities to a provider/agent who will reside outside the public sector. The services involved might be restricted to public space maintenance tasks, as is increasingly the case with the maintenance of parks and green areas in the UK, or might encompass a wide range of governance responsibilities including funding, policing and enforcement, as in many BIDs. It might involve just the management of an existing space, or it might involve the provision of a new one as part of a large, privately funded real estate development operation.

Early in this chapter, we defined public space governance as a four-fold process involving regulation, investment, maintenance and coordination. All four are directly relevant to the key publicness attributes of openness of access and use and a degree of collective control and accountability. Rules of use and codes of behaviour determine how a space can be used and by whom. Maintenance processes determine how accessible and usable it might be. The amount and type of investment in a space determines how fit for purpose it will be and therefore how it can be used. How all these dimensions are coordinated, who determines who undertakes them and how levels of power over all of them are distributed express the degree of collective control and agency by the various stakeholders. Consequently, which parts of those processes are transferred to third parties by contracts, the extent of the transfer and the manner in which it is done will all shape the resulting nature and level of publicness for any given public space. Contractual arrangements in formation of BIDs in the UK seem to encompass all four processes, transferring roles and responsibilities away from local government in all of them, albeit to different degrees. Planning gain agreements leading to the provision of new publicly accessible spaces can involve the four processes to an even larger extent, especially if those spaces are going to remain in private hands as in the case of the so-called POPS. Agreements to transfer the management of a public space to charitable trusts often focus on the first three while maintaining the coordinating role of local government. Straightforward contracting-out of public space management tends to focus on maintenance and occasionally on resourcing, while leaving regulatory and coordination responsibilities with the local government client. It seems therefore that in order to understand the impacts on publicness of emerging public space governance arrangements we would need also to explore the nature of these agreements, which governance processes they refer to and whether or not the way they deal with those processes has positive or negative impacts on publicness attributes.

Conclusion

This chapter has sought to define public space governance and suggest how different governance approaches might impact on publicness. We have defined public space governance as the broader process of strategic decision making about how to provide and manage public space, which includes the way the processes that comprise public space management should be carried out and by whom, and the role to be played by different stakeholders. In doing that, it determines the allocation of rights and responsibilities over public spaces and their attributes.

We broke public space management into four related set of processes and suggested how these have changed over the last few decades, and how, in doing so, they have reallocated rights associated with the management of public space, which in turn will have had an impact on the operational rights of access and use and the collective choice rights of control and accountability users would have, and which define publicness. We have also argued that context matters, as the particular location of any public space will determine what sort of attributes might be valued in them and which stakeholders and interests will be present and active, and that the nature of the arrangements between stakeholders, the contracts that have shaped the relationship between client and contractors in the multiple activities that make up public space governance and management also matter.

As we have suggested, the allocation of rights that make up publicness is not a static process, but instead a dynamic and constantly changing one. Changes in public space governance regimes that happen as societies try to adapt to new political, social or economic circumstances often lead to a rearrangement of those rights. Although not exclusively, this often happens because people with strong interests in particular attributes of a public space fear that the quality of those attributes might be compromised through lack of care or congestion, and to avoid that they exert their 'voice' power to gain rights over that attribute so as to protect it. Public space governance therefore comprises the constant rearrangement of allocated rights over the attributes of public spaces and in this way it also comprises the constant re-definition of publicness for any public space. At the end of the chapter, we suggest an analytical framework that brings together these considerations and provide a conceptual tool to understand publicness in its relationship with context, management forms and the contractual arrangements that distribute rights and responsibilities among stakeholders.

Having made more precise what we understand as public space and defined publicness on the basis of rights to attributes of public space, and explained how public space governance and management practices shape the allocation and extension of those rights, we now look at the systems of provision and management of public spaces in London and Hong Kong. In the next few chapters of this book we describe existing and emerging forms of public space governance in both cities in more detail. We look at how they have tried to tackle their own challenges in the provision and management of public space – how they have mobilised resources, engaged stakeholders, set out rules for their relationships with them and rules for the use and enjoyment of public space, and in the process of so doing have prioritised and recognised some stakes over public space and de-prioritised and ignored others, and have done so through reallocating operational and collective choice rights over different public spaces in different ways.

5

Public space management in London and Hong Kong

Introduction

This chapter provides an expanded overview of the recent history of governance and management of the public realm in general and open public spaces in both London and Hong Kong. In doing that, the chapter also provides a rationale for their selection as objects of study: their long-standing history of non-traditional forms of public space governance, which has acquired a new impetus with recent changes in urban governance worldwide. The emphasis is on how public spaces in these two cities have been produced and managed over time; the systems and institutional arrangements put in place to produce new spaces and to ensure that many of their publicness attributes fulfil their functions in the long run; the governance systems that represent the different interests with a stake in public spaces; how all these have evolved and the reasons for any significant changes. The chapter is divided into two parts, one dealing with London, the other with Hong Kong, both structured along similar lines. Both parts will describe and discuss public space provision, management and governance in each city. The chapter concludes with the challenges to both cities in how they provide and manage public space, which will be explored in the subsequent chapters.

Brief history of public space provision in London

The history of public spaces in London is long, although it should be kept in mind that our view of what these spaces are and what they are for is certainly not the same as the views of those who might have used them in the more remote past – as discussed previously in Chapter 2. Very little survives of the open spaces of the original Roman settlement apart from the routes of the old Roman roads radiating from London to other settlements of the period. The City of London, the historical core of the city, still retains much of the medieval street pattern on which a large part of public life took place, and many of the villages around London that were later absorbed into the city still have parts of their original village commons and village greens, a few still with ancient commons rights in place. The same applies to the large royal hunting grounds and some aristocratic estates surrounding London, some of which have become the contemporary London parks. Even if in some cases those areas had some form of public access from early in their history, they became open public spaces in the contemporary sense only much later (Clark 1973, Jordan 1994).

It would be proper to say that the history of open public spaces as we now understand the concept starts largely from the middle of the 17th century onwards. This was the period that saw the expansion of the city to surrounding areas and the development of a type of open space characteristic of London, the London square, in many ways the historical ancestors to subsequent green squares and gardens that characterise many areas in inner London. These were originally open courtyards, surrounded by residential buildings and whose original purpose mimics the arrival courtyards fronting stately homes, but soon took on the characteristics of leisure gardens enhancing the amenity value of the surrounding properties (Rasmussen 1948). These squares were not public in the modern sense of the word and were provided as part of development schemes helping to attract wealthier residents to new districts in the expanding city. Their ownership and maintenance remained – and in some cases remain to this day – in the hands of the original landowners, the aristocratic families who owned most of the land around London and who leased it out to developers who proceeded to build Georgian London. Many of these squares were gated early on in their existence, mostly through resident initiative, and it was only at the end of the 19th century that they began to be open to the public (Royal Commission 1928). Although a defining element of the landscape of central London, with undoubted public amenity value, many of these squares remain in private hands and a significant number have restrictions on access.

The early 18th century also initiated the period of the Pleasure Gardens, large open spaces for leisure accessible through a fee. These were places where the growing urban middle classes would find entertainment in what has been described as 'commercialised leisure' (Plumb 1982). These were privately provided and operated, and selective in terms of access, but by the mid-19th century many of those places had become less profitable and closed down, with the sites sold off for development.

Because of the way London has grown over the centuries, incorporating into the expanding city many surrounding villages, a significant proportion of open green space in the outer areas resulted from the incorporation into the urban fabric of what were previously rural common land and village greens (Figure 5.1). These were originally tracts of land in medieval landed estates over which particular people would have common rights of use. From the end of the 19th century several pieces of legislation were enacted to prevent the enclosure of common land and expand rights of access, and guardianship over most urban commons has been given to local councils (UK Government 1965), which now manage the majority of commons and village greens in London in their capacity as guardians.

Figure 5.1: Shepherd's Bush Green, formerly village common land

Figure 5.2: Trafalgar Square, a 19th-century urban square, seen at the end of that century

Source: United States Library of Congress

City squares as recognisable open public space, conceived to be accessible to all and managed by local government, were a product of the 19th century. Trafalgar Square was opened in 1844 as a civic and commemorative space (Figure 5.2). Next door Leicester Square, formerly part common land, part aristocratic enclosed garden, was transferred in 1874 to the Metropolitan

Board of Works, an embryonic and unelected form of London-wide government, to be used as a publicly accessible open space (UK Government 1874, Sexby 2014). Parliament Square was opened in the 1860s to open up space around Parliament, provide a civic open space next to the seat of government and improve the flow of traffic in the area (Burch 2002). The late Victorian and Edwardian years in the end of the 19th and beginning of the 20th centuries saw the opening of several squares with civic character in many of the boroughs around London, accompanying the building of monumental town halls across the city.

The next large expansion in the provision of open public space happened in the decades after the Second World War, until the 1980s, with the reconstruction of parts of the city and, especially, large housing estates following the modernist paradigm of separation of uses and towers in open parkland and ignoring street patterns – or more modest versions of the same when parkland was not available, with distinct buildings surrounded by open public space (Hannikainen 2016). A significant part of these open public spaces would later be redeveloped and repurposed as more confined and controllable open spaces as issues with maintenance, ownership and purpose of large tracts of anonymous open space became acute. This period also saw the opening of transport arteries cutting through the urban fabric to facilitate motor vehicle circulation, creating a different kind of public space which would become increasingly impermeable to pedestrians.

In the 1980s, as the economy of London changed, the pressing urban problem became the regeneration of large tracts of derelict land, especially around London's docklands, and the refurbishment of many of the post-war modernist social housing developments which had by now fallen into disrepair. This coincided with the height of Thatcherism and the belief in markets and the private sector as the best tools to reshape society. Not surprisingly, regeneration operations started to become increasingly dependent on private investment in real estate, whether or not in partnership with public bodies. Many large new developments from the mid-1980s onwards would have provided new public space, even if they remained in private ownership, with their publicness secured via contractual agreements with the public sector. Places like Canary Wharf or Broadgate did provide new public spaces where none previously existed, albeit under different rules of access, commercialisation and surveillance than those that had governed public spaces hitherto (Carmona and Wunderlich 2012) (Figure 5.3).

This dependence on privately led property development for the provision of new or refurbished public space has continued to the present, now with an increasing acceptance by larger developers that public space provision and adequate management can help maintain the value of their assets over the long term and therefore are an easily justifiable investment. The redevelopment of places like King's Cross, with its significant contribution

Figure 5.3: Exchange Square in Broadgate, among the first privately provided public spaces in commercial developments

Source: EBRD/Dermot Doorly

of new public spaces, or even Battersea/Nine Elms, seems to prove that point (see Figure 6.12). The idea of placemaking, now dominant in the discourse of urban regeneration, is certainly not incompatible with private investment in the public realm. This more recent period has also seen the proliferation of BIDs, with associations of local business starting to take over some public realm management duties for themselves.

Within this same logic, the most significant single addition to public space in recent times has been the Queen Elizabeth Olympic Park, the location of the London 2012 Summer Olympics. After the games, the Olympic Park was transformed into a complex with sporting facilities, business park, residential quarters, educational facilities and a large urban park. As befits the times, it was developed and is managed by the London Legacy Development Corporation, a mayoral development corporation created in 2012 and accountable to the Mayor of London, having on its board public and private sector representatives. Resources for this large-scale piece of urban regeneration have been largely secured through the lease of developable land to private developers, with most of the public facilities obtained through planning obligations and developer contributions.

Public space governance in London: who does it

To understand the current forms of public space governance in London we need first to understand how the government of the city is structured. As a governance jurisdiction, London is made up of 32 boroughs plus the

Figure 5.4: London and its 33 local authorities

1. Havering	9. Tower Hamlets	17. Brent	25. Wandsworth
2. Barking and Dagenham	10. City of London	18. Harrow	26. Sutton
3. Redbridge	11. Islington	19. Ealing	27. Croydon
4. Newham	12. Camden	20. Hillingdon	28. Lambeth
5. Waltham Forest	13. Barnet	21. Hounslow	29. Southwark
6. Enfield	14. Westminster	22. Richmond	30. Lewisham
7. Haringey	15. Kensington and Chelsea	23. Kingston	31. Greenwich
8. Hackney	16. Hammersmith and Fulham	24. Merton	32. Bexley
			33. Bromley

City of London, the square mile at the heart of the city on the site of the original Roman and then medieval settlement. The 32 boroughs comprise 12 inner-London and 20 outer-London boroughs. The former cover the area of what was the County of London, a former administrative unit for London created at the end of the 19th century with the introduction of elected county government in England, and abolished in 1965, when the 20 surrounding boroughs were incorporated into London for administrative purposes (Figure 5.4).

These boroughs are local authorities in their own rights, with planning powers, elected councils and responsibilities for delivering a whole array of public services and common goods, including the provision and management of most open public spaces including local parks and local roads. Local policies related to public space tend to be about maintenance and refurbishment of existing local open spaces and high streets and the provision of new spaces in private developments through planning gain instruments. There is no single officially agreed definition and categorisation of public space for the whole of London, nor formulas for how this common good should be distributed across the city, although there are quite sophisticated measurements of access to public spaces of different kinds per neighbourhood. There are also no specific quantitative targets of open space area per inhabitant, but open public spaces are seen as essential for place quality and local plans take that into account and consider the provision of new public space in any significant planning application.

Between 1986, when the Greater London Council (GLC) was abolished, and 1999, with the creation of the Greater London Authority (GLA), London did not have a level of government for the whole city coordinating the activities of the 33 local authorities. They would have had their own local plans, their own policies on planning, on public spaces and on other public services, framed by broader national policies and with only informal coordination mechanisms to make sure policies of neighbouring boroughs were compatible.

However, since 1999 London has had a citywide government with an elected London Assembly and a directly elected executive Mayor. The GLA does not replace or eliminate the 33 local authorities, but it has strategic powers over a number of public services, most importantly public transport, policing and planning, the latter through the statutory London Plan which frames the plans of the local boroughs. The Mayor also has urban regeneration powers, through the creation of Mayoral Development Corporations to guide and oversee the development of large strategic sites, with statutory powers related to planning, land ownership and infrastructure (UK Government 1999, 2011). In that regard, the Mayor of London in partnership with other public bodies and private interests has had a major role in the provision and management of the Queen Elizabeth Olympic Park already mentioned. The GLA has also had a role in provision and management of public space through its responsibility for main roads through Transport for London (TfL), its power to approve larger strategic planning applications and its role in urban regeneration.

Apart from the formal structures of citywide and local government, other bodies have an important role in the governance of public space in London. Many of the largest open green spaces in the city evolved from aristocratic estates. All large central London parks were hunting areas for royalty, some historically with public access such as Hyde Park, others not so, and became public parks in the 19th century. These Royal Parks, such as Hyde Park, St James's Park, Green Park, Regent's Park, Greenwich Park and Richmond Park were not taken over by local councils (Figure 5.5). They were managed until 2017 by a public sector body attached to central government but have since then been managed by a private charity, The Royal Parks Ltd, with some public sector funding but with operational independence. Some large

Figure 5.5: Hyde Park, one of the Royal Parks now managed by a private charity

aristocratic estates in the outer areas of London, with their parkland and woodland, are still in private ownership but are managed as public spaces by private and charitable trusts, such as the National Trust, sometimes with open access, sometimes with fee charges.

A similar management structure of charitable trust is responsible for the management of towpaths and public spaces around canals and rivers. The Canal and River Trust is a national charity in charge of managing canals, rivers and reservoirs, which in 2012 replaced a public corporation with similar responsibilities.

As mentioned elsewhere, the role of private property development in the provision of new public spaces has become particularly important in the last few decades. The type, size and nature of public spaces provided by private developments is usually the result of negotiations around planning obligations, based on section 106 of the Town and Country Planning Act 1990 – and known as Section 106 agreements. These are private and legally binding agreements between a local planning authority and a developer attached to the planning permission for a particular development to mitigate for its impacts and make it acceptable in planning terms. They are the product of complex and often lengthy negotiation processes and typically include the provision of a quantum of affordable housing, amenities such as open space, facilities for public services and other infrastructure. This negotiation will also decide on the long-term ownership of a public space and on management responsibilities, with some public spaces reverting to local authority control after the completion of the development and some being retained in private ownership. It will also define rules of access, openness and so forth which will secure that the space functions as public.

Specifically, in what concerns the management of existing public spaces, apart from the role of local authorities and other public bodies in managing spaces under their direct responsibilities, there are various legal instruments that allow degrees of transfer of ownership and management responsibilities to not-for-profit organisations that represent stakeholders in a particular public space. As discussed in further chapters in this book, there are several publicly owned public spaces in London over which governance and management responsibilities have been transferred to voluntary sector bodies. In many cases this happens through long leases to not-for-profit trusts (of 99 or even 999 years) which specify rules of access and openness and management responsibilities. The Housing and Regeneration Act 2008 set out the rules for Community Land Trusts, primarily designed to allow communities to have a more active involvement in housing provision, which can take over and maintain public spaces, as can other forms of community-led housing. Similar arrangements have been used to transfer management rights over some public spaces to BIDs, usually not-for-profit companies run by local businesses. Right to Manage legislation set out in the Commonhold and Leasehold Reform Act 2002 allows leasehold property owners to take over the management of a building and the upkeep of communal areas (including public spaces within a housing estate) and it has been used for that purpose by residents' associations in local authority housing estates organised in a Right to Manage company.

Finally, in the last 30 years approaches to public sector management prioritising value for money in public service delivery, combined with an actual decline in resources for those services, have encouraged the outsourcing of public space maintenance and some other management responsibilities to private contractors. The 1980s UK policies of compulsory competitive tendering to force public sector organisations to allow private contractors to deliver public services were followed in the early 2000s by Best Value policies, which encouraged local authorities up and down the country to outsource activities such as street and public space cleaning and security to private contractors, with some local authorities such as Lewisham contracting out the entire management of all their green spaces to a private company for blocks of ten-year, renewable periods.

This brief summary of the governance structure for public space provision and management in London is enough to highlight its diversity and fragmentation. Nevertheless, this structure has succeeded in delivering and maintaining a reasonable number of public spaces with variable quality.

Public space governance in London: how it is done

This chapter suggests that there are two interlinked but separate modes of provision and management of public spaces in London. For most of the 20th century and up to now, the management of public spaces in all English cities and all the activities it implies have primarily taken the form of a public service under the responsibility of local government. As a local public service, public space management has been provided through local government's hierarchy of operational structures, and has been responsive to users' needs, primarily through the direct and indirect accountability mechanisms inherent in local representative democracy.

By and large, the care of public spaces has traditionally been dealt with as an implicit part of the general environmental management responsibility of local authorities. Until quite recently, ordinary streets and squares had rarely been viewed as 'public spaces', a term which tended to imply green open spaces and iconic civic spaces only. Only more recently, as concerns with place quality have become more mainstream, have streets been recognised as public spaces with multiple functions other than just circulation (TfL 2017). Although this has somewhat improved, dominant practice has traditionally split the services addressing public space issues between functionally different departments organised around clearly defined activities: highway departments dealing with streets and public spaces in their roles as traffic corridors; parks and leisure departments treating public spaces as green and leisure areas; environmental services departments managing cleaning and cleansing functions; and so on. The functions of road sweeping, tree pruning, controlling traffic and so forth have been the focus of these services, whereas the public spaces of streets and squares have been merely the context in which those functions are exercised (Table 5.1). Local authority restructuring in the last ten years to cope with austerity and a decline in budgets, together with evolving understanding of the role of the public realm in economic and social matters, has led to the agglutination of the various public space services under broader public realm-focused departments, which in theory would be able to have a more holistic view of public space management. This is the case with, for example, the London boroughs of Hammersmith and Fulham, Hackney, Camden among others, where environment and public realm directorates now encompass almost the full range of public space-related services.

The mode just described is the dominant form of provision and management of public space in London: direct provision and management by local authorities and other public sector bodies in their role as providers and managers of public services. This is how the management of most open public spaces, squares, small parks, public green areas and streets operates. In this mode, public space provision and management is a public service,

Table 5.1: Fragmentation of public space management in England in the early 21st century

Local authority (% of total)	No of internal departments involved	Typical distribution of public space management responsibilities
24	1	Supra-departments discharging main public spaces functions under one director, typically subdivided into: • Planning/Transport/Highways • Parks/Leisure • Maintenance or: • Strategy • Operations
48	2	Public space services split between two departments, typically: • Planning and Environment/Highways (street services) • Leisure/Community Services (green spaces) or: • Strategy (Planning, Highways, Parks) • Operations (Management and Maintenance/Contracts)
19	3	Public space services split between three departments, more frequently: • Leisure/Parks • Planning/Highways • Contracts/Management and Maintenance
9	4	Variation of the three-department model, usually with a separation of planning and highways: • Leisure/Parks • Planning • Highways • Maintenance/Works

Source: Adapted from De Magalhães and Carmona (2006: 295)

delivered by the structures of elected local government either directly or through the use of external contractors.

In parallel and interlinked to it, there is a system of indirect provision and management of common good public space by third parties, either private organisations following a market logic, or voluntary and community bodies with a user-centred perspective, under obligation to do so by contractual agreements and similar legal instruments involving the provider or manager and the local authority. This might be in exchange for the right to develop a site or the opportunity to advance the interests of a group of stakeholders. This is the management mode responsible for the provision of a number of significant new public spaces in built-up areas of London through the use of planning obligations. It is also the mode adopted for the regulated transfer of management responsibilities for managing existing public spaces to charitable trusts, voluntary sector groups and users' organisations, which have become more common in London in recent times.

The following paragraphs describe in more detail how these two management modes approach the tasks of coordinating interventions on public space, regulate its use, define and carry out maintenance routines and raise resources to invest in public space and ensure it is fit for purpose.

Local authority-centred provision and management

Most public spaces in London are under the control of local authorities, which plan and deliver the array of services that make up public space management, with restricted and controlled use of external input from either private contractors or the voluntary sector. The key characteristics of this mode of management are hierarchical structures of planning and delivery; clear vertical lines of accountability both upwards to policy makers and downwards to service users; clear separation between service and use; a public service ethos with a commitment to the public interest. Apart from historical inertia, the main strength of this model is that it is based on visible and widely acceptable lines of accountability, as service planning and delivery are directly subject to established mechanisms of democratic participation in local government decision making. Moreover, it maintains clear lines of demarcation between the public and private spheres and therefore sets a clear, easily understood framework of responsibilities, of property rights, ownership and of public rights and duties.

Because of the already mentioned tendency of silo formation among specialised local authority departments, structures to secure horizontal and vertical coordination are very important in coordinating public space management. This can be translated into the creation of clear lines of management and responsibility for public space services at local authority level, bringing together a number of separate activities. In London the effort to better coordinate public space interventions has often meant restructuring local authorities to create more strategic structures, bringing the several dimensions of public space management under one roof. This has so far been easier in relation to open green spaces than in streets and public spaces that include highways, given the deep-rooted differences between transport and highway planning and engineering and parks and green space management.

As this mode of management is largely predicated on the separation between service providers (the local authority departments, which provide services to the citizenry in the public interest) and service users (actual public space users, with their preferences and expectations), an important issue for coordination is how the different aspirations, demands and actions of those users are factored into the management of actual public spaces. The normal channels securing the involvement of citizens in local government decisions in a parliamentary democracy obviously play a part. However, because of the centralised nature of local authority service provision, it has proven to be not sensitive or flexible enough to respond to changing demands or fine-grained contextual variety (Carmona, De Magalhães and Hammond 2008), and this issue has been one of the reasons for the proliferation of the other approaches to public space management discussed later.

The regulation dimension in this mode of public space governance involves mostly straightforward legislation on uses and their impact on public space, on how users should relate to public space and so forth, accompanied by enforcement action to secure compliance with legislation. This is expressed in local councils' by-laws, passed by councils' elected members on the basis of delegated power from Parliament, which regulate the use of public space and permitted behaviour in it. These by-laws are framed by common law and by accepted rules, norms and customs regarding public space. There will typically be restrictions on what time of the day a public space is open to the public (as many public spaces in London are gated), on riding bicycles and skateboards, on access to children's play areas by adults, on where ball games can be played, on trading or busking, on making loud noises and so forth. Enforcement action related to these restrictions will be carried out by either council employees, some with police powers (for example, the Law Enforcement Team in the Borough of Hammersmith and Fulham or the Parks Police Service in Kensington and Chelsea, or the Hampstead Heath Constabulary in the City of London), or by the London Metropolitan Police in case of more serious offences.

In this mode of governance, maintenance routines have been primarily technical and budgetary exercises within the local authority, confirmed by political sanctioning in policy instruments and public consultation to secure support when necessary. However, there has been an increasing awareness of the appropriateness and contextual sensitivity of maintenance routines (see, for example, Dempsey and Burton 2012). An increasingly important factor in the maintenance dimension of public space management is the way in which decisions on maintenance routines take into account public space users' views in the context of a formal separation between service delivery and use. This has become even more of an issue, given the shrinkage of in-house capability and the outsourcing of maintenance activities to private contractors as a way of buying in expertise or lowering fixed operational costs. Some councils like Hammersmith and Fulham or Lewisham have outsourced all public space maintenance to private contractors (in the case of the latter, this has included full management of all their public space since 2000). This means that maintenance routines such as cleansing, furniture replacement, graffiti removal, verge maintenance, tree pruning and so forth have to be specified in advance in contractual agreements, often with less flexibility to adapt to local aspirations and also adding another layer of complexity to the coordination activities already described.

The fourth dimension of public space management in this mode, investment, has traditionally been about capturing an appropriate slice of public sector budgets for public space services. As resources come mostly from within public sector service budgets, increases in the quantity or quality of public space services depend either on an increase in the amount of resources allocated to those services or on the optimisation and better use of those resources or a combination of both. Much has been written about how resources to parks and public spaces have declined in England in the last three decades (Wilson and Hughes 2011, Dempsey, Burton and Selin 2016, Whitten 2019), in a context of general decline of local authority budgets and skills, especially following the 2008 financial crisis and subsequent austerity policies. It was precisely the aim of accessing other sources of financial and technical resources in the private and community sectors that led to the emergence and proliferation of other modes of public space management which are described later. Although investment still comes predominantly from public sector budgets, many local authority-owned and managed public spaces have also benefitted from sponsorship from corporate organisations with a vested interest in that space, from the investment of time and labour from park friends' groups and other community organisations and from a few occasional capital investment grants from central or London-wide levels of government.

The devolved mode of provision and management

The second mode of public space management which we find in London is based on the allocation of responsibilities for provision and management of public space (that is, those of coordination, regulation, maintenance and investment) away from the public sector and towards other social agents. It comprises widely differing practices that range from the provision and management of public space by corporate organisations as part of the process of securing control upon externalities that might affect the performance of their business, to the takeover of public spaces by community organisations or interest groups, whose own interests become equated with the 'public interest'. There are two main variations in this mode: the first involves provision and/or management by private for-profit entities, whereas the second involves user-centred not-for-profit forms of both provision and management.

Private provision and management

As we have already mentioned, many new public spaces in London have been provided as part of private property development operations through the use of Section 106 planning obligation agreements, which regulate the size and other specifications of the new space. Further contractual dispositions might set out how the space is to be managed over the long term, whether it is to be handed over to the local authority or kept in private management and, if so, under what conditions the space should be managed so that it retains its function as a public space. This is done case by case and there is not a legally defined category of POPS. However, in 2021 the Mayor of London published the Public London Charter as guidance to the London Plan, which sets out principles to be followed by all developments in which public spaces are provided (Greater London Authority 2021). The Charter consists of eight principles that set out the rights and responsibilities for the users, owners and managers of new public spaces. The principles include issues of openness, restrictions on use, community involvement, possible charges, transparency and use of enforcement. The Charter requires developers to put forward a management plan setting out how those principles will be applied in the space. Until very recently, however, in the absence of the Charter, monitoring and enforcement of those contractual dispositions were done reactively, in response to complaints.

The privatised delivery of public space management and its constituent public services, dominated by contractual relationships, has important implications for the key dimensions of coordination, regulation, maintenance and investment. Whereas coordination might have been in the previous mode mostly a matter of devising better and more integrated links between public sector organisations at different levels, here it refers to the need to coordinate the outcomes of public–private arrangements and contracts. Therefore, coordination requires considerable attention to contract negotiation, contract drafting and contract implementation and monitoring. On the part of private managers of public space, coordination is about managing the space within the terms negotiated with a local authority and making sure actions are within the terms of the agreement. This is normally done by estate managers, in charge of managing the private estate in which the space is located, ensuring that subcontractors perform as required and that activities on the space do not infringe agreed publicness rules about access and so forth. This is the case with large private estates with significant public spaces such as Canary Wharf or King's Cross. In some other cases, when the public space results from a number of contiguous but separate developments, management is coordinated by private bodies created specifically to manage the public realm, with a board appointed by the surrounding property owners, as, for example, in the new linear park in Nine Elms.

Regulation in this mode of provision and management tends to have as reference existing by-laws about the use of public space, with adaptations to suit the location of the public space (such as a mostly corporate or a commercial environment) as well as the legal liabilities associated with managing open access locations. Previous research has suggested that factors such as insurance premiums explain some of the more restrictive rules for access and use in privately managed spaces (De Magalhaes and Freire Trigo 2017). Enforcement of access and use rules is normally done by private security guards, in cooperation with the police for more serious offences.

As expected, the definition of maintenance routines is the responsibility of the private managers of the public space, within the parameters of any dispositions of the initial agreements that might have been part of a planning obligation. Private managers of those spaces tend to have a clear vested interest in their quality – and that is the main reason why they retain ownership and management rights. They will establish maintenance schedules and routines, engage subcontractors and define and monitor outcomes according to their views of space quality, which are often higher than that in local authority-managed spaces.

On the last of the four key management dimensions, investment, there are significant differences compared to the previous management mode. Part of the rationale for private provision and management is precisely that it draws resources for public space, financial and technical, from outside the public sector. It does that by allowing those with a strong vested interest in a space to control how it is managed and pay for it. Privately owned and managed public spaces in London receive financial resources from the private estates of which they are a part or, where a separate management body exists, from payments from surrounding property owners and occupiers.

User management of public space

A variation of the devolved mode of public space provision and management in London that has gained prominence in recent years has been the devolution of management of existing public space (with partial transfer of ownership) to groups of users with vested interests in the space. Users in this case are not just individuals who access a public space for leisure, but surrounding residents and businesses with a direct interest on the space – because it is used by employees, or because it influences the quality of the location, the quality of everyday life and local property values.

Contractual relationships, especially those associated with planning obligations, define the nature of devolved service provision to private sector agents. However, given the variety of contexts in which public space management by users has evolved, it is difficult to define a single set of characteristics for the relationship between local authorities and organised groups of public space users. As mentioned elsewhere, and exemplified in detail in the next chapters, this includes private and charitable trusts which lease out a public space on long leases and take over management duties as prescribed in the lease instruments; shorter-term management transfers to residents' associations in public housing estates; and limited transfer of some management duties to organised groups of park friends.

Coordination in this mode of public space management often involves not only coordinating the activities of the various external bodies that have duties or contractual responsibilities in relation to the public space, but also keeping together the various groups and individuals that make up the users' body and making sure there is enough consensus for action. Unsurprisingly, this has been more effective in more formal bodies such as trusts and less so in weaker user bodies, which might crumble under pressure. This also depends to a large extent on how representative they are of their own constituencies, and how well they absorb and deal with the demands and aspirations of their members.

The regulation dimension also tends to rely on council by-laws and the police, although some trusts have added their own rules of access and use, to suit location, context and legal liabilities, in a similar fashion as in privately owned public space. The limits to these added rules are set in the lease terms and therefore local authorities do retain an oversight over them so that the space remains largely publicly accessible and limitations to use are acceptable.

As regards maintenance, the appropriate definition of routines, techniques and procedures is the role of the managing bodies, but often with performance targets included in the lease/transfer terms. Standards of maintenance and the consequent quality of the space will reflect the aspirations and resources of the organised group of users with management rights, and therefore vary from space to space. Similarly, the separation between service and user varies, with more organised trusts contracting out technical expertise to carry out maintenance routines and improvements decided by their members, whereas less formalised bodies will rely on the use of members' labour and time to do the same.

As with the private provision mode, investment and resourcing draws directly on the ability of those with a direct interest in the space to raise financial and technical resources and social and knowledge capital to invest in the space. Some trusts will have an initial endowment provided by a local authority on the basis of savings on the long-term maintenance of the public space, which needs to be managed and complemented by the trust. Many will have the right to organise private, ticket-based income-producing events to raise funds to reinvest in the space, and the rules for this are normally part of the lease/transfer agreement. Others will look for sponsorship, and others rely on donations and voluntary time and work from the communities they represent. As expected, this mode of management leads to a great variety of quality standards and typologies of spaces. Whereas this has proven problematic in some cases, it can also better reflect local priorities and aspirations than uniformly provided public spaces.

Brief history of public space provision in Hong Kong

Before embarking on a discussion of Hong Kong's much shorter history of public space provision, the context of this provision needs to be sketched. By 'Hong Kong' we mean the territory that is now known as Hong Kong Special Administrative Region of the People's Republic of China (HKSAR) and which was, until 1997, a British Crown colony. Hong Kong Island and Kowloon peninsula, which make up Hong Kong's 'urban' area, were ceded to Britain in 1842 and 1860, respectively, while the much larger area of the New Territories was leased for 99 years by the British in 1898. These three elements formed the British colony and, from 1997, the HKSAR (Carroll 2007). Some features of this context were there from its foundation in 1841 and shape the governance and, thus, the public space of Hong Kong today. Hong Kong's landform comprises a part of the Chinese mainland and over 230 islands. Today, Hong Kong's land area is 1,110 km^2, compared to Greater London's 1,569 km^2. Most of the territory is mountainous, with very little naturally flat land. The topography and restricted possibility for expansion limit the supply of easily buildable land (Figure 5.6). We first explore these factors and trace their consequences through a brief chronological account of public space provision in HK across three periods: from foundation to the Second World War (1841–1941), the post-war period to the handover to China and the creation of the Special Administrative Region (1945–97) and from handover up to 2019 (1997 onwards). The period of the Japanese Occupation (1941–45) is omitted.

History of provision from the 19th century to the Second World War: making ground, making space

In the first 100 years of Hong Kong's colonial history, the challenge was to physically construct necessary infrastructure to support port and trading functions, which involved creating an urban settlement in an area previously sparsely occupied by dispersed fishing villages. A number of factors, whether physical or social, that shape Hong Kong's urban landscape today have been influential since the very beginning of the colony. The extremely hilly topography with limited scope for expansion, and very little easily buildable land, together with a climate that sees strong tropical storms with torrential rainfall, are the physical forces that have shaped Hong Kong. For much of its life as a British colony, the effect of these conditions was exacerbated by its attractiveness as an economically liberal jurisdiction that promised various opportunities for immigrants. Hong Kong was a haven for Chinese refugees fleeing from civil and global wars, including the fall of the Qing Dynasty in 1911, the Sino-Japanese War (1937–45) and the Chinese civil war between the Communists and the Nationalists (1927–49) (Carroll 2007).

Figure 5.6: A complex topography leads to a densely built-up area with fierce competition for land for infrastructure, buildings and public space

With the return of the territory to British control in 1945 after the Japanese occupation came massive immigration, exacerbated by the civil war. The population of Hong Kong increased by 95% in the years between 1931 and 1941, and another 30% in the next decade (Hambro 1957). Space in Hong Kong was therefore even more limited than in other British colonial urban settlements in East Asia, which were also typically densely occupied. At the same time, Hong Kong's extended time as a colony has strongly shaped the 'social' and institutional aspects of its public space. The commitment of the colonial administration to 'public health, non-interference, and fiscal prudence' (Cheng 2012: 31), delivered by an established and hierarchical civil service, is still echoed in public space governance today.

These factors provide the basic circumstances for Hong Kong's subsequent high-density volumetric development and, consequently, its correspondingly physically and institutionally complex public space (Shelton, Karakiewicz and Kvan 2011). They also continue to explain the particular delineations between public and private space, the mechanisms that establish rights to access, use and collective decisions, and how they deliver 'public space' – defined as the contiguous space between private realms – in these spatially challenging conditions.

The lack of land had a direct influence on the governance approach by the first British colonial administration. 'Port colonies were intended to be self-funding' (Cheng 2012: 25), and land, despite its scarcity, was one of the few revenue sources the colonial administration had. The first land auction was held by the colonial administration in 1841, within five months of taking possession of the mountainous Hong Kong Island, and even before the formal ratification of the ceding of the colony. In the colony's first 65 years, approximately 38 km² were reclaimed from the sea to provide buildable land. These provide the foundation for two narrative threads in public space provision: the land management system, and engineering-led foundations of urban development.

The key problematic for initial public space governance was how to 'make ground', mainly for the link function (Jones, Boujenko and Marshall 2007), and to ensure that its inhabitation and occupation was safe, so that the colony could operate. It is also clear that there was at least two distinct 'publics' for which different spaces were intended: the colonists and merchants, who were predominantly European, and the local majority population, who were Chinese. In the early 20th century, public open space was included in planning of new development areas as a means of attracting residents. We look at the types of public spaces that were created, how they were managed, and how they fulfilled colonial, if not societal, needs more broadly.

Prior to the Second World War, public space was functional in supporting colonial aims: streets and 'gardens, squares and clubs', for the leisure use mainly of the non-Chinese inhabitants (Cheng 2012). Streets, of course, were first roads. The first acts that defined 'public space' in the colony were the twin actions of land auction (sale of private rights over land to generate revenue) and, to enable the setting up of the colony, the construction of strategic roads for both civilian and military purposes, the earliest being the shorefront Queen's Road, begun in 1841.

Until after the Second World War, Hong Kong's main public space typology was the street, which was ubiquitous simply because it was essential. Like most streets in pre-industrial cities, Hong Kong's served the dual purpose of being links and places (Jones, Boujenko and Marshall 2007). They were the locus for the everyday activity that had, in fact, characterised Chinese urban public space historically (Kinoshita 2001, Heng 2007, Cheng 2012). Streets were lightly regulated places for trading, socialising, celebrating, eating and even sleeping, and much of this activity carried on in Hong Kong's streets, from its early days onwards (Cheng 2012). The density found in most British colonial cities further encouraged the use of the street and alleys as an extension of what the evolving Victorian sensibility deemed as 'private' space (Savage 1992, Kinoshita 2001, Cheng 2012).

While the street was the main domain of the public life of the majority Chinese inhabitants, gardens, squares and clubs (this last, not strictly public), were seen as European-style public space. These gardens, squares and clubs had an almost exclusively 'place' function (Jones, Boujenko and Marshall 2007). The earliest such spaces were for recreation and not public in the sense of being open to all: the Happy Valley Racecourse, set out in 1845, and the Hong Kong Cricket Club, in 1851. The first park accessible to the general public was the Botanical Gardens, made fully open to the public in 1871. Its establishment in 1860 was 'criticized by the Colonial Office, which recommended the funds be used for sanitation improvements' (Endacott 1958). Blake Garden, opened 1905 (Ingham 2007, Farris 2018), was created only because 400 houses were demolished following repeated episodes of bubonic plague that began in 1894. A significant number of commentators have argued that, historically, parks were not enjoyed by, or made no sense to, the Chinese (Xue, Manuel and Chung 2001, Cheng 2012, see also Heng 2007).

Royal Square, now Statue Square, opened in 1896 to commemorate Queen Victoria's Jubilee. It was built on newly reclaimed land for the Praya – a promenade by the waterfront (now Des Voeux Road). Statue Square is notable because it is the earliest example of provision of public *open* space by the private sector in Hong Kong (Figure 5.7). It sits on land reclaimed in 1895 and leased to the Hong Kong and Shanghai Bank (Yeung 2001). This was not a public space for leisure (Farris 2018), but part of the configuration of ceremonial spaces that included Queen's Pier (Cheng 2012), in a city noted as being particularly deficient in monuments and ceremonial/symbolic colonial spaces (Lee 2008).

The 1920s saw the first incorporations of 'rest gardens' and other open spaces into comprehensive planning for the Kowloon Tong area, which was envisaged as a 'Garden City', designed for the civil service and professional classes (Forrest, La Grange and Yip 2004, Ho 2018). This was part of the early

Figure 5.7: Statue Square today

work of the Town Planning Committee, established in 1922, to plan 'New Kowloon', the area north of Boundary Street but south of the mountains separating the Kowloon Peninsula from the rest of the New Territories. Here again, Kowloon Tong's planning and public space were delivered by private enterprise (Kwok 1998, Ho 2018, see also Chu 2012).

History of provision post Second World War to 1997: high density, high rise, high intensity

In the years after 1945, shifting global geopolitics contributed to greater commitment of funds by the colonial government to longer-term planning and public works, including parks and open spaces. A major wave of immigrant influx sparked a surge of squatters in the early 1950s, and the Shek Kip Mei fire, which destroyed a large area of these squatters on Christmas Day in 1953, was a key turning point towards greater intervention from the colonial government in housing provision. Simultaneously, political pressures to justify continued colonisation of Hong Kong amidst the flurry of independence events in colonies around the world and the position of Hong Kong on the edge of the newly established People's Republic of China in 1949 (Smart 2006), pushed the colonial government to plan for longer-term urban development and to invest in public infrastructure. The first strategic plan, commonly known as the Abercrombie Report, was published in 1948 and from then on comprehensive planning led in the late 1960s to large public housing estates such as Wah Fu and Oi Man and satellite towns adjacent to the urban areas (Kwun Tong and Tsuen Wan), and from the 1970s onwards, with the advent of the Mass Transit Railway (MTR), New Towns or 'rail villages' (Xue 2016).

A key public space problematic in this period became to improve its link function to make movement possible in a city whose population was growing fast, and pedestrian congestion was seen as a major problem. Overcrowding on the street was seen as a problem in Hong Kong, and in line with local attitudes to governance, 'using the land twice' was seen as an 'efficient' solution (Tan and Xue 2016), especially in a city with difficult topography. The result was a network of elevated walkways and public escalators weaving in and out of private buildings and creating a 'grade-separated pedestrian network … a pedestrian-only precinct independent from vehicular traffic. It weaves through diverse outdoor and indoor pedestrian spaces in a continuous movement experience …' (Tan and Xue 2016: 689) (Figure 5.8). The corollary of grade separation of pedestrians and vehicles was the prioritisation of the ground for vehicles and the corresponding de-prioritisation of pedestrians. The development of the MTR, apart from furthering the construction of New Towns and their parks and open

Figure 5.8: Hong Kong's spatial complexity includes public escalators and lifts and underground and above-ground passageways at various levels, interweaving space for pedestrians and vehicles

spaces, also intensified the construction of networks of both elevated and underground pedestrian routes which had begun in the 1970s.

Another key problematic referred to the expected role of public space in enhancing welfare as part of a public housing programme in the context of a new urban form of high rise and high density. In the satellite towns, and especially the seven later New Towns, the evolution and full impact of the high-density rail-based planning vision was realised. These were comprehensively planned, self-contained settlements for which movement networks and open public spaces had to be created from scratch. It is in the New Towns' array of public spaces that we see an engineering- and public health-led conception of public space in which place identity plays a minor role (Figure 5.9). This is different from the new Victoria Park, Kowloon Park and Hong Kong Park, three major parks in the urban areas of Hong Kong Island and Kowloon created in 1954, 1970 and 1991, respectively, which have their own identities and character (Figure 5.10).

In terms of public space management, the Urban Council played an increasingly central role. The Urban Council was established in 1936 as the successor of the Sanitary Board (created in 1883) and carried out a range of municipal services through its executive arm, the Urban Services Department. The services included arts, culture, recreation (including parks and sports grounds) and sanitation services (including street cleansing,

Figure 5.9: Public open spaces in Tsuen Wan, a New Town

Figure 5.10: Victoria Park

refuse collection, pest control and also hawker control) (Lau 2002). Like its predecessor the Sanitary Board, the Urban Council was partially elected for most of its history, and from 1994 it was fully elected by universal suffrage. In the New Territories, management of all infrastructure, including open spaces, relied heavily on the District Office, with a local approach; and for the New Towns only, the Territory Development Department, which was much more engineering and 'modern planning' driven. These responsibilities were transferred in 1986 to a Regional Council for the New Territories.

History of provision from 1997 to 2019: places for people?

The sovereignty of Hong Kong reverted to the People's Republic China in 1997. In this post 'handover' period, the provision of public space took place in a context of highly built-up areas, the accelerated outflow of residents to New Towns and the beginnings of urban renewal. The year 1997 saw the introduction of the executive governance system in a new Special Administrative Region of the People's Republic of China (SAR). This replaced the British Governor with a Chief Executive governing under the 'One Country, Two Systems' principle. The administration has three branches. The Legislative Council is elected, although not via universal suffrage. The Executive comprises the Executive Council and various government agencies. The key ones are the Bureaux which make policies, and Departments and other agencies, empowered by relevant legislation, which implement those policies, including those related to public space (Table 5.1). The third branch of government is the Judiciary, which operates a common law system, with the 'Basic Law' as an explicit mini constitution. The system has interfaces with at least two other legal systems: first, with the national legal system of the People's Republic of China, and second, with Chinese customary law that govern land rights in the New Territories.

For public space provision and management, an important structural change was the abolition of the Urban and Regional Councils in 1999. Leaving aside what this meant for the enfranchisement of citizens, this was a loss of a key coordinating organisation with financial autonomy for many public space functions. Counter to the trend of devolution of urban governance powers around the world, almost all responsibilities for public space were, instead, further centralised into three SAR government departments, the newly created Leisure and Cultural Services Department (LCSD) and the Food and Environmental Hygiene Department (FEHD) as well as the Home Affairs Department (HAD) (Lai 2021).

Despite these governance developments, and the construction of three further New Towns, the pre-planned trajectory for Hong Kong's urban form did not radically change. Much of the foundations of its urban form, public space and ways of governing it had also already been laid in the late colonial era. The New Towns, the MTR, the grade-separated pedestrian systems both above and underground, the megastructures (multiple intensive land use, as described by Lau, Giridharan and Ganesan 2005) were already dreamed up in the 1960s and put into strategies such as the 1969 Colony Plan (Tan and Xue 2016).

Nevertheless, the emerging sense of local identity, the influence of community planning that was infusing planning practice elsewhere (for example, Healey 1997, 1998, 2020, Carr et al 2002), the resurgent role of civil society in public space production and new forms of cooperation between government, private and civic sectors did all have an influence on Hong Kong's governance of public space (Lee et al 2013). From the 1990s, around the world there was a renewed interest in cities as places to live, visit and in which to consume (Glaeser 2011, Ballas 2013). The rush towards consumerism and tourism, but also citizen responses to these and to the state of their (sometimes poor) urban experience, meant that there was an imperative to improve the quality of public space. As Hong Kong's de-industrialisation gathered pace, and the uncertainties of the 1997 handover receded, societal aspirations also reflected some of these themes, for example, in the work of the Harbourfront Commission (Lai 2021), in the community-supported work in small public spaces in Wan Chai in the 2000s and, more recently, in the work of NGOs such as Designing Hong Kong, Hong Kong Public Space Initiative (HKPSI), VeryHK, CollaborateHK, and Make a Difference Asia (Mad Asia) (Figure 5.11).

The key problem for Hong Kong's public space governance in this period was the difficulty in meeting citizens' demands – a necessarily political process – via technical solutions through 'un-reformed' governance mechanisms, both structural and attitudinal, and in the political context discussed earlier. While civil service reform happened to an extent under the SAR's first two Chief Executives (Wong 2013), this failed in instilling a results-led and effectiveness-driven culture in the civil service (Lee and Haque 2006). It

Figure 5.11: VeryHK Yuen Long Festival: an NGO-conceived public space with furniture and activities in an otherwise non-descript setting

Source: VeryHK

remained procedurally focused, empowered by public space legislation that was often outdated (Xue and Manuel 2001, Lai and da Roza 2018).

Public space governance in Hong Kong: who does it

We now turn to the procedures and responsibilities of public space provision. As we saw earlier, the provision of public space, including policy making and implementation of public space provision, lies largely with the SAR-level government bureaux and departments. The structural relationships of governance structures were discussed earlier, under the historical period since 1997, and remain unchanged. The policy-making Bureaux directly involved in public space provision include the Environment, Food and Health, Home Affairs, Transport and Housing, and Development Bureaux. In terms of implementation, a wide range of government departments and agencies are involved, including the Planning Department (PlanD), the (LCSD, Lands Department (LandsD), Buildings Department (BD), the FEHD, Transport Department (TD), the Civil Engineering and Development Department (CEDD), the Drainage Services Department and the Highways Department (HyD).

Despite centralisation of provision, the spatial nature of public space logistics means that District Councils continue to play a critical role in public space governance. The District Administration system operates under the supervision of the Home Affairs Department and comprises District Offices and fully and directly elected District Councils of Hong Kong's 18 districts (Lam 2012, Electoral Affairs Commission 2020) (Figure 5.12). The District Councils are very different from London's Borough Councils, as they have no policy-making nor executive power, only an advisory role, and act as communication channels between citizens and the relevant government departments which execute public space work. In 2013, the District Councils were given one-off grants to execute signature projects through the Signature Project Scheme, some of which were public space improvement projects. In addition to District Councils, there are District Management Committees, Area Committees, Mutual Aid Committees, Owners' Corporation, whose roles are to enhance communication among core governments in districts, residents of a building and owners of private buildings (HAD 2021). The Hong Kong Housing Authority and Hong Kong Housing Society are responsible for providing a not insignificant proportion of Hong Kong's public open space within their estates, but through arrangements that are separate from what is described in the foregoing, although its quantum contributes to 'countable open space' for planning purposes.

As for indirect provision, the range of non-governmental bodies is much less diverse than in London. These are usually private sector actors such as property owners and developers. For example, the elevated walkway system around Jardine House in Central, usually recognised as the earliest part of

Figure 5.12: Hong Kong's 18 administrative districts

1. Islands District
2. Kwai Tsing District
3. North District
4. Sai Kung District
5. Sha Tin District
6. Tai Po District
7. Tsuen Wan District
8. Tuen Mun District
9. Yuen Long District
10. Kowloon City District
11. Kwun Tong District
12. Sham Shui Po District
13. Wong Tai Sin District
14. Yau Tsim Mong District
15. Central and Western District
16. Eastern District
17. Southern District
18. Wan Chai District

the elevated walkway network in Hong Kong's central business district (CBD), was constructed and is maintained by Jardine's, now Hong Kong Land (Cuthbert and McKinnell 1997). However, they may be responsible for providing a range of publicly accessible spaces, from private streets to POSPDs (which refer to both the spaces and the mechanism for management), some parks (such as West Kowloon Art Park, provided as part of the West Kowloon PPP (Lai 2021), some waterfront spaces, or public passageways through private buildings. This provision of public goods and services by non-governmental bodies, whether from the private or charity sectors, has been accepted practice from early colonial times (Cheng 2012, Ho 2018), and while the government owns all the SAR's land, and provides public housing and a public health service, there has never been a government-driven trend towards 'nationalisation' of common goods and public services. Notably, some major private sector players are oligarchs (Wong 2016), and with privileges granted to them comes implied responsibility to provide common goods. Arguably, the relationship between citizens and major private sector players is not simply one of the provider and customer, but one in which a duty of care may be seen to be owed to the citizen.

There have been few 'third sector' organisations, NGOs, in Hong Kong, such as charities or community-led organisations, focused on public space provision. However, with increased interest in heritage protection and civic participation, there have been a few examples of this, even if public space provision has been ancillary to other activities. For example, Collaborate HK has supported community groups in obtaining short leases from government to enable projects to happen, such as Friends of the 30 Houses Neighbourhood on Shing Wong Street Community Living Room, Hong Kong Young Women's Christian Association on Tin Shui Wai House of Stories, and Tin Shui Wai Community Development Network on Tin Shui Wai Neighbour-Wood. More recently, the Development Bureau (DEVB) has worked with two NGOs to deliver two POSPDs on the Victoria Harbour Waterfront (Lai 2021), in an experiment in new forms of public space management.

The key elements of the legislative framework for public space provision, set out in Table 5.2, underpin all formal direct public space provision, and have influence over indirect provision. Various government departments and agencies are empowered by different Ordinances and Regulations that invest them with duties and powers over different aspects of public space. This strict compartmentalisation in a governance culture that is procedurally compliant (Lee and Haque 2006) leads to difficulties in responding to emergent issues and to coordination of governance actions. Any delay in the ability of the Legislative Council to make new laws or amend existing ones also results in inability to modify governance actions appropriately (Lai and da Roza 2018).

Extending the legislative framework are contractual arrangements that commit various non-governmental public space service providers to a wide range of responsibilities that constitute indirect provision of public space. The most well-studied of these are the POSPD arrangements formalised in the 1980s (for example, DEVB 2011, Lai 2021, Rossini and Yiu 2021). Others include various agreements between the government and private developers, whether incentives-supported or otherwise, and also PPP arrangements. These will be discussed in greater detail in the following section.

Public space governance in Hong Kong: how it is done

While there are two main modes of provision – direct and indirect – in Hong Kong, as in London, the boundary between private and public in these two places is constructed quite differently. Hong Kong's mode of societal service provision was far less influenced by the nationalisation trend that gripped Europe post the Second World War, even though the provision of public housing, public health services and public parks took off at the time. Nevertheless, Hong Kong does retain in the civil service a strongly Weberian approach to governance, which impacts on direct public space provision.

Table 5.2: Selected examples of Hong Kong ordinances for the four management actions of public space

Management action	Type of public space	Ordinance	Organisation
Regulate	All types of public spaces	Public Order Ordinance (Cap 245) • Granting no objection to public processions • Control public assemblies and gatherings • Punish offenders for disorder in public places and unlawful assemblies	HKPF
	Public land; public pleasure grounds; streets; public places	Public Health and Municipal Services Ordinance (Cap 132) • General behaviour, including personal cleanliness, littering, begging and so forth • Issuing itinerant and temporary hawkers' licences • Opening and closure of public pleasure grounds	LCSD FEHD HKPF
	All types of public spaces	Summary Offences Ordinance (Cap 228) • General behaviour in public, including annoyance or obstruction, sales, performances, throwing filth or rubbish and so forth in any public place	HAB SWD HAD
	All types of public spaces	Places of Public Entertainment Ordinance (Cap 172) • Issuing licences for places of public entertainment • Restricting unauthorised sales of tickets	HAB FEHD
Maintain	Roads; streets; street parking	Road Traffic Ordinance (Cap 374) • Power to erect and place traffic signs and road markings • Establish zebra crossings • Removal of vehicles	TD HyD
	Public open space within West Kowloon Cultural District	West Kowloon Cultural District (Public Open Space) Bylaw (Cap 601A) • Temporarily close any part of a public open space to the public to facilitate repair or maintenance works in a closed area • Advise and remove equipment of performer if they obstruct pedestrian movement (Guidelines – no statutory power)	HAB WKDCA
	Public place; street	Public Health and Municipal Services Ordinance (Cap 132) • Seizure of abandoned hawker equipment and commodities • General management and control of public pleasure grounds, including exclusive right to amenities provision of any kind • Protection of grass and flower beds • Require occupier of a street or public space to remove litter or waste found	FEHD LCSD

(continued)

Table 5.2: Selected examples of Hong Kong ordinances for the four management actions of public space (continued)

Management action	Type of public space	Ordinance	Organisation
Invest	All types of public spaces	Town Planning Ordinance (Cap 131) • Outline Zoning Plan for land-use zonings including public open spaces, comprehensive development areas (POSPD-related) and green zones • Development Permission Plans (DPA) • Lease modification (when proposed land uses are different from the permitted lease conditions)	PlanD LandsD

	POSPD; public passage; public access	Buildings Ordinance (Cap 123)
		• Deeds of dedication and lease
		• Practice notes for authorized persons, registered structural engineers and registered geotechnical engineers
		  • APP-002 Calculation of GFA and non-accountable GFA
		  • APP-108 Dedication of land/area for use as public passage
		  • APP-151 Building design to foster a quality and sustainable built environment
			BD
			Private Developers

	Public pleasure grounds	Public Health and Municipal Services Ordinance (Cap 132) • Set aside places for use as public pleasure grounds • Provide and demarcate public pleasure grounds for different activities • Provide facilities for physical or other recreational purposes within the public pleasure ground	LCSD (for this cat.)
	Roads; pedestrian priority zones	Road Traffic Ordinance (Traffic Control) Regulations (Cap.374G) • Designate pedestrian priority zones (TD) • Road closures (HyD)	TD HyD
Coordinate	MTR areas	Mass Transit Railway Ordinance (Cap 556) • Granting the franchise to the MTR Corporation • Obtaining information from the MTR Corporation • Make regulations and by-laws to confer power upon the Corporation; or upon TD and THB to direct the Corporation	MTR Corp. THB* TD HKPF

Note: *THB = the Transport and Housing Bureau of the Hong Kong Government, which existed from 2007 to 2022, when it was split into the Transport and Logistics Bureau (TLB) and the Housing Bureau (HB)

The indirect mode has two sub-modes. First, there is a continuation of cross-sectoral arrangements in Hong Kong to provide common goods, for example, through POSPDs, deeds of dedication or other land lease agreements, as discussed earlier. The second is user management of public space. Here, the situation in Hong Kong is very different from that in London. It in effect continues a long tradition stretching back to colonial times of being almost completely informal, but highly visible and very characteristic of Hong Kong's public spaces. It can be characterised as 'commoning'. This is where public space users share, whether explicitly or otherwise, resources such as the ubiquitous 'discarded/rescued chairs' that are found everywhere in the city, or public space being used for the essentially private activity of sorting cardboard by waste pickers. Alongside this, there is an intricate spatial interweaving of management regimes, the result of Hong Kong's intensive space use.

Government provision and management

As in London, most public space is provided by the government. The key feature of this provision is the central role of the legislative framework, which in turn underpins the strong organisational structures. The PlanD has the responsibility for checking whether there are sufficient open spaces for a set population in any area. If there is a surplus, planned open spaces can be allocated to other uses. If there is a scarcity, possible locations and sources of open space will be identified. These new spaces will be then provided by government directly as some form of 'public open space', usually implemented by the LCSD, or by the private sector as POSPD. The latter involves the LandsD in the land lease agreement. The BD is responsible for agreeing with private property owners, space dedicated for public movement. If we include highways as public space, the TD, HyD and the CEDD are also responsible departments. In terms of management of government-provided space, a further range of departments are involved, including the Home Affairs Bureau (HAB) via the District Offices, DEVB, LCSD and the (FEHD).

This strict organisational and legislative framework, together with the conservatism of Hong Kong's governance attitudes and the low penetration of New Public Management-type reforms means a governance style characterised by rigid hierarchy, procedure rather than results-orientation and strict division of labour between departments. This exacerbates problems of poor coordination and the lack of purchase of legislation on specific problems on the ground (see, for instance, Rossini 2022).

Two types of ordinances underpin public space management, those that focus on managing particular user actions, and those that address particular types of spaces. The action-based legislation regulates collective actions (for example, public procession, gatherings under the Public Order Ordinance), individual behaviour (for example, littering, sales, annoyance under the Summary Offences Ordinance) and specific activities (for example, public events involving entertainment under the Places of Public Entertainment). Cheng (2012) argued that since streets were, in the early colonial period, the primary public space type in Hong Kong, and since public health and hygiene were major concerns, 'public space management' historically was largely about 'managing streets for public hygiene' and, in particular, hawker regulation. While relevant legislation for street regulation is scattered across a wide range of ordinances (Lai and da Roza 2018, Lai 2021), we see this focus on 'hygiene' in both the organisation and legislative structures for public space management today.

Given Hong Kong's historical discourse of minimal governmental intervention and, as discussed here, outdated legislation that does not fully respond to contemporary issues, coupled with the intensity of public space use, public space management is characterised by quite a broad arena of action, in which rules can be interpreted quite creatively by users and by street-level bureaucrats, out of necessity. This becomes evident when we discuss the user management of public space later, which has significant interface with regulation.

The FEHD is responsible for maintaining general hygiene in public spaces; much of the labour is subcontracted to private cleaning companies. Nevertheless, full privatisation of such services was not achieved due to push-back from unions. Specific duties in LCSD-managed public places and regarding street hawking are communicated through the Public Health and Municipal Services Ordinance. Repair of facilities depends on the department responsible for that particular type of public space. For instance, the HyD and TD oversee traffic signs, road markings, removal of vehicles and so forth under the Road Traffic Ordinance. At district level, funds for district minor works are provided to upgrade and improve district facilities as well as for realising community involvement projects.

The government's role in investment is focused on such activity as the commission, design and construction of public open spaces, and the design and building of movement infrastructure such as roads, streets and public footbridges. Depending on the type of space, the lead is taken by different departments empowered under the relevant Ordinance. 'Public Pleasure Grounds' constitutes the largest part of urban public open spaces in Hong Kong delivered by LCSD. The Public Health and Municipal Services Ordinance empowers LCSD to set aside land for its provision, demarcate and provide facilities to support different activities within the spaces. When it comes to footbridges or streets, it is variously CEDD or HyD who lead. The TD has also been implementing pedestrianisation schemes on a permanent or part-time basis to provide vehicle-free zones on roads. The government, however, plays a major role in enabling all investment in public space, whether public or private. This is not direct provision, but it is a critically important part of coordination of investment, and we will discuss this next.

For coordinating investment, this is addressed at urban and individual development project scales by different mechanisms. At the urban scale, and for investment and delivering on the provision target of 2.5 m^2 of public open space per inhabitant, the Town Planning Board (TPB) supported by the Planning Department (PlanD) are the statutory bodies that prepare and update the Outline Zoning Plan (OZP) under the Town Planning Ordinance. The plan shows land-use zonings of different urban areas, including sites designated for public open space. Although the OZP system may appear a relatively comprehensive tool to coordinate public space investment, in practice, many spaces that are effectively public fall outside its remit, including Space Left Over After Planning associated with infrastructural planning such as elevated highways, railway embankments or drainage. At the scale of single developments, land lease-related matters, including modification, are helmed by the LandsD as already mentioned. Areas dedicated for public use, such as public passages, street widening, footbridges/subways, are the result of agreements made between the BD and private property owners via deeds of dedication; all of which are granted gross floor area (GFA) concessions as incentives.

For coordinating regulation and maintenance, two features would suggest that coordination is not embedded into public space management activities. First, the structure of the Ordinances reviewed suggests limited explicit legislative support for inter-departmental coordination. Many of the regulations focus on clearly demarcating responsibility boundaries, and thus strictly distributing them to particular departments, rather than encouraging cross-departmental cooperation. The difficulties discussed earlier in updating legislation in a culture where rule-following and organisational hierarchy is important means that any necessary management actions not explicitly authorised are unlikely to be enacted. District Offices and Councils are supposed to work together as a bridge between the government and citizens, to effectively provide place-based coordination. Representatives from government departments are present in District Council meetings as part of the District Management Committee (Lam 2012, HAD 2021). Effective coordination, however, requires highly delegated authority that is responsive, and District Councils can only provide 'advice' and do not have implementational authority.

Provision by private and non-governmental organisations

Due to the density of form, topographic complexity, spatial interweaving of property ownership regimes and a shortage of open spaces in older urban

Figure 5.13: A POSPD in the Lee Tung Avenue development

areas, the provision of both public open space and public thoroughfares for movement through privately owned space is a necessity. Several mechanisms enable the government to formalise such arrangements. Although there was a moratorium on POSPDs in 2009 (Lai 2021), they are still occasionally the basis of provision. Many of the POSPDs in the latest large-scale developments are planned under Comprehensive Development Areas and Open Spaces for active and/or passive recreational uses (Figure 5.13). Apart from POSPDs, there are established mechanisms by which the private sector provides space for pedestrian passage, for public transport interchanges and for MTR facilities and for road widening (LandsD 2011). These are governed by a range of lease conditions and other contractual documents. For example, the 'Deed of Dedication' process that usually secures private land or space for public thoroughfare and which is sometimes incentivised with favourable additional GFA and Floor Area Ratio (BD 2008, 2022). There are also numerous PPP arrangements, where the private partner may be either a for-profit or non-profit organisation (Lai 2021). A high-profile example of this is the West Kowloon Cultural District Authority's (WKCDA) jurisdiction over the Art Park and the West Kowloon Waterfront Promenade (Lai 2021).

The DEVB published guidelines for the design and management of POSPDs in 2011, but most POSPDs were built before these were implemented and many studies demonstrate that the guidelines are not enforced. Maintenance of privately owned public spaces is usually provided by the owners. In special cases like the West Kowloon Cultural District, which is actually provided via a PPP arrangement (Lai 2021), statutory by-laws and non-statutory guidelines are put in place to regulate and to manage performers and facilities in the public open space.

Regulation here refers to two things. First, the regulation of user behaviour in the privately provided public spaces. If the public space remains under provider management, regulation is most often provided by the property owner (LandsD 2011), although, if needed, the police may be involved in enforcement. In the case of the public–private joint development and management of the MTR, the Mass Transit Railway Ordinance clearly stipulates the conditions of granting franchise to the MTR Corporation and establishes regulations about the use of the space. Second, regulation can be in respect of the government enforcement of lease conditions that created these privately provided spaces in the first place, to ensure they are delivering the public benefit that was intended. There are numerous examples where accessibility to these spaces is limited via regulatory or maintenance pretexts, for example, the lifts to POSPDs being often 'under maintenance'. However, as Lai (2021) has pointed out, leases are poor instruments for the lifetime management of public space, as lease conditions reflect only those issues imaginable at the start of the lease and cannot be modified in response to changing conditions. Lease conditions also tend to be generic and will unlikely be suitable to every eventuality in every place.

As discussed earlier, any private sector investment is also coordinated via the interrelated planning, land lease and building control processes (LandsD 2011). In terms of coordinating maintenance and regulation of indirectly provided spaces, there appear not to be standard mechanisms. However, if a space was under the jurisdiction of a single owner, this might ameliorate the difficulties of inter-organisational coordination that have such a major impact in the direct provision of public space by different departments in a government bureaucracy.

User management of public space

Finally, user management of public space in Hong Kong is quite different from that in London, mainly because it happens almost completely informally. It would not be inaccurate to describe it as 'commoning'. What characterises Hong Kong's public spaces is the ubiquity of all sorts of commercial activity, often microscopic in nature, though not always, that fill their every corner. Some of this involves activities already regulated by government, such as shop display of goods on the street (called 'shop front extensions'), street markets and mobile hawkers, the last of which are now a dying breed, as new licences are no longer issued. Others, such as the ubiquitous waste pickers or recyclers working individually with human-powered hand carts, and who are very often elderly women, hence the term 'cardboard grannies', or the second-hand chairs that appear at bus stops or at various street corners where seating is much desired but not provided by the government, are often tolerated, and have historically been so, given the history of Hong Kong's street culture discussed earlier (see also Cheng 2012) (Figure 5.14). While some of this tolerance is enabled by laws or regulations being silent, or even

Figure 5.14: Waste pickers and cardboard recyclers play an essential role in Hong Kong's waste management, and the street is their workplace

enabling, some involves those rules being not enforced. For example, many chairs which are just left to effectively act as public seating could, in theory, be removed because they are obstructing the highway, but are not because no one has yet complained about it and they may actually be providing a service for the local elderly population. Other arrangements, such as an informal agreement between waste pickers over each one's space for sorting their cardboard, may be considered exertion of 'customary rights' set out in the unsaid agreement between them.

Probably the most high-profile example of non-enforcement behaviour by the authorities is the 'Instagram Pier', discussed in the next chapter, which was for over ten years until 2021 one of Hong Kong's favourite waterfront spaces. The Marine Department's non-enforcement of the rule that only persons with official business could enter the Western District Cargo Working Area, which still functions as a cargo pier during the day, meant that this space functioned as a park, but one that was not subject to any of the safety design standards, such as waterside railings, or strict regulations that governed open spaces managed by the LCSD. While this space was legally not 'public space', an effective public space was created by the commoning behaviours of users and authorities. The implementation of enforcing exclusion from this space finally came about when the government opened an official waterfront space nearby and closed the Pier.

Conclusion

We have seen in the previous sections/chapters what the systems are for provision and management of public space in both London and Hong Kong. We have seen that for both similar and dissimilar reasons (pressures on public sector budgets, costs of land in dense central areas and need to make most of a scarce resource, ideological and policy approaches, public sector inefficiencies) both cities have to a larger extent transferred the initiative on public space provision and, to smaller extent, public space management, to real estate developers or other corporate actors. In London, there has been also a devolution of management responsibilities over existing publicly owned public spaces to not-for-profit associations of stakeholders, thus transferring management responsibilities and the rights that come with them away from the public sector.

Overall, the reality is that in both cities the common good public space with all its attributes has been provided and managed in ways that do not entirely fit what is usually regarded as the expected mode of provision, whereby this sort of good should be provided by the public sector and managed from public sector budgets, on behalf of the communities represented in a particular polity. Both cities – and they are not alone – have resorted to modes of public space provision and management that require that we interpret what public spaces are and what makes them public in a different light, as explored in the initial chapters of this book. In both cities, the challenges associated with public space provision and management have often been tackled through increased private provision and devolved management.

As can be inferred from this chapter, these challenges are, firstly, the provision of sufficient public space and of sufficient quality, especially in densely occupied areas (an issue of straightforward availability of land in Hong Kong, given the scarcity of easily developable land in Hong Kong Island and Kowloon, a more nuanced issue of providing public space in areas of high land costs in both cities). This might be a clear objective of policy as in Hong Kong, or not so as in London, but it is certainly associated with long-standing views about the desirability of public spaces because of their amenity value, and also the more recent emphasis on the health benefits of public space, leading to policies to make public space more accessible to a larger part of the population, recognition of the importance of public space in urban regeneration efforts and so forth.

The COVID-19 pandemic has put a new emphasis on the availability and distribution of public space, highlighting the correlation between easy access to open space and well-being, with those in worse housing conditions, living in denser neighbourhoods without access to open spaces, doing substantially worse in terms of physical and mental health than wealthier residents with easy access to private gardens, public parks or promenades (see, for example, Honey-Rosés et al 2021).

Another factor at play is the increasing acceptance in policy circles, but also among developers and large commercial occupiers, of the role of good and well-maintained public spaces in placemaking, in making locations desirable for occupiers and their employees. Both cities have increasingly relied on well-designed commercial environments with public spaces and other amenities to remain competitive in attracting large corporates to their business districts. Planning and urban design policies in both cities emphasise place quality as a way of attracting both businesses and their potential workforce.

An important part of this 'quantitative' challenge involves the costs and difficulties over time of maintaining a large number of public spaces to acceptable levels of quality, and of adapting these spaces to changing user needs. We have already mentioned that economic policies of austerity have led to the reduction of public sector budgets, with resources diverted to essential statutory public services such as health, education and social security. This applies more to London than Hong Kong, where bureaucratic inflexibility is more of an issue, but it is a challenge that exists in many other cities throughout the world. As the quantity and quality of public spaces increase, and their usage becomes more intense – especially in densely occupied and intensely visited neighbourhoods – the costs of maintaining and adapting public spaces increase significantly and they must be met without compromising the ability of public authorities to meet their other obligations. As we saw earlier, this has been behind the search for resources outside the public sector to manage and maintain public spaces.

The second challenge, more of a qualitative nature, results from the increasing diversity of lifestyles, cultures and associated needs that impinge on public spaces in culturally diverse global cities. On the one hand, this raises issues of varied and conflicting aspirations for public spaces, differentiated across public spaces, which are difficult to address with standardised provision and management systems. This is visible in London, especially through conflicts between different user interests, and also in Hong Kong through attempts at making homogeneous provision more adaptable to the needs of particular places. On the other hand, it raises issues of exclusion as particular groups of users of public space, defined by their culture, ethnicity, age or gender feel systematically less welcome in public spaces dominated by lifestyles and aspirations that feel alien to them (Ruddick 1996, Low, Taplin and Scheld 2009). On the other hand, it presents a challenge to large public bureaucracies which have been more efficient in delivery bulk homogeneous services and have often showed little flexibility in adapting them to localised demands. The pressure for more user and stakeholder involvement that we see in both cities, and the process of management transfers we see mostly in London, but also in Hong Kong in a more limited form, are all ways of tackling this particular challenge.

Associated with the issues already mentioned are fundamental questions about user involvement and accountability around public space decisions. As we saw in the earlier part of this book, one element that instinctively defines publicness is the capacity to have a say in what happens to the attributes of a public space that users might value – which we called collective choice rights. In complex and diverse cities, with equally diverse sets of interests and aspirations, the challenge is how to ensure users feel connected to their public spaces, how expectations can be managed and conflicts negotiated and solved. As the diversity of provision and management regimes for public space increases, multiple forms of user involvement and accountability emerge.

A third challenge therefore revolves around managing a public realm made up of different kinds of public space, provided and managed under different regimes and keeping some sense of continuity and homogeneity that avoids a sense of fragmentation and ghettoisation among public space users. This relates to the perception of public space provision and management as a public service, a common good in itself – regardless of issues of ownership and use regulations. This is a challenge that is manifest in plans and strategies in both cities, which aim at improving users' experience of public spaces and ensuring that they feel and operate as 'public', regardless of their ownership or management regime.

How cities tackle these challenges has impacts on how rights over publicness attributes are allocated and therefore what sort of publicness landscape emerges. By adopting a variety of provision and management arrangements, public authorities in both cities have been rearranging and reallocating the rights to attributes of public spaces that define publicness. We suggested in Chapter 3 that publicness is an expression of how operational rights of use and access and collective choice rights – rights of agency over the attributes of public space – are allocated to the various stakeholders in that complex common good. Therefore, by facing the quantitative and qualitative challenges in the ways summarised earlier, both cities are creating a varied and complex landscape of publicness rights. The following chapters examine in more detail the implications of that for common good public space and for the societal task of managing it.

6

The quantitative challenges of public space provision and management

Introduction

This chapter discusses the first set of challenges to the provision and management of public spaces in London and Hong Kong, through empirical cases in both cities. In the previous chapter we termed these quantitative challenges, as they refer to the challenges of providing enough public spaces of appropriate quality in the neighbourhoods where they are needed and, subsequently, of finding the resources to maintain those spaces over the long term to standards that will not compromise their viability and usefulness. The chapter looks first at the issue of provision in Hong Kong, and the ways capital investment on new or refurbished public spaces has been sought outside public sector investment budgets, and primarily from private property development operations. The chapter looks at the production of public facilities in private developments or on privately leased land, including public passageways and public open spaces and the land leasing and deeds of dedication mechanisms that make these possible. In London, the chapter discusses the use of planning obligations to obtain new public space as a planning gain from development operations of different types and the mechanisms used for it. This is followed by a section that examines the challenge London faces of maintaining existing and new spaces to the standards expected both by government and users. The chapter discusses the types of negotiation between local authorities and property investors, the transfer of management rights to public space stakeholders of various sorts and various forms of outsourcing management responsibilities to private and voluntary bodies. The chapter concludes with a discussion of how both cities' responses to the quantitative challenges can potentially affect the more immediate operational rights associated with publicness, the rights of access and use.

In the previous chapters we saw how city authorities have sought private resources to help deliver improvements in the public realm. If the creation of new or refurbished spaces through municipal investment might still be viable at a small scale or in more peripheral neighbourhoods, or where municipal landownership is significant, it is a far less attractive proposition in highly dense central areas where land prices are prohibitive and the opportunity costs of allocating public land for public space are high. Similarly, the costs of maintaining public spaces in popular areas with high footfall and high tourist influx can be various orders of magnitude higher than the cost of maintaining regular local public spaces and can consume a significant proportion of public space budgets. All this militates against the idea of a well-balanced and equitable distribution of public spaces across the urban fabric and can skew the distribution of public space maintenance budgets in favour of higher-profile and more visible spaces.

In London, over the course of the past four decades it has become accepted that the dominant archetypal mid-20th-century ideal of public space provision by the state sector was not able to deliver either the quantity or quality of public spaces required, or indeed to do so equitably, given resource constraints. The response of city authorities has been to seek private resources. In Hong Kong, the private sector has always been widely involved in delivering public space. On the one hand, public open space as a publicly provided amenity only became a reality in the 1950s. On the other hand, stemming from the early colonial era, the attitude of the private sector as a source of common goods has never been repudiated. In both cities, a wide range of value-capture mechanisms have been used by public authorities to ensure profits generated by private property development projects are added to municipal resources, while also delivering something of value to private sector actors involved. These mechanisms are especially common in the case of larger urban regeneration or development projects in which whole urban quarters are being created and the funding of common goods is predicated on market success of a real estate operation. In London, this is also becoming increasingly common in smaller developments with predominantly local impact, although this has always been the case in Hong Kong. Whether or not these value-capture processes are being driven by municipal government-led planning systems or PPPs, private interests are also increasingly waking up to the benefits of providing those public goods themselves, as they can be capitalised over the long term in real estate values.

It stands to reason that an increasing reliance on the input of private resources for the provision and management of public space will have direct implications for how the publicness rights we discussed in Chapter 3 are allocated and exercised. By transferring the financial responsibility for provision of public spaces to private and often corporate stakeholders, public authorities are changing the character of the stakes in those spaces, with implications for the rights each stakeholder will have over them. We now look, in London and Hong Kong, at the drivers and justifications of such practices, the mechanisms that have been used and the types of rights and responsibilities that have been reallocated over public spaces. We go on to reflect on the implications of these reallocations for publicness, on the design of mechanisms to ensure delivery of publicness and on whether the conceptualisation of public space set out in Chapter 2 stands up to the task of working well for public space governance debates. A range of cases help us discuss the general implications for the public realm of both cities and for others that adopt similar practices.

The publicisation of private space: private capital and public space in Hong Kong

As we have seen in Chapter 5, both London and Hong Kong have come to rely to a great extent on the provision and management of new public space through planning and land-use mechanisms. However, this takes different forms in both cities, which are largely shaped by the nature of their respective planning system, as that system itself determines what sort of rights related to development (how much, where and what) are allocated to the main stakeholders, who they are and what obligations/premiums can be requested to accommodate the impact of development.

It would not be technically accurate to describe the private provision of publicly accessible space in Hong Kong as privatisation as is often argued about London. Rather, it may be described as the re-publicisation of private space, since land in Hong Kong is owned by the state and leased out to private developers.

'Overall, there are 1932.9 ha of countable open space (COS) in Hong Kong, excluding country parks, green belts and coastal protection areas, of which ... 49.4 ha (2.55%) are classified as (Public Open Space in Private Developments) POSPDs' (Rossini and Yu 2021: 6). This gives us an indication of the private sector contribution, at least to open space, if not to public spaces in general. According to Yiu (2018), the majority of public space on privately leased land provided by some combination of the mechanisms listed in Table 6.1 is in Hong Kong's urban areas, where most land is controlled and was developed privately – as opposed to the New Towns, whose development was less piecemeal and more government led.

The policy to increase public open space and facility provision on privately leased land was first regulated in the Building Regulations in 1962 (Yu 2018), which underpin the 'incentivised process' of dedication of land for public passage or street widening, formalised with a deed of dedication. The policy regarding public open space – that is, space for leisure, not just passage – did not take shape until the 1980s (Rossini and Yiu 2021) and was made more transparent and refined around 2010. These spaces are known as 'public open spaces in private developments' (POSPDs) (DEVB 2011).

While the 1962 launch of Section 20B (1) may seem to follow the 1961 policy for POPS in New York City, similar arrangements for private provision have long been made ad hoc. They and were responsible for important spaces such as Statue Square, the result of an unwritten agreement made at

Table 6.1: Mechanisms for indirect private sector provision of public space in Hong Kong

Typology	Provision mechanism	Regulation, maintenance
Public open space in private developments (POSPDs)	Land lease (written contract between property owner and the government)	Arrangements subject to the relevant provisions in the respective leases in respect of their management, maintenance and opening to the public. The enforcement of the lease conditions is administered by the HKSAR LandsD.
Public facility in private development: typically, pedestrian passage and vehicular access	Land lease (written contract between property owner and the government)	Arrangements subject to the relevant provisions in the respective leases in respect of their management, maintenance and opening to the public.
Public transport terminus	Land lease (written contract between property owner and the government)	Usually assigned to the Government upon completion.
MTR facilities in non-MTR privately owned building	Planning gain via statutory planning process	Usually assigned to the Government upon completion, and in turn are disposed of to the railway corporation.
Private provision of open space on government land	Planning gain via statutory planning process	Assigned to the Government upon completion (to the relevant government department, LCSD, as all other 'public open space' on government land).
Dedication of land for public use	Deed of dedication (written contract between property owner and the government)	Rights and obligations of the property owner set out in the deed of dedication appended to the lease, in respect of their management, maintenance and opening to the public. Enforcement of the deeds of dedication is administered by the HKSAR BD.
Public–private partnerships	PPP agreement (contract between the service-providing partner and the government)	Arrangements subject to the relevant provisions in the respective leases and partnership agreement, sometimes relevant ordinances covering the agreement, in respect of their management, maintenance and opening to the public.
Public open space provided by private memorandum	Deed of dedication (written contract between property owner and the government)	Rights and obligations of the building owner set out in the deed of dedication, in respect of their management, maintenance and opening to the public.
Open space in private developments	Planning, building control	Rights and obligations of building owners set out in law and condominium regulations.

the turn of the 20th century to dedicate this land, over which HSBC holds a long lease, for public use in perpetuity (Yu 2018).

Today, apart from ensuring critical public passage over private land, which takes a wide range of forms, from public passageways, whether pedestrian or vehicular, elevated or subterranean, to the provision of public transport termini or the provision of facilities for the MTR (for example, access to MTR stations), the Hong Kong government also has a scheme to regulate the provision of public open space (POSPDs) provided by the private sector. 'Public open space' in Hong Kong means spaces for leisure. These, together with many elements of the 'public facilities', fall within our definition of 'public space'.

The government has at its disposal three mechanisms for delivering public space: the highly interwoven land leasing, town planning and building plan regulation processes. Which mechanism or combination of mechanisms are used depends on the development situation. Due to the peculiarity of state ownership of all land in Hong Kong, the land-leasing process is also essentially wielded as an instrument of 'planning' regulation (Cuthbert and McKinnell 1997), albeit one that turns on the contractual negotiating power of the seller and ultimate owner of the lease. When a land lease is granted, renewed or modified LandsD can impose requirements for public facility provision, which may include management arrangements, without providing compensation, leading Yu (2018) to label these 'mandatory', despite being planning by contract. These conditions are then incorporated into the lease. Where no lease operations are involved, new buildings require either one or both of planning permission and building plans approval. Whether planning approval is required is set out by the relevant planning policies over which the TPB, supported by PlanD, has jurisdiction. The TPB may request developers to provide public open space/recreational open space. Even when planning approval is not required, new buildings often require building plans approval via a process managed by the BD, leading to a 'Dedication of Land/Area for Use as Public Passage'. The planning and building plan approval processes are not mandatory but instead are incentivised by government, and therefore negotiable. The incentives mean that developers may also put forward proposals to provide public facilities and space, so long as these are for a public purpose and have the support of the relevant government department. They become means for gaining permission to increase the GFA allowed for the development. This means that the way deeds of dedication are used in Hong Kong is closer to that of mechanisms often found in zoning-based planning systems, for instance, the POPS mechanism in New York as discussed by Kayden (2000). In Hong Kong, developers can exchange floor area given to public use for added floor area between two and five times that amount or 20% of the development GFA. Such exchanges are recorded in a deed of dedication appended to the land lease and enforced by BD. They are legally distinct from any agreements in the lease.

The lease conditions and deed of dedication processes can be seen as the formalisation of a negotiation and rights and responsibilities transfer process between different parties. The way that the operational jurisdiction of each component process is allocated to LandsD, the TPB, PlanD and BD reflects the logic of this process. Apart from government departments mentioned, the private sector developer and their consultants (almost all non-government provision of public space is by private developers) the other key participants of the process are TD and HyD and, in some cases, the MTR Corporation or the Urban Renewal Authority. Both of these operate in some instances as private sector bodies, although publicly listed, but in other instances, as quasi-governmental organisations.

These mechanisms have been instrumental in creating the complex public realm of Hong Kong, including the multi-level network of pedestrian passageways in many areas, such as in some parts of Central and Admiralty, Hong Kong's CBD (Tan and Xue 2015). There, these constitute weather-protected pedestrian routes at a separate level from the car-congested streets, and to some extent retrofitting an existing fabric. The privately provided elements of that network take it inside commercial buildings and shopping malls and are integrated with internal mall plazas and public transport MTR stations. The same formula has also been extended to the centres of New Towns and areas around MTR stations in new comprehensive development, very often built under shopping malls the profits of which fund the transport infrastructure. This is Hong Kong's well-known 'rail and property model' (Leong 2016), which is itself a variation of the provision of common goods – in this case, public transport – in exchange for development value. Although the main right the general public has in these privately provided public spaces is access for the purpose of movement, in a city with very hot summers, typhoons and a heavy rainy season as well as a difficult topography, many of passageways and plazas have come to function as streets and town squares, and to some extent perform functions one would expect in those places, even if not fully prescribed in use rules.

PPP or similar design–build–operate–transfer contracts are yet another, less common variation of private provision of public goods, which may include public space. It is a label for arrangements whereby the public sector procures assets and/or services from the private sector. This typically involves an agreement between a private consortium and the HK Government whereby the consortium builds a park or a public promenade, operates and manages it for the time stipulated in the agreement and at the end transfers the ownership back to the government. It can mean a 'full service' contracting-out of urban management of a part of the city to a private entity. It generally includes revenue-raising activities that justify the private investment. Included in this group are short leases of potential public spaces by government departments to private companies or not-for-profit bodies to equip and run particular public spaces. The oldest and of such spaces is the Avenue of Stars, a part of the Victoria Harbour waterfront promenade, initially privately developed with the support of the HK Government, and since 2015 redeveloped and managed by a not-for-profit PPP involving the original developers and the HK Government's LCSD.

Other non-PPP agreements are also known to exist, which might be design–build–transfer only. Examples of these include public space provided as part of new town development carried out by private developers – such as Tin Shui Wai and the provision of Tin Shui Wai Park – by private (confidential) memorandum between the developer and the HK Government but then handed over to the government to be managed as public spaces. Finally, there is the provision of shared space in private developments and private land *not* for general public access but for the use of residents or occupants of those developments as open space or access roads.

In the following paragraphs we show how various publicness rights have been allocated on paper and in practice. As noted by Lai (2021), leases in Hong Kong are usually for 50 years or longer and are not ideal mechanisms for the ongoing management of public spaces, which needs responsive management actions, including mechanisms for realistically enforcing breaches of lease conditions.

The following examples illustrate the POSPD and public facilities in private developments (PFPD) processes. The latter includes public transport termini, MTR stations and other types of facilities.

POSPD and PFPD and private provision of public spaces

The POSPD process has been used for a wide range of sizes, shapes and locations of privately provided public open space, including around single-building developments in dense built-up areas. The examples shown in Figures 6.1 to 6.3 are in Kwun Tong, a densely built, former industrial district in the eastern part of Kowloon. These are small to medium-size landscaped open public spaces around newly developed office buildings required by lease conditions. In all these cases, long-term management is the responsibility of the owners of the developments object of the land lease deal.

The first case, International Trade Tower, now called 'Manulife Place', is a small, single-ownership ground floor space in the setback of, and around the curtilage of, a new office building with a landscaped garden and a few sitting places that opens up the narrow pavement along Kwun Tong Road, a busy trunk road and bus corridor (Figure 6.1). It also adjoins Yan Yip Street and Hang Yip Street. This space is 1,006 m². The well-kept public space shows clear signage designating it as such, but there are signs of over-management

Providing Public Space in a Contemporary Metropolis

Figure 6.1: Kwun Tong Road landscaped garden around the International Trade Tower, now called 'Manulife Place' – private land, private investment, private management

Figure 6.2: Kingston International Centre POSPD

Figure 6.3: Landmark East Development signage indicating the physical integration of public and private space under the mechanism of providing PFPDs

that could be interpreted as a deterrent against real public use. The second case is 4,400 m² single-ownership space that wraps around the Kingston International Centre, a new office building. A relatively simple space with trees and water features, it is clearly signposted and physically integrated into an existing public space, the Lam Hing Street, Wang Tai Road and Lam Fook Street sitting out areas, which together, form a green air ventilation corridor (Figure 6.2). This series of spaces cuts through the Kwun Tong Industrial area, which is currently being transformed into a post-industrial CBD. The third case is in a recent office development called Landmark East, which has two towers, an open-air public concourse of about 3,300 m² and pedestrian walkway, both at ground level and open to the public at all times and provided as public facilities (not public open space). It adjoins a small park and playground, the Tsun Yip Street playground, and the physical and functional connection with this recently renewed public playground reinforce the public space character of the privately provided space (Figure 6.3).

The Pacific Place complex comprises a high-end shopping mall, office towers and several hotels, and is located in the Admiralty area of Central Hong Kong, owned by Swire Properties. It is an example of a large development with both POSPD and non-open space public facilities. There are two POSPDs, a 3,000 m² at Level 6 of the complex (but being on a sloped site, this is actually at ground level) and 696 m² which is a ground-level

Figure 6.4: Pacific Place, part of its PFPD passageways

landscaped area on a slope beside a road running alongside the development. The public facility elements are: (1) an access driveway that goes into the heart of the development, (2) a footbridge connecting the neighbouring Queensway Plaza and the MTR station, (3) a covered pedestrian walkway and precinct, escalator and stairways linking the footbridge from the large and busy Admiralty MTR station to neighbouring buildings and a major park on higher ground as well as the next-door government offices and (4) a landscaped public pavement along the major road fronting the mall (Figure 6.4). All elements of the public open space and the passageways are at least partly or fully on government land. All elements are open to the public at all times.

This arrangement may have resulted in Pacific Place taking the role of what some scholars might call a 'true' public space, in which rights of use covers also public protest. Normally just a set of busy passageways, during the 2019 Extradition Bill protests the mall and its spaces effectively became part of the public streets and squares of the city. Protesters were allowed to congregate inside the mall, and for the Silver Hair Rally in July 2019 (Dapiran 2019) - a demonstration of Hong Kong elderly citizens in support of the mostly youth-dominated protests – the demonstrators were allowed to march through the mall towards their rallying point protected from confrontation with the police outside. This picture, on the face of it, is a stark reversal of roles for 'the shopping mall', which in the West, has long been demonised as an emblem of a privatised, purely consumerist urban space. In fact, due to the spatial arrangements guaranteed public access, many of the shopping malls with these arrangements became the loci of protest gatherings (as the International Finance Centre [IFC] and Sha Tin New Town Plaza – see later – were, also). In some shopping malls (although not necessarily in the ones named here), mall security was actually keeping the police out and away from the protesters within (Ho and Wan 2021).

Another example of a large development with both public open space and non-public open space public facilities and an MTR station is the IFC, a prominent landmark in high-rise, intensely developed Central, Hong Kong's CBD. The Hong Kong Station Development, of which the IFC elements are a part, was constructed between 1996 and 2003 and is owned by a consortium of the firms Sun Hung Kai Properties, Henderson Land and Towngas. Tower Two IFC is the second-tallest building in the city. There are also a high-rise hotel building and a shopping mall situated on top of the Hong Kong MTR station, which serves as the central HK terminus of the Airport Express train service. As part of the land lease agreement and planning permission terms, the development provides two POSPDs (9,600 and 3,400 m^2), various public access infrastructure (footbridges that connect IFC with the General Post Office and with Exchange Square, footbridge supports and connections), public pedestrian passages at ground and Podium Level 1 of IFC Mall) that connect it both to elevated networks and, finally, the MTR Hong Kong station itself, its ancillary facilities and station carpark. The landscaped roof gardens on levels 3 and 4 of the shopping mall are surrounded by bars and restaurants. The second POSPD on the first floor is in part situated on government land. All the public facilities, except the MTR station, are open to the public 24 hours/day. The POSPDs are privately managed by the IFC, and the rules and regulations that made them formally public open space in Hong Kong law are clearly visible and made explicit on noticeboards at the entrance (Figure 6.5). The regulations include rules of behaviour in the space, such as no demonstrations, no busking or hawking, no ball games, keeping off the grass. Notably, such rules are not uncommon in HK public spaces, whether publicly or privately managed, and in POSPDs they would

Figure 6.5: The IFC POSPD

have been negotiated and agreed by the developers and LandsD and are included in the land lease terms. The obligation to keep the public spaces accessible at all times means that the public needs to have access to them through the shopping mall corridors, escalators and lifts, which need also to be accessible. These public spaces are well maintained, and adherence to use rules is monitored by private security. They are used mostly by shoppers or workers from the adjacent towers who will know of their existence, and at the weekends sometimes by foreign domestic workers. Access is unimpeded, but getting to them requires users to know they are there and how to get to them, a common issue in many of these internal public open spaces.

Outside the densely occupied CBD, POSPDs have been used for the creation of public spaces in new towns in the New Territories, especially around the shopping facilities and in connection with the MTR stations. The Sha Tin New Town Plaza shopping mall was the biggest shopping centre in the New Territories when it was completed in the 1980s and is part of a larger development that includes commercial and residential buildings completed in several phases (Figure 6.6). The complex constitutes a large part of the centre of Sha Tin New Town, and in fact is the main pedestrian link between the Sha Tin MTR station and Sha Tin's many residential developments. In this regard, of the six items of 'public facilities' in its lease, three – the footbridges, footbridge connections and passage areas – serve this pedestrian link purpose almost solely and are open at all times. As far as the configuration of public

Figure 6.6: The Sha Tin New Town Plaza landscaped roof decks, which are PFPDs

access facilities is concerned, New Town Plaza is very similar to Pacific Place, as it is one of the only routes, if not the only route, between an MTR station and the surrounding land uses, and the internal spaces of the mall are also public passageways, whether on private or government land. Similar to Pacific Place, during the 2019 protests, these internal corridors and atria came to resemble and be used as spaces of demonstration and protest as if they were public streets and squares, especially after a battle between the police and protestors in July 2019 took place inside the mall and the management was accused of conniving with the police to attack protesters inside and restrict their legally guaranteed rights within the mall (Cheung 2019).

The landscaped roof decks, open from 0700 hrs to 2200 hrs, act both as open space (although not classified as a POSPD) and as pedestrian links at high levels (level 3 and above). In their various levels the roof decks contain play facilities, also explicitly covered by the lease as 'recreational facilities'. The roof decks were popular and well used for a time, but awkward access and restricted interpretation of their potential function, including enforcement action taken by LandsD regarding outdoor restaurant seating that contravened the original lease, have returned it to poor usage in spite of good levels of management and maintenance. The whole ensemble is managed by Kay Shing Management, the estate management arm of the original developers, Sun Hung Kai Properties.

As mentioned in the previous section, more recently the HK Government has used PPPs for the provision and management of public space. This form of engagement of private providers has been mostly used in the creation of waterfront promenades along Victoria Harbour (Lai 2021) and involves a design–build–operate agreement between private developers and the government. They can involve provision and management of public spaces for profit or otherwise, the latter with a more intensive involvement of public bodies in management. The Avenue of Stars is actually a segment of the Victoria Harbour promenade in the Tsim Sha Tsui district and is the most well-known case of a not-for-profit PPP already in operation (Figure 6.7). It was completed originally in 2004 by the developers New World Group, which developed and owned adjacent property, and had the support of several departments of the HK Government. In 2015, as the original ownership and operation contract was about to expire, a new one was drafted for the redevelopment and extension of the promenade, this time a PPP with the same developers and LCSD jointly contributing to the development (Govada et al 2020). The redeveloped promenade reopened in 2019 and is a popular open space, although there are issues concerning its permeability to the surrounding areas.

Planning and building control and deeds of dedication

We now discuss two cases of spaces provided under 'deeds of dedication' via the planning and building control processes, both of which are very well known.

Figure 6.7: The Avenue of Stars, an example of public space delivered via a PPP

The first is the ground floor space in the iconic HSBC headquarters building in Central; the second is a series of street-level spaces in the popular Times Square mall in Causeway Bay. The various episodes of use, occupation, clearance and legal contestation over these two spaces touch upon many issues of not just what publicness *is* for public space governance, but also what public space is, at all, in Hong Kong.

The space on the ground floor of the Norman Foster-designed HSBC headquarters building in the centre of HK's CBD is probably the most high-profile subject of a deed of dedication (Figure 6.8). It is an open space conceived mostly for circulation between Queens Road Central and Des Voeux Road Central, and access to the first-floor banking hall inside the building. Management and maintenance as well as enforcing use rules and regulations are the responsibility of the building managers. This case is important as a good example of how those formal rules and regulations which form the basis of the legal agreement between the HK Government and the public space managers can end up diverging from the actual use of the space and be superseded by a different set of informal practices with their own rules, which might be tolerated and accepted if the political and social cost of enforcing the original dispositions becomes too high. Although conceived mostly as circulation and access space, and regulated for those functions, as a public space sheltered from the weather and across the road from an open public space exposed to the elements, it became very popular with Filipino

Figure 6.8: The HSBC atrium, a public space delivered through a deed of dedication for public passage

Source: Wpcpey

domestic helpers on their Sunday day off (Cuthbert and McKinnell 1997). From the time of the completion of the building in the late 1980s, they began to congregate in the plaza in large numbers to socialise with each other and enjoy their limited free time together, away from their cramped living conditions and punishing working hours. Typically, they would take up most of the space with cardboard mats and tents for the whole of Sunday, and it would all be gone by the end of the day. Initial attempts to limit their access and gathering as irregular and not-prescribed forms of use of the space were later relaxed as political pressure to the contrary materialised and the weekend concentration of domestic helpers became part of the cultural landscape of Central Hong Kong (Law 2001). The same space was again occupied irregularly for a different purpose for almost a year in 2011–12 by the anti-capitalist Occupy Hong Kong movement until their eviction by a court order in September 2012 (Yu 2018). This was longer lasting than any other occupation by the Occupy movement in Europe and North America, and once again suggests a degree of tolerance, even if limited and temporary in this case, to breaches in formal rules and regulations. After the eviction of the Occupy activists, the atrium was boarded up and closed off to public access for a period, but it has since been refurbished and reopened and has once again become occupied on Sunday by scores of Filipino domestic helpers.

The publicly accessible space on the ground floor of the Times Square shopping complex in the densely built Causeway Bay district is a rare example of a public space not solely for passageway purposes provided by a deed of

Figure 6.9: Times Square, open public space secured through deed of dedication, with a history of controversy

dedication (Figure 6.9). It also an example of a product of a bonus floor ratio in a location devoid of public space alternatives which has become a legal battleground of conflicting interests. Times Square is a vertical shopping mall with offices on top, completed in the mid-1990s. Under the terms of the agreement between the developers and the HK Government around 3,000 m² of the ground floor should have been made publicly accessible for circulation, passage and also passive recreation, even if the estate managers still retain the rights to organise temporary paid events and exhibitions in that space (Luk 2009). However, the pressure for profitable use of the space in a high footfall area soon led the owners to extend commercial uses into the dedicated public space, and to discourage the public from lingering in what had become a popular resting space. In 2008 the HK Government sued the developers for non-compliance with the terms of the original agreement, but more recently the estate managers won a court order to ban buskers from the space, as this use was not contemplated in the original deeds of dedication and therefore is not part of the activities that should be allowed in it. It was this case that triggered the further formalisation of the POSPD process, in pursuit of greater public accountability.

Private/communal open space in private developments

Finally, a widespread way of producing green open space but not necessarily publicly accessible open space is the encouragement of provision of

Figure 6.10: Recreational area in podium of private residential complex in Ap Lei Chau

recreational open space within private residential developments. These are a key component of local open spaces and have their own planning standards. A common typology of housing in Hong Kong typically includes a podium with facilities such as landscaped roof gardens, children's playground, recreational facilities, barbecue areas and so forth, topped by several high-density residential towers (Figure 6.10). The open space is accessible only by the residents, it is managed and funded through service charges and the quality and quantity of facilities as well as levels of maintenance depend on the willingness of owners and residents to pay for them. Although these recreational spaces are definitely not public space in any sense, they are fulfilling the standard requirements for public open spaces for the residents of the estates. They are a form of provision of open space for a restricted public that can often be in excess of a thousand or many thousands of people, depending on the size of the residential complex.

The arrangements already described summarise the ways in which the challenge of funding public space provision has been met. The management challenge involves finding the resources to maintain an increasing number of public spaces to the required quality standards. Differently from London, reduced public budgets do not constitute a major issue and the HK Government, through its departments, is still by far the main responsible for maintaining all kinds of public space, from roads to parks, to seaside promenades, to recreational spaces and to sitting-out spaces. The transfer of management responsibilities and contracting-out practices that have become increasingly common in London (and are discussed later in this chapter) are rare. The exceptions are those examples already discussed in which lease terms of deeds of dedication specify so, especially those spaces inside private developments (for example, roof terraces, internal plazas), whose management and maintenance remain in private hands. Similarly, public spaces created through PPP mechanisms will remain privately managed for the duration of the PPP agreement, reverting to public ownership and management once that agreement terminates.

Civil society involvement in public space management and maintenance is also not common, in spite of the wealth of NGOs focusing on public space issues mentioned elsewhere in this book. Episodes of community-led management of public space tend to be unplanned and fragmented where they exist and last for a short period only, with management of the space reverting to state control. The implications of this for how public space responds to local needs and aspirations are dealt with in Chapter 7.

The privatisation of public space: provision and maintenance of public space by private entities in London

Tackling the quantitative challenge of provision in London through planning gain

The quantitative challenges in the provision and management of public spaces in London, and hence the involvement of the private sector, are of a different character from those in Hong Kong. London is well regarded for its open green spaces, with a good network of easily accessible squares, greens and parks spread over its territory, and although its street network is still in many regards over-dominated by motor vehicles and, despite common law rights of way, pedestrian permeability across private land has not systematically been safeguarded by policy, unlike in Hong Kong. However, traffic-reducing policies like the Congestion Charge and Ultra Low Emission Zone, together with incentives to cycling and urban design interventions in the last two decades have started to question the role of streets and consider their function as public spaces and places (TfL 2017). The quantitative challenge in London is therefore not necessarily one of provision of new spaces to make up for local scarcity, but mostly one of managing and maintaining a large network of existing public spaces to the level of quality expected by users, coupled with ensuring the provision of new spaces in areas of significant redevelopment.

In Chapter 5 we discussed changes in modes of provision of public space in London, and the increasing reliance on private resources for the construction and long-term management of public spaces. In that chapter, we suggested that this continues a tradition of private provision of public space dating back to the end of the 18th and the early 19th centuries, and although this tradition subsided in the late 19th century and most of the 20th century, with a much stronger role for local authorities and other public bodies, it re-emerged in the 1980s with large commercial redevelopments and the simultaneous decline in local authority resources. A count by the *Guardian* newspaper in 2017 shows more than 50 privately owned and managed public spaces in Central London, all built in the last 30 years (*Guardian* 24 July 2017). Actual numbers are hard to ascertain; the lack of a legal definition for privately owned public spaces in England makes inclusion on a list far less straightforward than in Hong Kong, where those types of spaces are clearly defined. It is useful to mention here that lack of legal definition also means that there is no obligation or accepted practice for making visible through signs the conditions of access and rules of use as there is in Hong Kong.

This is not to say that large new public spaces have not been added to London's existing list by either the London Boroughs or by the London government, directly or through their associated organisations. By far the largest new public open space in many decades is in the Queen Elizabeth Olympic Park, a legacy of the London 2012 Olympic Games implemented under the auspices of the London Legacy Development Corporation, an entity created by the Mayor of London in 2012. However, this is an exceptional case, in a location that is still in the process of becoming an urban quarter, and many public spaces that most Londoners will come across in their daily experience are more likely to be provided and managed differently.

A good early example of the 1980s privately provided and managed set public spaces is Broadgate, on the fringes of the City of London. It was one of the first modern commercial developments in London to deliver privately owned public space as a result of a planning permission requirement. Developed from the mid-1980s and modernised and adapted since, it is a large office- and retail-based estate developed on railway land using the air space over the access to London's Liverpool Street station and the site of the defunct Broad Street Station, covering an area of 13 ha. The development provides four open public spaces at ground level (Finsbury Avenue Square, Broadgate Circle, Broadgate Place and Exchange Square) in a layout that replicates the urban tissue surrounding it (see Figure 5.3). Given the commercial nature of the development and its location, the public spaces are well used, mostly by office workers of surrounding buildings for relaxation and eating, and, like similar spaces in shopping malls, are dominated by food outlets. To make them lively, the space managers run a programme of arts and other events throughout the year. As one of the earlier and more significant privately provided and run set of public spaces in Central London, conceived and developed at the height of Thatcherism, Broadgate was controversial at the time and the discussion about it paralleled that taking place in New York at the time around the subject of POPS (see, for example, Punter 1990 and

Figure 6.11: Cabot Square, one of the many private public spaces in the Canary Wharf estate

Source: Mattbuck

Minton 2006). As part of a private estate, public spaces in Broadgate are patrolled by private security and there is a strong emphasis on consumption and circulation, even if the spaces are in principle open to everyone as part of the legal agreements embedded in the original planning permission.

Another example of privately provided public spaces amid a commercial development is Canary Wharf in the Docklands area, whose development started a few years after Broadgate. Though much larger in scale, covering 39 ha, the formula is similar: large office blocks and shopping facilities distributed according to a master plan that created spatial focus through a series of squares and gardens, all within the private estate and managed by it (Figure 6.11). The various public spaces are mostly used by office workers, although there are a few public facilities that are intended for the use of local residents. Although the public spaces are open and accessible to the public, the relative insularity of the estate, with its poor connections to the surrounding districts and intensive and ubiquitous security and surveillance – a consequence of its office towers having been a high-prestige target for terrorist attacks in the 1990s – makes the spaces feel and behave a lot more like private corporate spaces, and they are poorly used at weekends and out of working hours. Although the public's operational rights of access and use are to some extent guaranteed, collective choice rights of agency are visibly absent, in a way that is stronger than the other cases described here.

A more recent and arguably much more successful example of a similar process of public space provision is Granary Square. This is a *public* square provided as part of the King's Cross area redevelopment which saw the

Figure 6.12: Granary Square, privately provided and managed within the King's Cross estate

Source: Bex Walton

transformation of a disused railway yard into a large mixed-used quarter with new public streets, parks and squares, and among them Granary Square. This is an open public space on the banks of the Regent's Canal and adjacent to a historical granary building which now houses an arts college (Figure 6.12). Due to its position in relation to the existing urban fabric, to the rest of the development and the canal, the interactive fountain in its middle, the presence of the arts college, a larger area for relaxation and a less conspicuous presence of retail and food outlets, it has become a very successful public space notwithstanding being privately managed and patrolled by private security. As in Broadgate or Canary Wharf, the provision of public spaces was a requirement of the planning permission agreement between the developers and the local authority. However, at King's Cross the new streets and squares it created are better integrated to the existing urban tissue and not just internal connections within the development. Therefore, there was no physical impediment for them to be transferred to the local authority after completion so they would be publicly managed. The fact that they remain privately owned and managed was the outcome of a prolonged negotiation between the London Borough of Camden and the developers, in which the developers managed to retain ownership of all public spaces within the estate and the right to manage and maintain them to the standards they deem appropriate (Bishop and Williams 2019). The

Figure 6.13: Privately provided public spaces around the Westfield London shopping centre

public spaces in the development are indeed maintained to a much higher level of quality than the surrounding public realm by King's Cross Estates Services, which also provides security, and is part of the strategy of capturing the externalities generated by the new urban quarter and ensuring a higher value captured through rents over the long term.

Whereas the new privately provided public spaces already discussed are all within a private estate, even if permeability with the surrounding urban fabric is high, others will surround a new development and will constitute an extension of the existing public realm, only under private ownership and management. The public spaces and public areas around the Westfield London shopping centre in Shepherd's Bush are a case in point (Figure 6.13). This is a very large development in one of London's Opportunity Areas (areas earmarked for regeneration), centred on a large shopping mall but with a significant residential component. As part of planning gain arrangements, the developers have provided new open public spaces (squares, pedestrian connections, landscaped street space), public transport infrastructure, affordable housing and community facilities. The fact that many of the privately managed public spaces open onto and are a continuation of the existing public realm erases to some extent the distinction between them and makes their pattern of usage not fully distinguishable from that of the publicly managed areas around them. Although there are formal differences in how rights of publicness are allocated in both types of spaces, in practice these form a gradient in which the more formalised allocation implicit in the private management of public spaces by the Westfield management is more likely to be applied the further into the estate the public space is.

Whereas all the examples given refer to privately provided public spaces within large single developments, the same types of mechanisms have also been used in the provision of new public spaces going through multiple development sites and therefore of a more strategic importance. The Nine Elms Park is a linear park being implemented through the redevelopment of the relatively central Vauxhall, Nine Elms and Battersea neighbourhoods. These are classed as Opportunity Areas for comprehensive regeneration and have been redeveloped under a strategic framework set out in 2012 guiding several separate private property development operations, led by multiple developers (Mayor of London 2016). The linear park is part of the master plan for the area, and it is being provided through planning gain agreements with the developers of individual sites along it, as part of the conditions for their planning permission. As each development parcel is completed by its developers, so is a segment of the park, and once all sites along the park are developed, so will the park be. Its long-term management was still in discussion at the time of writing, especially whether it should be absorbed by the two local authorities that cover the three neighbourhoods, but the most likely outcome was that it would be privately managed by a trust set up by the multiple developers, property managers and the two local authorities, to avoid fragmentation and ensure the resources to maintain the park (Carmona 2022). The planning permission agreements require the park to be publicly accessible at all times but allow for parts of it to be used with by retail and food outlets to serve as the hub of the new neighbourhood that is expected to emerge from the redevelopment of the whole area. Although rights of access and use by the public at large are guaranteed at least nominally, the distribution of collective choice rights in this case will be shaped by the nature of the trust that is set up to manage it.

If all the foregoing cases refer to efforts to secure the provision of large new public spaces through planning gain, there are plenty of examples of how the same mechanisms are used not only for the provision of small and localised new public space, but also for the redevelopment and refurbishment of existing public space, replacing the need for capital investment in them on the part of local authorities. This is typical in the redevelopment of decaying local authority-owned social housing estates, many built in the 1960s to modernist designs and master plans. The costs of modernising these estates have led resources-poor local authorities to form partnerships with private developers, with transfers of property rights to the latter, who then redevelop the open spaces associated with these estates as part of their planning gain obligations. This use of private investment to provide common goods implies a trade-off between private profitability and public interest which has proved difficult to get right. There is evidence of exclusionary impacts of these arrangements, not the least through gentrification (Figure 6.14). The same mechanism has been deployed to refurbish publicly owned and

Figure 6.14: The 10,000 m² main park in the Elephant Park development in South London still under construction

Note: 45,000 m² of public space are the planning gain from this controversial redevelopment of a former social housing estate that many equate to outright gentrification.

managed public space on its own or in conjunction with public money. It has been used in the revamping of squares, street markets, the landscaping of streets and street pavement. In many cases, that provision of private capital has become a precondition for the renovation of those public spaces. Often also, planning gain monies are pulled together to contribute to a programme of funding for public space improvements, as for instance in the Street Scene Challenge programme in the City of London (see Carmona and Wunderlich 2013). Although in these cases local authorities have more power over the outcomes of the planning gain trade-off with private developers, there is still a sense that often these arrangements curtail pre-existing operational and collective choice rights.

Tackling the quantitative challenge of managing and maintaining public spaces in London: management transfers

As already mentioned, one of the biggest challenges in London is the adequate management of public spaces of all kinds. Local boroughs and the Greater London Authority are responsible for the management of the vast majority of local parks, streets, squares, playing fields, greens and commons. Public space management is not a statutory duty, and this service competes for resources with others that are, such as education, environmental protection, waste management, public health, housing, welfare and so forth. Chapter 5 refers to historical challenges in funding the maintenance of public spaces in England in general and London in particular, and how this lead to a continuous decline in the quality of many publicly maintained public spaces. The multiplication of privately provided and maintained public spaces is itself a result of that situation, as a way of securing levels of maintenance that do not compromise the intended quality of the space.

A way of facing this particular challenge that has become more widespread over recent years is the takeover of the management of parks and other public areas in London by not-for-profit organisations from the voluntary, community and private sectors, as well as the emergence and multiplication of BIDs. This off-loading of governance and management responsibility over public goods in general and public spaces in the UK has a long history, with its fair share of controversy and opposition. This process was given a considerable push with the 2008 financial crisis and the austerity measures that have come to dominate many Western economies (see, for example, Peck 2012, Raco 2013, Hasting et al 2015). Local authorities have used this devolution of power framework to transfer in part or as a whole governance and management responsibilities for local public services to interested parties in civil society, under what some have termed contractual governance (Vincent-Jones 2000, Peel et al 2009). For public spaces, this has been substantiated in many forms: in the proliferation of long leases to allow the transfer of public land containing, or designated to contain, parks and green space, to not-for-profit trusts; in the increasing use of the 2002 Right to Manage legislation to transfer the management of local authority housing estates and their grounds to resident-led bodies; in the use of PPPs and private finance initiative (PFI) mechanisms in build–operate–transfer contracts to secure private capital investment for redeveloping and then managing public facilities for a specified time. This is in addition to the wide use of simpler contracting-out instruments transferring all or some public space governance responsibilities to a contractor and the multiplication of less formal arrangements incorporating stakeholders in governance decision making (De Magalhães 2010).

Some of these transfers of management responsibilities are between local authorities and private entities, which are taking provision and management of publicly owned public spaces for profit, operating under contractual conditions. Others are between local authorities and not-for-profit organisations (trusts, community bodies), which, although legally private, represent the interests of local residents, businesses and interest groups. These organisations are in some cases allowed to generate profit, but this must be reinvested in the public space. In a few cases, those transfers imply the transformation of public sector organisations into not-for-profit entities, able to generate income to become financially self-sufficient.

A very visible example of the latter is Potters Fields Park, an open public space just across the river Thames from the historic Tower of London and next door to what was the Greater London Authority headquarters (Figure 6.15).

Figure 6.15: Potters Fields Park, trust-managed space on public land

Source: Paul Farmer

The area was previously part of the Port of London, with wharfs, docks, warehouses and even a burial site. In the 1970s, as the port moved east, it was temporarily occupied by an urban ecological park set up and run by a charitable trust, and then returned to the London Docklands Development Corporation in the mid-1980s and later leased to a private developer as part of a master plan for the riverside. By the mid-2000s it was in the hands of the local authority, Southwark Borough Council, as a park, but poorly equipped and used mostly as a source of income through hiring the prominent location for private events (De Magalhães and Freire Trigo 2017). However, the redevelopment of the adjacent sites, and especially the More London estate, making the area a destination for office workers and tourists created challenges for the future management of the park that a financially overstretched local authority could not cope with. To address those challenges a not-for-profit trust was set up in 2005, with an initial endowment of money from the More London development Section 106 agreement. It received the lease of the park from Southwark Borough Council for a period of 30 years, renewable for another similar period, and was tasked with redesigning and redeveloping the park and managing it for the duration of the lease. The Potters Fields Park Management Trust is run by a board of directors made up of two representatives from the local authority, one from the Greater London Authority, one representative from each of the two neighbouring residents' associations, one from the adjoining More London business estate and one representative from the local BID. The lease gives the Trust full autonomy to manage the park, including the right to raise income to reinvest in the park through hiring out parts of it for private events. As with other leases of this kind, it is accompanied by a service level agreement with detailed specifications on cleaning, health and safety, maintenance, gardening and hiring the park for events. Under the trust management, the old park was closed in 2006 for redevelopment and reopened in 2007. In spite of occasional disputes with local users about the frequency and timing of closures related to the hiring of the park for private events, the park has fulfilled its function as a well-managed new public space in a densely built-up part of London without equivalent alternatives. In fact, it has been so successful that in 2017 the Trust was asked to take over from Southwark Borough Council the management of a nearby local community park, St John's Churchyard. This small local park surrounded by mostly local authority housing was also in need of a major upgrade and an improved management regime, which are now being provided by a not-for-profit organisation with more flexibility to raise and spend resources than the more rigid and regulated local authority.

Other public spaces with similar management arrangements can be found in more central areas of London, with the rationale that stakeholders there are more able to raise resources to invest in public space and free overstretched local authorities to concentrate investment in more deprived areas further away. Accordingly, a number of new or renovated open public spaces in Central London are managed by trusts, some run by local businesses, some by local residents, some by interest groups and most by a mix of all those.

Waterloo Millennium Green is a small park located just south of Waterloo station, one of the main London railway stations. Situated on a former derelict site in a heavily built-up area, it opened to the public in 2001 as part of the Millennium Gardens project, a government initiative funded mainly by the National Lottery that aimed to create 250 new green spaces across England to celebrate the turn of the Millennium (Figure 6.16). This was the only urban green in the whole project, as the other 249 were all located in rural areas, and it was the first new park in the London Borough of Lambeth for 20 years. Once the construction of the green space was finished, Lambeth Council granted an exceptionally long 999-year lease to Waterloo Green Trust (WGT), a small local charity that would work alongside the community in the management of the park, according to the requirements of the Millennium project. WGT partnered with Bankside Open Spaces Trust (BOST) in 2009, after some time struggling to find enough funding to maintain the park, and in 2014 the lease was fully transferred to BOST, which has managed the space ever since. BOST is a well-established charity set up in 2000 that supports and services a broad network of community-managed

Figure 6.16: Waterloo Millennium Green, community trust-managed park on public land

green spaces and has itself managed a portfolio of open public spaces across neighbouring Southwark. It is governed by a board of 12 trustees with connections with several residents' groups in the neighbourhoods on the south bank of the Thames, where the Millennium Green is located. The contractual relationship between BOST and Lambeth Council is framed by the 999-year lease agreement and its accompanying service level agreement. It transfers to BOST the responsibility for the maintenance of the park, from cleaning and waste collection to gardening and small improvements, as well as securing revenue funding and empowering the community to take on greater responsibility for the maintenance of the park. The lease agreement also entitled BOST to receive some financial support from the Council for maintenance and enhancement of the park and its facilities until 2024, from a series of Section 106 contributions Lambeth Council agreed to assign to the park. Most of the resources have come from other sources including the local BID, local donations and revenue-generating activities in the park.

If Waterloo Millennium Green represents a trust based primarily on resident participation, the Jubilee Gardens represent a trust with significant involvement of large local businesses. Jubilee Gardens is a highly visible landscaped open park by the river Thames, across the river from the UK government buildings in Whitehall and the Houses of Parliament and next to the London Eye (Figure 6.17). The park was a patch of grass in land that had belonged to the disbanded Greater London Council, was subsequently transferred to the Arts Council of England and then leased out to the Southbank Centre (a not-for-profit complex of theatres, concert

Figure 6.17: Jubilee Gardens, trust-managed public space with strong private sector input

halls and exhibition spaces), which gave it on a 135-year sub-lease to the Jubilee Garden Trust in 2012. The lease gives the Trust full responsibility for managing the park, including enforcement of rules and regulations, but significantly not the power to generate income from the park. The Trust itself is a charity set up in 2008 to take over the management of the park after it was redesigned to its present form. Its board is composed of up to 16 trustees representing neighbouring landowners, local businesses, residents and up to four co-opted members (the local authority being one of them). It is chaired by the chief executive officer of the South Bank Employers Group (SBEG). SBEG was a major player in both the renovation of the park and its management under the Jubilee Garden Trust. It is a partnership of 17 of the major private and public organisations in South Bank, Waterloo and Blackfriars neighbourhoods to promote the area as a destination for leisure and business. It has been directly involved in delivering or coordinating capital improvements to the public realm and was instrumental in the creation of the South Bank BID in 2014. Under the banner of the BID, SBEG delivers a series of public realm services such as the South Bank Patrol, graffiti removal, street cleaning and so forth and the management of the Jubilee Gardens under a contract from the Jubilee Gardens Trust. In spite of the strong private presence in its management, Jubilee Gardens is an open space with no physical barriers and there are no restrictions on access. Rules concerning the use of the space are set out in a 'code of behaviour' that details activities and forms of use permitted and those prohibited. The regulations are published on the Jubilee Gardens web page and reproduced in signage in the park. Restrictions on use focus on activities that, according with the understanding of the Trust, can either impinge on the rights of other users to enjoy the park, pose safety problems for some users (for example, represent a risk to young children) or cause damage to the gardens or the facilities, or those that would infringe on the terms of the lease of the site. Prohibition of assembly and demonstration falls under the latter category, whereas restrictions on cycling, skating and ball games would fall under the first three. The regulations and the forms of restrictions on use, exclusions and limitations they contain are enforced by the Trust and its management contractors, SBEG and its the South Bank Patrol.

If all the foregoing examples refer to the use of lease instruments and not-for-profit trusts to secure the long-term management of relatively small open public spaces, the case of the Royal Parks – the great London parks already referred to in Chapter 5 and shown in Figure 5.5 – shows the use of similar mechanisms at a much broader scale. Until 2017 they were managed by an executive agency of the Department for Culture Media and Sport of the UK Government, which managed the Royal Parks under powers derived from section 22 of the Crown Lands Act 1851, and public use of the parks – not a legal right – was secured through a permission to use for recreational purposes derived from the agency's statutory management function. Funding for the parks came from a central government grant and income from commercial activities. In 2017 that executive agency, the Royal Parks Agency, and an existing charity, the Royal Parks Foundation which supported the funding and management of the parks, were subsumed into a trust, The Royal Parks, which took over the management of all eight London Royal Parks and a few other public spaces, together with the fundraising and education functions of the Royal Parks Foundation. The Trust is led by a board of trustees of 12 members, some of whom are appointed by the UK Secretary of State for Culture, Media and Sport, some by the Greater London Authority, which is charged with managing the parks on behalf of the government. As a not-for-profit entity technically separated from government, Royal Parks has some flexibility in relation to public sector procurement rules and has far more flexibility to raise income from commercial activities, receive donations and so forth. It still receives a grant from government, but the creation of the Trust was meant to compensate for declining government funding with more active fundraising in other forms.

Apart from lease agreements transferring management responsibilities, other legal instruments have been used with the same purpose. The management of public spaces in several adjacent housing estates in the Leathermarket neighbourhood in Bermondsey in South London is the result

Figure 6.18: Resident-led 'Right to Manage' public space in the Leathermarket neighbourhood

of the transfer of full management responsibilities from Southwark Council, the landowner, to a tenant- and resident-led body, the Joint Management Board (JMB), on a five-year renewable contract originally signed in 1996 (Figure 6.18). JMB is Southwark's largest resident-led housing management organisation, overseeing 1,500 housing units alongside the grounds and facilities of their respective estates. It is run by a board of directors made up of ten residents, appointed by the participating tenants' and residents' associations. The contract with Southwark Council is based on the Right to Manage legislation, which set the terms for the residents' takeover of management of council housing. It gives JMB responsibility for managing the housing stock, including redevelopment and tenant allocation, as well as the surrounding grounds and public spaces. In this case, rather than a fee for their services as with other Right to Manage agreements, JMB keep all the rent and service charge income from the housing estates they manage in return for a 30-year investment plan and for taking over the Council's housing debt related to the original capital investment in those estates. The investment plan includes the maintenance and renovation of the mostly post-war housing stock and of the associated public spaces within and surrounding the estates.

Whereas all the foregoing cases involve giving public space management powers to not-for-profit organisations, whether made up of residents or local businesses small and large, in other cases contracts to manage public space were given to private for-profit organisations, especially when capital investment was required to renovate, redesign and re-equip an existing public space. As with Hong Kong's PPPs, PFI-type arrangements – that is, build–operate–transfer contracts – have been tried, although only exceptionally, and the results have proved controversial (see, for example, Hodkinson 2011). In the redevelopment of the Myatts Field North estate in South London, public space management is included in a 25-year contract between Lambeth Council and a PFI consortium. This is a complex contract for the redevelopment of the whole estate and its open spaces, signed in 2012 after six years of negotiations, with works completed in 2017. The consortium was responsible for the capital investment in redeveloping around 1,000 social and market housing units and related facilities – including a large park and smaller squares – recouped through the sale of the market housing and through service charges from the management of both the housing stock and the open spaces. The parks and grounds management part of the contract is based on a set of standards and performance indicators included in the PFI contract, which specify the nature of the management and maintenance service the consortium is expected to provide.

Far more common than the necessarily over-complex PFI arrangements have been the contracting-out of management responsibilities to private contractors. These have been either limited to particular services, such as cleansing or grass mowing or general gardening, or much broader in scope, and in one case encompassing the management of the entire portfolio of open spaces and parks under local authority control. The London Borough of Lewisham has an all-encompassing open space management contract, which was awarded to a company called Glendale in 2000 for a ten-year period and has since then been renewed. The wholesale transfer of management responsibilities to a private contractor came out of recognition in the late 1990s that the open space infrastructure in Lewisham was in a poor state of repair and in need of investment. The solution adopted by Lewisham Council was a PFI-style contract awarded to Glendale. The contract also transferred the risks associated with public space management and their financial implications to Glendale, which became responsible for insurance claims, liability and so forth. The contract includes grounds maintenance of over 300 housing estates and management of around 50 parks and open spaces. The initial agreement included a £1.5 million up-front investment to upgrade parks and infrastructure over its first three years, payable back by the council over the duration of the contract. The renewed contract included a 3% yearly efficiency saving component, to be achieved with income generated from the parks through income-producing activities.

Conclusion

Provision of public space through the various legal instruments described in this chapter in both cities is clearly part of an effort to increase the amount of public space through private investment. By requiring public space as a condition for leasing public land or for giving planning permission, municipal authorities in both cities are able to capture part of the value generated by private development and use it to try to meet their needs for public spaces in terms of quantity, quality, spatial distribution and improving accessibility within the urban fabric. By transferring management responsibilities over public spaces to trusts, PFI consortia, residents' organisations, in London and in Hong Kong, to private sector entities such as developers or the MTR Corporation, municipal authorities are seeking to fulfil their own public responsibilities by enlarging the pool of resources available for public use.

In London, it is the need to find resources to provide and manage its open spaces that has led to an increased reliance on non-state agents. For provision of new/redeveloped spaces, this has meant an increasing dependence on the private sector, and especially the development industry, with the common good character of those spaces increasingly dependent on contractual instruments, mostly shaped by Section 106 agreements. For long-term management, that process has meant the involvement of stakeholders of various kinds, from residents to businesses and interest groups, through the use of lease instruments and other contractual forms to transfer management rights. This system relies on those with the strongest stake in a particular space responding to these as opportunities to see that resources are brought forward to manage the spaces they care about. The transfer of rights and responsibilities takes diverse forms, and the terms are highly bespoke to each place and the relative bargaining powers of the private provider, the municipal authority and civil society organisations and actors, and, as the cases show, there are, unsurprisingly, also different levels of success in terms of perceived performance and political acceptability.

In Hong Kong, the drivers for the involvement of the private sector in public space provision and maintenance are more the need to finding sufficient space to ensure continuity of public passage in intensely developed and used built-up areas and to get the most value from scarce buildable land, although public resource constraints (manpower, budgets and funding) also play a part, especially in what concern open spaces. LCSD as the relevant department can initiate only a small number projects a year, and many open spaces that have been included in plans remain unrealised for years and often decades, with private provision filling the gap. This is done through closely intertwined statutory and contractual means of lease conditions, planning and building control. Here the bargaining of rights and responsibilities is mainly between the government and the developer and often hidden from public view, with far less input from the community or civil society sector. This long-standing tradition of cooperation between the public and private sectors also means that it makes less sense to talk about the transfer of rights and responsibilities *from* the government *to* private actors, than to characterise this as the redistribution of rights and responsibilities between them. The rights and responsibilities of each party that are finally arrived at are set out in either the land lease or deeds of dedication, even though earlier arrangements may be reliant on unwritten agreements. The legal conditions in today's agreements that deal with POSPDs or public facilities do set out which activities are permissible in the space and what should be the operational standards (hours of opening, maintenance and upkeep). Some activities are supposed to be always permissible, such as walking, relaxing and temporary stay (sitting), whereas others will need to be specified and permissible or will be allowed at the discretion of the space managers (Yu 2018). Enforcing all these publicness elements in the case of POSPDs is the task of LandsD through its role in awarding and monitoring lease agreements. In recent years, there has been a greater focus on precisely this enforcement, that is, whether the government is able to hold those private sector actors to account on behalf of citizens.

What are the implications of these arrangements for publicness?

In both cities, it must be noted that, in relation to rights of access and rights of use, the mechanisms in place do not confer systemically different *levels* of such rights, even if they may lead to a *different configuration* of them, compared to those available to the public in publicly provided public spaces.

The question of how similar 'private' arrangements affect 'publicness' has been the subject of huge public debate in London, reflecting similar controversies in the United States and in the academic literature (see De Magalhães and Freire Trigo 2017). These controversies tend to centre on the rights to political action, actions that, as Qian (2014) notes, are also present in 'non-Western' public space. Nevertheless, even London's publicly owned and provided public spaces do have on them restrictions of access and use, such as the by-laws about prohibition to play musical instruments in that most public of public spaces, Trafalgar Square. In London, as far as legal instruments for public space provision by private sector actors are concerned, Section 106 obligations are formal documents, deeds on the land, which identify the relevant land, the person entering the obligation and their interest and the relevant local authority that would enforce the obligation. If the obligation is not complied with, it is enforceable by an injunction against the person that entered into it and any subsequent owner of the land. Therefore, non-compliance with the physical provision of a public space with its agreed design characteristics is relatively rare, as are significant deviations of agreed rights of access and use by the public. Similarly, lease agreements as forms of ownership transfer to not-for-profit trusts can be rescinded if lease terms related to rights of access and use are not respected, and the same applies to other contractual transfers of management rights, even if these processes are all costly and time consuming.

Historically, the most notable aspect of government–developer negotiations in Hong Kong has been conceptualised as the rights transferred to the private sector to create a more privately valuable development, via the developer gaining concession to increase the GFA of the development, or, indeed, the right to develop at all, through a classic 'planning gain' mechanism. In recent years, however, the issue of publicness has become more visible. The high-profile case of Times Square kicked off the re-formalisation of POSPD policy around 2010, and then significant research by the NGOs such as the Hong Kong Public Space Initiative (HKPSI 2018) and, latterly, the Civic Exchange (Lai 2021), has contributed to this move towards greater public accountability on issues of publicness. Accordingly, this has started to move the focus from simply 'right of access' to 'right of use', including the considerations of experiential quality. Even so, apart from the basics of pedestrian passage, other uses are still allowed only to the extent that the interests of the private owners and managers coincide with those of space users in, for example, having a lively public space around their property, or a comfortable outdoor space for office users. When these interests diverge, or the pressure to use the space for other activities becomes too intense, public use is secured only if the bodies responsible for enforcing the public character are active and effective.

The reallocation of rights and responsibilities over public spaces in both cities has a direct impact on the 'publicness' nature of those spaces. This reallocation is captured in various formal documents, whether land lease agreements, planning permissions or PPP/PFI contracts. On paper, this secures operational rights of access and use for the general public, during specified hours and for the purposes specified, and also the transfer of management rights and responsibilities to a variety of stakeholders. However, the rigid and fixed contractual clauses alone are inherently inappropriate for responsive monitoring and enforcement to secure publicness functions. For example, a study in Hong Kong, where recent leases are typically a relatively short 50 years, has suggested that lease-based conditions there are not ideal for public space management, since lease terms can be modified only when the lease comes up for renewal or a redevelopment of the land requires changes in the lease terms, so there is little agility in the system to deal with partial compliance with land lease terms (Lai 2021). These are only really enforceable if the non-compliance is serious enough to warrant taking back the land into government possession, a lengthy and complex legal process. For those spaces provided through planning policy or building regulations, based on deeds of dedication and incentives of greater floor area, taking a developer to court for breach of contract is slightly easier, but not by much, although this did happen in the case of Times Square, summarised earlier (Lai 2021). In other words, the high cost of enforcement means that routine or emergent failures of publicness may go unaddressed.

The actual extent to which intended rights of access and use can be exercised on an everyday basis seems to depend on two things. First, on the coincidence between the interests of the private managers of a public space and those of the users to whom those rights have been formally allocated. There is, indeed, some evidence to back this up. For example, such coincidence is more apparent in the connecting spaces inside shopping malls and commercial buildings, at least in what regards the right of movement and lingering (Xue, Ma and Hui 2012). Such meeting of interests seems to be far less the case in some of the POSPDs in which public use is not actively encouraged or in planning regulation-produced spaces where the interests of the managers in having more commercial space and that of the users of keeping the relaxation character of the space clearly conflict with each other (Rossini and Yu 2021).

Second, for the public to enjoy rights of access and use in practice requires a management arrangement that is responsive to the interests of stakeholders, including individual managers or management bodies that are amenable and responsive. The main challenge in London, and to some extent also in Hong Kong, is the ability of government departments, local authorities and other public bodies to translate the multiple functions public space might acquire, the variation in those functions over time and the different needs of users into relatively rigid and fixed contractual clauses, and to devise and implement adequate monitoring systems to ensure a transferred public space continues to meet its intended publicness functions as the context around it evolves. The more successful cases include mechanisms that ensure that the management body is permeable to the interests of all the main stakeholders and that conflicts between them can be successfully negotiated.

These sorts of issues highlight the limits, in practice, to the operational rights of access and use in both cities. Whether they do restrict the publicness of public spaces relates to how the collective choice rights, the agency rights discussed in Chapter 3, are shaped as those cities address the qualitative challenges of public space management. This is the substance of the next chapter.

7

The qualitative challenges of public space provision and management: quality and responsiveness

Introduction

This chapter discusses the qualitative challenges associated with the provision and management of public spaces. The previous chapter discussed how both cities have mobilised resources, public and private, to meet demand for new public spaces and to make sure that new and existing spaces are maintained to appropriate standards. Now we look at how the two cities try to adapt public spaces to meet evolving needs and how users' aspirations for public spaces are incorporated into provision and management so that these spaces can fulfil their roles as common goods. The chapter looks at the issue of diversification, that is, how public space provision and management systems in each city deal with the challenge of addressing the different functions public spaces have in different contexts and any changes in those functions over time. We discuss the mechanisms through which public spaces are shaped and reshaped in each city to adapt to the needs of their users and how this affects the allocation of those rights that make up publicness. These are mechanisms through which users and more generally all those with a stake in a public space can engage with public space providers and managers to make their aspirations heard – so that public spaces perform the functions those users and stakeholders expect of them – and through which multiple and occasionally conflicting demands are brought together and compromises produced. Whereas the previous chapter addressed issues that had a direct impact on the operational rights that make up publicness, responses from both cities to the qualitative challenges summarised earlier have a direct impact on the agency rights, the collective choice rights that are at the root of what it is to be 'public'. The chapter concludes with a typology of how these qualitative challenges have been addressed in both cities and what this says about the public realm in both cities, which will be explored in the following chapter.

As we saw in the previous chapter, London and Hong Kong have responded to the challenge of providing more public spaces through the increasing use of private resources, capturing value generated by real estate development. At the same time, especially in London, resources for the long-term management of these new public spaces, but also increasingly of existing public spaces, have been sought outside the public sector and within civil society. All this has relied on the use of contractual instruments as a way of securing that those spaces provided and managed by third parties, whether corporate or voluntary, can perform as public spaces and ensure that the general public has access to the operational rights of access and use that are an essential component of what we define as publicness.

However, as we saw back in Chapter 3, publicness is also defined by collective choice rights, the rights of agency through which public space users can influence decisions on public spaces in which they have a stake, make their demands and aspirations over them heard and have their concerns addressed through accountability mechanisms that directly or indirectly connect them and the managers of those public spaces. In a context in which much of the provision and management of public space is shaped by contractual instruments between public sector agencies – the traditional guarantors of accountability over common goods – and a variety of private bodies and interest groups, then a number of challenges arise.

The first is the challenge of adapting public spaces to local needs, that is, having the capacity to diversify provision and management mechanisms so that public spaces respond to local contexts and to the particular needs and aspirations of those more likely to use them. The common good we lump together under the category of public space is actually a collection of spaces with different characteristics and functions, catering for different publics and combinations of interests, which might require different designs, maintenance regimes, combination of facilities and equipment, rules and resources to match even minimally what users expect of those spaces.

However, this capacity to diversify provision and management is a direct function of another related challenge, that of engaging users and stakeholders in public space provision and management so that the space does meet local needs and is therefore well used, and of establishing the accountability and mechanisms that allow for meaningful user input into those processes. As we suggested in the earlier chapters of this book, in many public spaces there has been a replacement of the nominally homogeneous and equitable form of engagement and accountability of public space users with local authorities and other public bodies through the forms of representation that characterise elected government. In an increasing number of public spaces there is a more heterogeneous arrangement in which some stakeholders have direct lines of accountability to the management of a particular public space, whereas the rest of the citizenry has a far more indirect and often residual line of accountability through the public bodies that represent the public interest in contractual instruments with third-party public space managers and providers.

Those two challenges express therefore the ability of those cities to understand and accept the localised public space needs and demands of their population and to translate those needs and demands into a diversified portfolio of public spaces that addresses them. As a consequence, facing those challenges requires some form of permeability to bottom-up input so that demands from public space users can shape public space management. As we shall see in the examples from both London and Hong Kong, bottom-up input can take a wide variety of forms and degrees of institutionalisation. In most of the literature (Fraser et al 2006) the notion of bottom-up is associated with the idea of community and community involvement, focusing mostly on organised groups of citizens, mostly residents and seen as in opposition to top-down state action or corporate influence. Bottom-up input could indeed come from people living around a public space, who see in that space a place for exercise and play, or relaxation and quiet contemplation, and who might seek to get involved in its management as a way of securing that the qualities that allow for those uses are maintained. However, the property-owning sectors of that community might see that public space as an externality that might enhance or reduce the value of their homes, depending on how it is managed, and might influence its management for precisely that reason. Their rationale for engaging in public space provision and management would be very similar to that of corporate stakeholders engaging with placemaking, but is it less 'bottom-up' because of that? Moreover, user input can be indirect rather than the result of the direct actions of users. Many user-triggered interventions in the management of their local public space might take place indirectly though the actions of their local authorities trying to respond to perceived demands. Other interventions of this kind are mediated by professional voluntary sector organisations acting on behalf of users, according to their interpretation of the latter's needs and aspirations.

As we shall discuss in this chapter, the kinds of actions involved in tackling the qualitative challenges already described, whether initiated and sustained by public space users themselves, by voluntary sector bodies or interest groups representing users, by local government or by a combination of some or all of those are behind the emergence of a range of public spaces and public space management practices. At one end, there are the mostly temporary spaces that emerge from activist takeover of public spaces and political movements. The occupation of the area around St Paul's cathedral in London for a few days by the Occupy London movement in October 2011, or the space under the HSBC building in Hong Kong occupied for almost a year in the Occupy Central protests of 2011–12, are examples of transient spaces that for a limited period express approaches to public space use and appropriation by the groups associated with those movements and their supporters, independently and often in opposition to established public space governance systems. Then there are longer-lasting temporary gardens created and maintained by residents' groups with support from local authorities in bits of left-over land, such as the Sawley Road gardens in London, discussed later, that might temporarily suggest alternative ways of using and managing them (see De La Latta 2021). Going towards the other end of the scale there are the more permanent forms of contractual transfer of public space management to organised community groups and voluntary sector organisations, in which the aspirations and demands of these groups are formally recognised and to a negotiated extent given the right to be incorporated into the management of public space for long periods. Then at the very end of the scale are spaces in which the demands and aspirations of users influence public space management indirectly, as part of the undifferentiated general public interest, either as third parties in privately managed public spaces without direct access to management structures, or through the bureaucratic structures of local government.

This chapter therefore discusses how public space provision and management are shaped in both cities to incorporate the needs and aspirations of residents and users of space, by desire or by necessity. We look at how the various demands and aspirations regarding public space are expressed, how they are acted upon and, especially, what are the mechanisms and practices in both cities that make it possible for those demands and aspirations to shape public space and, by doing so, to shape the overall public realm of both cities. In this process, collective choice rights of agency and accountability are allocated to different groups of stakeholders and to individual citizens forming the texture of public spaces found in both cities.

Engaging with public space users' aspirations in Hong Kong

We have argued earlier that direct involvement of users in the provision and management of public space reflects the channels open to different types of stakeholders to get involved in the provision of common goods in a particular political system. As depicted in Chapter 5, Hong Kong has a centralised administration with a chief executive and powerful government bureaus and departments, vertically structured and operating under strict hierarchical rules. It also doubles up as state government (the HKSAR) and city government. Public spaces of all kinds, from roads to sitting-out spaces to public parks are clearly defined in plans and zoning ordinances, and this is accompanied by clear prescriptions of how these spaces should work and therefore their function and roles cannot easily change without a formal change in their designation. As seen in the following paragraphs, Hong Kong has very few public spaces that have diverged from the norm, and significant changes in function are rare. We mentioned previously the failed pedestrianisation of a small number of streets in the densely populated Mong Kok area, the only such case to date in Hong Kong in which the change from traffic-dominated to pedestrian-only uses was reversed – probably the only case, ever, of bringing back traffic as a noise-management strategy.

Management of most public spaces is the responsibility of LCSD, with the Housing Department in charge of public spaces in public housing estates, although some management decisions will involve other departments (for example, FEHD for the operation of food and drink outlets in public spaces). Provision of new spaces reflects decisions from LandsD, which sets out the terms whereby land is leased out to private and public bodies for development, and PlanningD, which might impose conditions on planning permissions, as required by the city's approved physical plans. There are very few direct channels for stakeholder/user engagement with those bodies other than through the 18 elected District Councils, whose function according to the Hong Kong Basic Law is to advise the government on matters that affect the well-being of residents, and the adequacy and priorities of government programmes. District Councils have access to limited funding but can undertake minor projects of public space improvement suggested by the district residents to district councillors, although the resulting public spaces will then be managed by LCSD and follow the same rules and codes of use as standard across the city.

For privately owned public spaces such as those described in the previous chapter as a result of lease conditions, planning incentives or PPPs, there is a clear dual system of allocation of collective choice rights. Developers and the interests they represent have direct access to the shaping of lease terms and planning incentives, and within the limits afforded by those mechanisms they have some power to shape the management regimes for the public spaces they provide. For other users and stakeholders, their rights of agency are exercised indirectly through the actions of government departments. These are defined in principle through the substance of negotiated lease terms or planning incentives and are made effective or otherwise through the enforcement of those terms and incentives in cases of non-compliance. There is very little room for actual agency on the part of those users and stakeholders, who must rely on their interests being interpreted correctly and acted upon by government departments, and on the agility of the instruments available to those departments to make sure agreements with private providers of public space are enforced. As we saw in Chapter 6, this is not a given, and in fact there is little expectation by citizens that government will act on their behalf.

Transfers of rights to manage public space to user-led bodies (trusts, community groups and so forth) seen in London are not found in Hong Kong. The ability of users to negotiate with local government the rules for maintaining, using and accessing a particular public space is not formally

Figure 7.1: The now closed Instagram Pier, a spontaneous public space

present. The few cases in which users have taken over the management of public space have been temporary, spontaneous and mostly ad hoc, with individual interventions of many disconnected users rather than the expression of organised collective activity. Collective choice rights, the rights of agency over public space, are mostly vested in the Hong Kong Government departments, and formal interactions between them and users and stakeholders are not based in any significant reallocation of those rights.

This is not to say that collective choice rights will never be appropriated by public space users, but that when this happens it has been mostly spontaneous and lasts for as long as the city authorities tolerate it. Instagram Pier in Sai Wan is emblematic of a spontaneous bottom-up public space in Hong Kong (Figure 7.1). Officially the Western District Public Cargo Working Area, it served (and still does) as a cargo loading area for boats transporting goods from Hong Kong to the surrounding islands. It is not an official public space recognised by the city or marked as such in city plans, but instead it is a boat freight pier managed by the Marine Department. Two processes led to its increasing use as a public space from 2010, more intensely since 2015, and its closure (public access blocked) in 2021: the decline of smaller freight companies, leading to far less intense use of the pier, and the lack of alternative open public spaces, especially along the shores in the areas west of Central Hong Kong. With a reduced intensity in the freight use of the pier, locals started to use its large surfaces for jogging and dog walking, despite the formal interdiction of access to anyone not involved in boat loading and unloading. From then on it started receiving larger numbers of non-locals and tourists attracted by the exceptional views of Kowloon and Victoria Harbour and of its sunsets. It became popular with families, wedding parties and photo shoots, and in 2013 it won an 'Outstanding Public Space Award', organised by a number of public space and urban design NGOs, who praised its spontaneity and freedom of use in contrast with the heavily regulated environment of official public spaces.

At the same time, literally next door, the official Central and Western District Promenade was implemented alongside the Western Wholesale Food Market. This new public space uses a sequence of former piers and docking areas which will link in the future Sai Wan to Central Hong Kong through a series of shoreline public spaces. The promenade is a formal public space, designed and furnished with play equipment for children, exercise equipment for the elderly and resting spaces, planting and facilities, all carefully zoned, and is managed by LCSD and subject to the usual rules of use and behaviour that apply to all Hong Kong public spaces (Figure 7.2). Very quickly both the official top-down promenade and the non-official bottom-up pier began

Figure 7.2: The Central and Western District Promenade, the official alternative to the Instagram Pier

Source: Biganoach Buoodz

to cater for different publics: the elderly and older families in the former, young people, tourists and young families in the latter.

However, the pier was always a non-official public space, not recognised as such in legislation and subject to plans for different uses and the inevitable redevelopment pressures in a city with severe scarcity of developable land. Over the years, several plans were put forward to redevelop the area and requests by NGOs and district councillors to officialise its use as a public space were turned down. Finally, in March 2021 the HK Marine Department closed the pier to public access, enforcing accessibility rules to which it had turned a blind eye for a decade. The justification for that was based on safety concerns, real and exaggerated, of people moving around a working pier without safety barriers at the edges, misuse by members of the public and potential and real conflicts between freight operators and the visiting public, all underpinned by the pending incorporation of part of the site into the approach of a planned road tunnel linking Hong Kong Island to the proposed artificial islands of Lantau Tomorrow. This largely unregulated bottom-up public space ended up as a victim of its own popularity, without the possibility of any mediating forum to sort out potential conflicts of rights among users and stakeholders.

As with the Instagram Pier, most such bottom-up spaces in Hong Kong are temporary in the sense that they emerge as the spontaneous ad hoc use of a location as a public space by locals. By virtue of that unplanned appropriation, they don't conform to official rules for public space. This is tolerated for a while by the authorities until their perception of the risks for potential conflicts involved in an unregulated space becomes such as to make them act and enforce the rules that return the space to the status quo ante. Another good example of this process is the public space that emerged on top of Bishop Hill, in the location of the deactivated Sham Shui Po underground freshwater reservoir, in Shek Kip Mei, New Kowloon. The reservoir was built in the first decade of the 20th century on top of the hill but deactivated in the early 1970s. The hill is mostly covered in vegetation and is marked in zoning maps as green open space. It is situated in a densely populated part of the city, very close to the first high-rise social housing projects built in the mid-1950s to replace the extremely dense shanty towns occupied then by refugees and migrants from mainland China. The flat area on top of the hill – and on top of the underground reservoir – belonged to the city's Water Supplies Department (WSD) and was technically off limits to public access. Since deactivation, the reservoir site was largely ignored by WSD, with vague plans to return ownership to the city's LandsD for a change in use and redevelopment. In the meanwhile, local residents had been ignoring access restrictions and transforming the abandoned hilltop into a local park. They built their own fitness and exercise stations, improvised with materials carried to the top of the hill, a little temple and a communal hut and managed the area as their community park. This situation persisted for some time until the mid-2010s, when the WSD alleged structural risk and obtained a licence to demolish the reservoir. This would have been the end of another spontaneous bottom-up public space, had it not been for the fact that heritage NGOs realised the historic value of the reservoir and its brick structures and initiated a campaign to retain it. In December 2020 the WSD formally recognised the importance of the reservoir structures and halted all demolition work. The area is now scheduled to become a formally designated park and will no longer be managed in an ad hoc fashion by the local community but instead will be incorporated into the official structure of Hong Kong parks and open spaces. If, on the one hand, bottom-up activities by local residents gave them the right to shape the status of this piece of land in way that met their aspirations, on the other hand, by succeeding in that process, they lost much of the right to directly influence in the future as management responsibilities for the public space are absorbed into the rather rigid municipal bureaucracy.

The same degree of spontaneity in the shaping of existing public spaces by users and the ensuing change in the nature of those spaces can be seen in the Sunday takeover of public spaces of different kinds by the around 300,000 domestic helpers all over Hong Kong, but especially in the Central district around Statue Square, which on Sundays becomes Little Manila (see Villani and Talamini 2021 for a similar discussion on pedestrianisation). Living in cramped conditions and without access to private leisure space, these helpers, mostly Filipino and Indonesian women, have for years congregated in groups in sheltered parts of public spaces on Sundays, sitting on sheets of cardboard, plastic mats, and more recently in small tents, to socialise, share a meal, groom each other, sing and enjoy themselves. This happens in publicly owned public space – parks and streets – but also in privately owned public spaces and the many covered walkways in Hong Kong Central. A lot has been written on how these women use the space, how they temporarily demarcate spaces for their groups and the meanings this form of socialisation has for them (see Law 2002). For our purposes, the interest is in how a spontaneous form of appropriation of space, of temporary reallocation of rights of agency that happens repeatedly every Sunday, has managed to survive and be tolerated in spite the rules regulating how those spaces should be used and who has the right to decide on that. Law (2002) shows the restrictions and barriers to their use of public space in the 1980s and 1990s, both from public and private landowners, with barriers being erected on Sundays to prevent those women from doing anything other than circulate, how anti-hawking regulations were mobilised by the authorities to prevent them from cooking hot food or selling homemade products to each other. However, as their numbers increased and they became more organised, and as their Sunday presence became a part of the landscape of Central Hong Kong, they became

Figure 7.3: Foreign domestic helpers meeting and socialising on Sundays in the HSBC atrium

gradually accepted. Their presence and their use of public space is now part of the city's traditions and image. This is now equally so in private public spaces, with the plaza underneath the HSBC building, a privately owned public space, having been a traditional gathering space on Sunday, with the exception of the near year-long occupation of the site by the Occupy movement in 2011–12 (Figure 7.3). This spontaneous appropriation and use of public space in an unplanned form and in breach of official regulation highlights again how bottom-up, user-led forms of appropriation of rights of agency – albeit in an unofficial and fragmented form – can still happen even within a rigid and bureaucratic top-down context. The system itself and the rules governing it might not change, but the need to have some tolerance of uses and activities that escape the norm provides the necessary flexibility (Rossini 2019).

This form of sanctioned or tolerated rule breaking in the use of public space and consequent reallocation of collective choice rights over it happens also on an everyday micro scale and is actually one of the characteristics of public space management in Hong Kong. Residents might put a chair or any relatively inconspicuous piece of furniture or equipment in a small public open space and, although they do not have the right to do so, it will be tolerated by the authorities in charge of managing that space. In a city in which the formal management of public spaces is overregulated, rigid and relatively impervious to localised demands, this gives residents a small degree of agency over spaces they use frequently, and, even if in a very restricted sense, makes them co-managers of that space. Examples of this nature are widespread throughout Hong Kong, from the creation of small resting spaces through the addition of spare chairs, to unofficial overnight parking and storage arrangements for the ubiquitous hand-pushed carts that perform multiple functions in the city and the belongings of

Qualitative challenges of public space provision and management

Figure 7.4: Informal resting space created through chairs on the pavement

Source: Another Believer

the people pushing them, to more structured interventions by some of the NGOs discussed later (Figure 7.4). However, this tolerance is limited to interventions that do not directly infringe on any law or regulation, or more likely until someone complains. Informal hanging of banners – for which a set of specific permits are required – or the selling or consuming of food on streets or pavements with the attending street furniture – highly regulated and not generally supported by the city's FEHD – are very unlikely to survive for long.

Differently from London, with its different forms of possible contractual agreements between government and public space stakeholders, most bottom-up, user-led action in public space to assert stakeholders' collective choice rights in Hong Kong takes the form of NGO activity. There are a large number of NGOs focusing on public space and urban design, bringing together university students, urban design, planning and architecture professionals and district councillors, often interconnected. They organise events, interventions, community activities, petitions, competitions and so forth and function as lobby groups, trying to influence the agenda of the city authorities. Although in practical terms their material interventions in the provision of public space might not have the lasting presence that, for example, transfer agreements have in London, their impact is on the thinking about public space from the public and the authorities. In essence, what they do is to instigate new ways of thinking about public space provision and management through real-life interventions, and slowly change the top-down culture of public space discussed in previous chapters (Figure 7.5).

As an example, Nullahplace the temporary space illustrated in Figure 7.5, was designed by a team from the Chinese University of Hong Kong, together with Collaborate Hong Kong and other local NGOs, with the objective of demonstrating how the use of temporary urban design interventions could be an effective bottom-up tool to reactivate abandoned and residual urban spaces and create new areas for social interaction.

Figure 7.5: Nullahplace in the densely populated Prince Edward area of Kowloon, new temporary public space created by university staff and students in collaboration with a number of local NGOs

Source: Max Au

Another example is the work of HKPSI, another of the many NGOs concerned with the public realm. As with similar NGOs, it is run by a large contingent of young volunteers, predominantly graduates in planning, architecture, geography, urban studies, urban sociology, landscape architecture and related disciplines. Created in 2011, its work focuses on disseminating the values and benefits of public space to the population. This has involved disseminating information and increasing awareness of public spaces. HKPSI was instrumental in creating a directory of publicly and privately owned public spaces in Hong Kong, so that the public know where these are and what they offer – especially important in the case of some of the POSPDs discussed in the previous chapter, which tend to be hidden away and not easily accessible. They organise symposia bringing together stakeholders from government, the private sector, academia and resident communities to discuss topics relevant to public space, and they are behind the Hong Kong Public Space Awards, a biannual event that aims to engage the public in assessing the quality of public spaces. More recently, they have also started to intervene directly in public space design, through their placemaking laboratory, which organises bottom-up projects in existing public spaces to experiment with innovative ideas. The first of these projects was the 'Design Our Dream Park' Yau Ma Tei Community Project, which lasted from March 2014 to May 2015. The project took the opportunity that some public spaces in the Yau Ma Tei area were to be redeveloped to engage with the local community and elicit their views on what sort of public space they would like to have. The reported lack of sitting areas led to a focus on chair design and sitting arrangements, with inputs from professionals and the communities, with moveable chairs being placed in public spaces for users to organise them at will and create spaces in a much more spontaneous way than traditionally found in the somewhat rigid and formulaic designs of most sitting-out spaces in the city. This project and other similar interventions in public spaces by HKPSI were tolerated by LCSD and other city departments with responsibility for types or uses of public spaces (HyD, the FEHD and so forth) or at least for a while. As with other similar NGOs interested in public spaces, HKSPI have explored that temporary tolerance to intervene guerrilla-style, adding elements to public spaces that users can interact with and suggest new ways of looking at the space. They have also taken advantage of grey areas of responsibilities, for which it is not clear which city department is responsible, to prolong that temporary tolerance for alternative, bottom-up solutions for public space.

The challenge of responding to users' demands and of accountability in London

London has a tradition of voluntary groups involved in the provision and management of common goods, through which stakeholders in those groups influence and shape how those goods are provided, and which demands they meet. In the early chapters in this book we mention how this active role of stakeholders in the provision of common goods was partially replaced over the 20th century by a more professionalised local government machinery, which ensured that direct stakeholder demands were tempered by a public interest focus that subsumed specific interests within what were perceived as the general interests of all citizens in a particular local constituency.

This translation of user demands for public space into more abstractly formulated public interest objectives became, by the middle of the 20th century, the norm of how local demands for public space were considered by local authorities. Greater professionalisation of local authority staff meant the translation of potential demand into quantifiable indicators of ideal and universal square footage of open space per inhabitant, ideal distances between homes and different types of parks, ideal composition of public space facilities and equipment and so forth. Direct public participation in the provision of public space would happen through a consultation process preceding the approval of local development plans. Direct participation in management would have been more restricted. The exception would have been local parks with park keepers, which would have allowed for some direct interaction between users and park management, with more direct feedback and accountability for the response to users' demands.

This is a somehow simplified description of the way collective choice rights over public space were allocated for most of the second half of the 20th century in London, but the main point here is the formalised interaction between users and providers and managers, mediated by technical standards and the subsumption of local interests into the wider public interest. This to some extent still informs state provision. However, the increasing emphasis on public participation in planning in the UK since the 1970s has created more opportunities for direct public participation in public space provision, not just through public involvement in the approval of local plans, but also through the right to be consulted in planning applications, as manifested in the obligation of local authorities to produce Statements of Community Involvement (Planning and Compulsory Purchase Act 2004). This means that there is a statutory guarantee that local communities should be heard about development proposals in their area, and that includes the amenities that new developments should provide.

In what regards provision, with the roll-back of the mid-century state machinery, public space users and stakeholders in the last few decades have found ways of expressing their demands directly and negotiating them with local authorities. The last two or three decades saw the implementation of a number of community gardens, created through the work of local neighbourhood associations in some kind of partnership with local authorities and funded by government grants and donations from businesses

Figure 7.6: Marchmont Community Garden, a small community garden in Central London

and individuals. Often these community gardens are implemented on derelicts sites left over from adjoining developments, and their design and use directly reflect the demands and aspirations of organised local communities. As an example, Marchmont Community Gardens are a small urban garden in the Bloomsbury area opened to the public in 2011, situated on a piece of land left over from the development of the social housing complex Brunswick Centre in the early 1970s, which remained undeveloped (Figure 7.6). The construction of the garden was a result of the work of the Marchmont Association, a group representing the residents and businesses of that neighbourhood, together with Camden Council and several residents' associations brought together under the Marchmont Community Garden Partnership. They managed to secure a peppercorn lease on the site and obtained funds from a grant from the UK Lottery Fund, the local council's Section 106 (planning gain) budget and donations from private sponsors. Places like Marchmont Community Gardens are the direct result of the demands and aspirations of local stakeholders and therefore suggest their ability to exert collective choice rights in a much more direct way than any other potential stakeholders and the London citizenry at large.

A similar process has taken place in relation to the management of council-owned parks and green spaces. Associations of stakeholders such as friends of parks groups have multiplied in London from the early 1990s, with the London Friends of Green Spaces Network, a network of such groups counting with around 600 members at the time of writing. These groups will demand a say in what happens to green spaces, raise funds to ensure green spaces are properly resourced and will occasionally take over

Figure 7.7: Sawley Road gardens: community management of public green areas

some green space management tasks. In doing that, they are exerting their collective choice rights by making their demands heard and acted upon.

An example of such groups is the Friends of Wormholt Park in West London, created in 2011 to have a direct voice with the local authority on the management of their local park and to ensure that the facilities and landscaping are properly maintained and improved. The Friends raise donations and organise voluntary work, and over the years have managed to reinstate a playground, added sculptural elements to the park, redeveloped and maintained flower beds and increased the use of the park. In parallel, the Wormholt Residents Association, which congregates residents of the surrounding area, took over of a number of small green spaces in road junctions facing the park, hitherto grassed areas of undetermined use, and transformed them into small community gardens (Figure 7.7). They have used voluntary work, private donations and local council resources to create little gardens on previously neglected public land which are now actively cared for by the local community.

More developed forms of the same process have already been discussed in the previous chapter with the examples of Potters Fields Park, Waterloo Millennium Green and Jubilee Gardens, in which the financial and operational burdens of management have been largely transferred to voluntary associations of stakeholders. In all these cases and others like them management rights were formally transferred through lease instruments to charitable trusts composed of local stakeholders: local residents, local businesses and local associations of various kinds. Although this is circumscribed by the terms specified in the lease terms, which try to ensure that these spaces function like 'regular' public spaces, those stakeholders are given extensive rights to manage their public space, with powers to set regulations for access and

Figure 7.8: Rules and regulations for users of the Jubilee Gardens

use of the public space and its facilities, determine how it is maintained and who has a voice in those decisions and how this happens. Trusts can set restrictions on activities taking place in the parks they manage, which typically can include restrictions on cycling, using skateboards, ball games, large and/or political gatherings, rough sleeping. While these restrictions may have their origin in concerns about legal liability, they also express the views, needs and aspirations of the stakeholders those bodies represent. In Potters Fields and Waterloo Millennium Green, for instance, such regulations are the result of complex negotiations between the local authority freeholder and the managing trust to keep them as close as practically possible to the by-laws applying to other surrounding public spaces, but at the same time meeting the concerns and demands of the stakeholders represented in the trusts. In places like the Jubilee Gardens, where the freeholders are not the local authority but other public bodies, trusts may have more latitude in formulating use and accessibility regulations (Figure 7.8).

Collective choice rights in these cases are allocated in a way that is quite different from that found in 'traditional' public space, which assumes a locus of those rights within the local authority structure and an equal allocation to all citizens. The management body constituted as a trust with its board is the main locus of accountability, of allocation of collective choice rights, which determines to a large extent the rights of agency of those with a stake in that particular public space. Trust boards provide a forum for all those stakeholders to voice and negotiate their aspirations. However, this does not apply to all socially relevant stakes. By their own constitution, these boards privilege the interests of particular groups of stakeholders, who have formally received the right to oversee the management of 'their' public space on behalf of themselves and the public interest.

Local residents are clearly recognised in almost all the arrangements. They are those living in the immediate vicinity of a public space, whose interests in it as users or property owners are recognised as those of the 'local community'. In the foregoing examples, they are directly represented on the boards of two of the three charitable trusts (Potters Fields, Jubilee Gardens), albeit with different strengths. They also have seats in the steering group overseeing BOST, the managers for Waterloo Millennium Green. Locally based businesses and commercial property owners small and large can also be part of the 'local community', and in all the three foregoing cases they are represented in their respective trust boards.

However, other potential stakeholders and the wider public have no direct access to those forums. Any line of accountability to them largely depends on the mediating role of the local authority and is therefore less direct, and so is their capacity for agency. Again, using those three cases as examples, the local authority has a seat by rights in the board of the Potters Fields Trust, is a co-opted member in the Jubilee Gardens Trust and works in close partnership with the charity BOST in the Waterloo Millennium Green. As the freeholder in two of those cases, the local authority has set the scope and the limits for the trusts' power through the drafting of lease terms. Nevertheless, this still constitutes an indirect form of representation of those interests not directly represented in the trusts and contrasts with the direct accountability benefitting the stakeholders represented in them. Its effectiveness depends on the local authority's interpretation of the 'public interest' at any moment in time, on a match between that interpretation and the interests of any particular section of the public, on the local authority's negotiating ability, on the effectiveness of the lease terms and accompanying service level agreements, and the strength and effectiveness of sanctions for non-compliance with them.

What these examples suggest is a particular case of public space governance and allocation of publicness rights, and more particularly of collective choice, that we have termed elsewhere as self-regulated (De Magalhaes and Freire Trigo 2017). The exercise of key publicness rights is to a large extent directly shaped and controlled by surrounding residents, businesses and landlords, to whom a wide array of governance rights has been transferred. Their managing bodies formally incorporate a range of local stakeholders, and the arrangement secures the fullest possible transfer of governance rights to them, including defining operational rules of access, codes of conduct and, in most cases, the right to raise revenues from rental of the space and facilities. The result is a form of self-regulated openness/

accessibility and of accountability mechanisms that are complex but direct and inclusive of the 'key' stakeholders (that is, those formally recognised in the management agreements). Other interests and stakes are indirectly represented by the relevant local authority in their role as representatives of the 'public interest'.

The foregoing cases represent a form of stakeholder involvement in public space management – and therefore of allocation of collective choice rights, whereby these rights are largely vested in a body that represents those stakeholders. In a larger number of London public spaces, stakeholder involvement and the ability to exercise their rights of agency in public space management happen in the context of contractualised mechanisms, in which operational decisions of various degrees of latitude are delegated to third parties and regulated through service contracts. These contracts establish a client–contractor relationship between the public body that owns the space and the management body and the interests it represents. Whereas the strategic aims of a public space in terms of the purposes it needs to serve, its general accessibility and its broader management regime will be specified by the local council in service contracts, a varying range of operational decisions with impact on how that space will be used by the public will be taken by the contractors. In these cases, bottom-up demands from users have to be expressed through the normal channels of citizen involvement with local authority decision making, as summarised earlier in this section, with the added complication that their actual implementation depends on their inclusion in contractual dispositions and the effectiveness of those. On the other hand, the clients and the interests they represent, be they shareholders or partners, in the case of corporate, entities or users and/or residents in the case of voluntary sector organisations, will have some latitude to exert collective choice rights directly within the operational decisions which contracts transfer to them.

A good if extreme example of this type of public space management regime is the London Borough of Lewisham. As mentioned in the previous chapter, it has an all-encompassing open space management contract, which was awarded to a company called Glendale in 2000 for a ten-year period and has since then been renewed. The contract includes grounds maintenance of over 300 housing estates and management of around 50 parks and open spaces. The wholesale transfer of management responsibilities to a private contractor came out of a recognition in the late 1990s that the open space infrastructure in Lewisham was in a poor state of repair and in need of investment. The solution adopted by Lewisham Council was a PFI-style contract awarded to Glendale, levering £1.5 million worth of up-front investment to upgrade parks and infrastructure over the first three years of a ten-year contract, payable back by the council over a longer period. The contract also transferred the risks associated with public space management and their financial implications to Glendale, which became responsible for insurance claims, liability and so forth.

In this case, the interests of local users, residents and businesses and the public interest in general are represented through the role of the local authority as the client. While there is no formalised representation of those stakeholders in the running of the contract, there are mechanisms for residents' groups to engage with the management body, Glendale, which also has the responsibility for liaising with the public when formal consultation is required. As with many other local authorities in which public space management in the whole or in part is contracted out to third parties, the incorporation of bottom-up demands and the allocation of collective choice is set by the client–contractor agreement, and it depends on the ability of the local authority to devise contractual clauses in a way that reflects the public interest. The contractors undertake to provide a service (that is, the governance and management of public spaces) whose details are specified in the contract, albeit with the necessary operational freedom to make day-to-day decisions. On the whole, and in theory at least, this should ensure that the public space managers, as contractors, are accountable to the client which represents the public interest and local, bottom-up demands.

All the foregoing examples refer to public spaces which are legally in public ownership – even if in the case of leased-out spaces this is much diluted, and therefore not fully outside local authority control in the specification of who has a say in management and how this should work. How are then stakeholders' interests and demands incorporated or otherwise ignored in the management of fully private-owned public spaces?

In the previous chapters we saw various examples of public space provided through the planning system, the result of planning gain mechanisms. In some cases, the newly provided public space is transferred back to the local authority, becoming as a result part of the portfolio of publicly owned and managed spaces. The incorporation of bottom-up demands and the related allocation of public choice rights in these cases will be the same as described earlier in this section.

However, and especially the larger cases discussed in Chapter 6, ownership and management responsibilities for the new public spaces are retained by the development owners. Management of the public space is often the responsibility of the estate management arm of the development owners, as for instance in the public spaces of the King's Cross development, managed by King's Cross Estates Services. The same applies to Canary Wharf, where the public spaces within the private estate are managed by Canary Wharf Management, the estate management arm of Canary Wharf plc. In a few cases, management responsibilities for the public space are transferred upon completion of the development to a body set up for that purpose. In the New Nine Elms linear park, which is emerging from the coordination of a number of independent developments and their planning gain requirements, the management of the park is proposed to be entrusted to a trust incorporating the various developers/estate owners and the local authorities, operating under a charter to secure the publicness of the space.

In all these cases, involvement of other stakeholders than the surrounding property owners and occupiers is shaped in the creation of the public space through the rules, procedures and negotiation processes embedded in the planning system. As we have mentioned already, the English planning system is discretionary, as each case is discussed on its own merits, albeit this is framed by policies included in local development plans, national planning policy and guidelines and other incidental pieces of legislation. For many decades it has also required community involvement, even if this can often be formulaic and tokenistic (Zakus and Lysack 1998). Therefore, the location, size, shape and characteristics of public spaces created through planning gain agreements, together with decisions about long-term ownership, management regimes, are all shaped in the context of negotiations between different players, which will necessarily incorporate the demands from local communities. Local councils will participate in these negotiations as representative of the general interests of local citizens expressed in more or less democratically approved plans, and several local communities – residents, business interest groups of all sorts – will be involved in consultation exercises with the potential to shape the nature, size and number of the facilities provided by a development.

A relevant illustration of this process, which summarises the complexity of the way bottom-up views on public space influence the nature of private public spaces produced through private developments is the already mentioned King's Cross development, which resulted in the creation of a number of new public spaces. Whereas the main parties negotiating the public facilities coming out of the development were Camden Council and the developers, Argent, during the six years it took for the development to get planning permission it is estimated that more than 100 different local groups of various kinds were consulted through forums, debates, letters and so forth, with tens of thousands of letters sent to local residents and businesses (Bishop and Williams 2016). Whereas consultation did not fundamentally shape the development and its public spaces, there is evidence to suggest that it did influence decisions on the location and character of public space, either by reinforcing the position of the Council in the negotiations with the developer, or by directly influencing revised planning applications. In this particular case, the long-term management of those private public spaces has remained in the hands of the development owners. Camden Council had the option to adopt the network of streets and open spaces other than the larger formal squares, therefore obtaining public control over most of the public realm. However, it hasn't exerted that option and public control is now subject to the contractual arrangements agreed as part of the planning permission.

What this suggests is that even in the case of private provision and management of public spaces there is scope for bottom-up input and, with it, the exercise of collective choice right to shape the nature of those spaces. This goes beyond statutory mechanisms through which stakeholders have their interests represented by local authorities as defenders of the public interest.

The growing incidence of privately provided public spaces in London has led to more strategic efforts to secure that the allocation of both operational and collective choice rights over those spaces does not diverge fundamentally from those associated with local authority-provided and managed ones. In October 2021 the Mayor of London published the Public London Charter, to guide planning authorities in London on the requirements to be applied when securing public spaces from private development. The Charter sets out the rights and responsibilities of users, owners and managers of new public spaces so that these operate as real public spaces, are open and accessible, encourage public use, are well maintained and serviced regardless of ownership (Mayor or London 2021). The Charter is new, and its impact is still in the future, but it is indicative of the recognition of the need to ensure an appropriate allocation of publicness rights throughout an increasingly complex pattern of provision and management of public spaces.

While all the discussion in the previous paragraphs refers mostly to open space, the mechanisms for the exercise of collective choice rights in other types of public space are also there, albeit in a more limited form. As an example, the Play Streets initiative, established in 2008 on the basis of much older 1930s legislation, allows for a community to request the closing off of a residential street to traffic for a few hours either on a specific occasion or on a regular basis (for example, every week) for a year to function as a play area for children or a venue for communal celebration of events. A group of residents can apply to their local authority and, if approved, they take charge of the closing off and the management of the newly created public space. This is linked to an increased acceptance generally that streets are public spaces with roles and functions that go beyond circulation, and especially motor vehicle circulation, and of the role of street life in creative community cohesion. Currently around two-thirds of London boroughs have Play Street policies in place, and this suggests the growing potential residents have in shaping the role of road space, even if only temporarily.

Conclusion

This chapter suggests that while both London and Hong Kong have a similar pattern for allocating operational rights over public space, they differ substantially in how collective choice rights, the rights of agency, are allocated among different stakeholders, reflecting the history and nature of urban governance in both places. To understand how both cities adapt their public space to changes in demand and respond to them, we have focused on how bottom-up demands from users and other stakeholders are absorbed by public space managers.

London has a history of more structured and long-lasting users' involvement in the provision and management of public space, which happens mostly through the engagement of residents in arrangements with local authorities of various degrees of formality. As we saw, this varies from voluntary participation in friends of a park group helping with specific management tasks (planting, helping with safety, fundraising and so forth), to highly formalised management transfer contracts which might lease out the public space to a not-for-profit trust made up of individual and corporate users with varying combinations of rights over the space.

The channels for user engagement are structured and formalised and there are clear ways through which engagement can take place. The system is well codified but flexible enough to admit variations on the standard local authority ownership and full management regime. User groups with limited ambitions to engage in public space management can come together and negotiate with a local authority to take over or help with particular tasks. More organised and permanent groups can use legal dispositions to get local authorities to have management powers transferred to them. Others, notably more complex and organised groups of stakeholders, can constitute a trust and negotiate a lease of a public space which will give them almost full ownership rights and a very large degree of freedom in deciding how the space is managed over the long term, even if this power is constrained by terms and conditions set in the lease in relation, especially, to the operational rights of access and use.

This is a highly formalised system of participation, with several recognised channels that seem to have the capability to respond to the aspirations of users of public space that are organised and articulate enough to have their voices heard. Formalisation constrains spontaneity, and therefore the individual interventions in public space found in Hong Kong are rarely seen. Formalisation also crystallises the rights of those groups and interests who are part of the transfer of management powers and differentiate between them and other interests in that public space, whose rights are diluted among others that compose the generic 'public interest'. In a sense, this is more akin to privatisation in the sense of public space management rights being transferred to a group of private citizens and organisations in their capacity as users/stakeholders, whose aspirations and interests are now recognised formally to have precedence over others.

Within that system, in London we could characterise two main types through which collective choice rights are passed from local authorities to groups of stakeholders. In a previous work we have described these as a vertical and a horizontal break-up of public space management rights, depending on the extent of the transfer, the relative power of user/stakeholder groups vis-à-vis local authorities and the stability of the arrangement, which are also a function of the institutional capacity of user/stakeholder organisations. These result in either a self-regulated mode of public space governance which we mentioned earlier, in which groups of users and other stakeholders are allocated a substantial degree of power to decide on how a public space is managed, or what we have termed as a contractual mode of public space governance, in which groups of users and stakeholders have a relative power of decision over a public space, acting as management contractors to a client local authority.

In Hong Kong, the chapter suggests an absence of formalised mechanisms for allocating collective choice rights over public space to users/stakeholders that could allow for stable bottom-up take-up of public space management. Attempts by users/stakeholders to mould public spaces to suit their demands tend either to happen spontaneously in an ad hoc fashion, often the result of the accretion of several individual interventions, taking advantage of gaps in the regulations or in enforcement dispositions, or to follow a protracted process of negotiation between voluntary bodies and local authority, whose result in public space management tends to be experimental rather than more permanent.

In terms of collective choice rights, spontaneous interventions on various scales represent a temporary and unofficial appropriation of the capacity to shape, but without any changes in ownership rights on formal public space management structures, or of channels of accountability associated with that. The public space is still formally managed by a city department, but users have added physical elements or new forms of use that are not formally incorporated into management plans or routines. Consequently, there is a temporary disjuncture between a formal and an informal management regime. In the case of programmed intervention, NGOs, community groups or other users are allowed experiments in public space, time-limited and under control of public authorities. Limited management powers are allocated to those conducting the experiment, which are then withdrawn as the allocation of rights goes back the status quo ante. The first case could be defined as a tolerated temporary allocation of restricted collective choice rights, while the second case could be described as an experimental transfer of restricted management responsibilities. In both cases groups of users/stakeholders might gain de facto rights over public space, their ability to enjoy those rights is not secure and depends on the willingness of the city authorities to permit and/or extend what remains an irregular situation.

The coexistence of these different forms of treating collective choice rights over public space, as well as the different ways of managing operational rights, contributes to a complex public realm, which inevitably characterises cities such as London and Hong Kong. How can such a complex public realm be managed? This is the substance of the next and last chapter of this book.

8

Conclusions and the sketch of a practical theory of public space governance

Introduction

As we argue in the initial chapters of this book, public space scholarship has grown rapidly in the last couple of decades. However, scholarship on public space management and governance is still underdeveloped and undertheorised. How should we be thinking about how cities manage their public space and face challenges such as the ones discussed in the two previous chapters? How should we talk about it and how do we conceptualise this? A discussion about the management of governance of public space such as that developed in this book must have as its aim to support effective performance of public space management in practice. We ask, therefore, what would a practically useful theoretical basis for public space management look like? How can a complex public realm, as we have set out in the preceding chapters, be managed and public spaces challenges be solved?

In this concluding chapter we draw together the conceptual discussions and empirical evidence from London and Hong Kong to propose a practical theory of public space governance. The ubiquitous nature of public space has meant that conceptual development for public space governance has sought to build upon diverse theoretical sources, from law to institutional economics, public administration and urban design, and directly from the experience of practice itself. In this book we have drawn on these to suggest the theoretical underpinnings of public space governance in a way that can bridge scholarly theoretical work and the challenges of practically governing and managing public space in cities around the world. Since cities and their public space are diverse, fluid and locally specific, for any practical theory to be useful, it needs to be sufficiently general to apply in a wide range of cities, but sufficiently situated to inform operational decisions. The selection of London and Hong Kong as developed cities with similar legal systems, some similarities in governance structures, but very different political cultures and physical morphology, provided opportunities to counterpose practice and space, and to probe questions about the similarities and differences that arise from their experience. Since theorisation of public space governance is still limited, and a significant gap exists between practice and scholarly theorising, the book draws on practical knowledge of public space governance in the two cities.

This chapter summarises the conceptualisation and explorations of public space governance theory to date, before suggesting some grounds for a practical theory of public space governance.

What the book has argued so far

In Chapters 2, 3 and 4, we developed the theoretical bases of public space and publicness, in ways relevant to public space governance. In this final chapter we try to unpick the terminology and concepts deployed in the literature and in 20th-century governance practice as conducted in London and Hong Kong, to suggest the underpinnings of a practical theory of public space governance.

In Chapter 2 we sought to define public space and emphasised its complex nature, with it being a catch-all term for physical space performing a variety of functions depending on the particular context of their location. We said that a fundamental dimension of public space is its nature as a contiguous spatial field between private realms, fundamental for a city's very existence and functioning. This is the foundational public space concept for theorising its practical governance. Because of the role public space in its various incarnations plays in the life of the city it is and needs to be managed as a common good. As we saw earlier, common goods are those goods that a community provides to its members to fulfil the relational obligations that justify its very existence. They are the embodiment of the interests those members have in common. In this case, that common interest is being able to get around the city, to meet others, to relax, to perform functions that don't belong in the private realm and all the things that flow from that. The city could not exist otherwise. Since a common good requires the active or tacit agreement of a community, public space is a socio-spatial construct, which depends for its existence on sufficient societal agreement, which reflects the power dynamics within society.

Following from our definition of public space as the physical embodiment of a common good that provides a series of attributes valued by members of society, we explored the idea of publicness as the set of qualities that define that common good 'public space'. In Chapter 2 we discussed the fact that the public space literature and 20th-century practice of public space governance have often conflated and made normative several meanings of the term public such as public-as-non-exclusive, and public-as-provided-by-the-state. We tried to disentangle these to clarify how public space as a common good fulfils its various context-specific functions and how it has been and can be governed. For that purpose, we proposed an understanding of publicness based on the nature of key rights allocated to those with a direct or indirect stake in a public space. We grouped those key rights into the operational rights of access and use and the collective choice rights of agency accountability, whose allocation and extension will necessarily vary according to the context of each individual public space. The corollary of that proposition is that since public space serves diverse publics in diverse situations, and since publicness is meaningful only if defined in relation to its societal context and to the needs and demands of the relevant stakeholders, the publicness of a public space may be defined as the extent to which different interests in it are contemplated and met in relation to other interests and needs. Publicness is therefore about how and to what extent sets of urban spatial functions valued and agreed by a community of different stakeholders are achieved, rather than about variations on a scale of some absolute standards.

In Chapter 4 we discussed the governance and management of public space as the governance sphere in which rights and responsibilities associated with public space are allocated and the common good qualities of public space are agreed and implemented. The fundamental mechanism for governance is the allocation of rights and responsibilities associated with public space. Governance goals are enabled by the allocation of rights of access, use and collective choice to the various stakeholders. The processes of investment and resourcing, maintenance, regulation and coordination that make up public space governance and through which various rights over the space and its management are allocated (which impact on operational and collective choice rights) can take several forms. They have historically evolved, in the recent past from a more hierarchical system within the public sector to a more contracts-based form involving public and voluntary sector stakeholders. These evolving governance arrangements allocate publicness rights differently and, in doing so, address the challenges of providing for the common good character of public space in ways that can be more or less effective, more or less equitable, more or less capable of maintaining or expressing the societal agreement on what roles public spaces should play, how and for whom.

The case study-based Chapters 5, 6 and 7 provide an overview of how London and Hong Kong have addressed the key public space governance challenges of providing enough public space to meet the demands of their citizens in the quantity, quality and locations required, and of understanding that demand in terms of the functions, facilities, activities, nature and symbolism citizens want from the spaces they have a stake in. In those chapters, we have explored changing forms of governance that allocate rights differently, and which are defined by institutions such as funding arrangements, rules and regulations, contracts and agreements, and customs. In doing so, we have tried to understand what this means for the allocation of publicness rights and, consequently, the resulting 'publicness' attributes of public space as a complex common good.

In this concluding chapter we try to bring all those strands of discussion together to reflect on how we should think normatively about public space governance and management. The challenge is to reflect on how the theoretical framework used in this book to understand public space, publicness and public space governance, and which has been applied to interpret public space management in two cities, could provide a conceptual language that could inform the practice of governing and managing public space.

Meanings of public space governance: evidence from London and Hong Kong

What can the evidence from London and Hong Kong tell us about public space governance in general, thus helping to theorise it? Is there a general meaning of public space governance that we can surmise? In turn, what might that tell us about the meaning of public space to society? Juxtaposing literature with empirical data reveals how the co-evolution of public space meanings with new forms of governance has corresponding implications for the meanings of public space governance. We can identify four such meanings, which, although they emerged at different times in history, all remain in play today.

The first meaning is public space governance as preventing enclosure of common space and enabling access. This is based on the early modern meaning of public space that we identified, that is the recognition of public space as a common resource for circulation and access, which calls for spatial contiguity between private realms. This is simply a basic necessity for a city to function. This is public space irrespective of its institutional status and who provides it. In dense or densifying settlements, space needed to be designated as public space to prevent encroachment by private interests and to retain its common good function. In England prior to this recognition, our contemporary understanding of publicness as access and use open to all may have had a forerunner in the common law right of way, but there was little that could be consider the equivalent of modern collective action rights. In London, as demand for space increased and congestion threatened the provision of spatial goods, private entrepreneurs stepped in to solve a spatial problem and grasp a business opportunity at the same time, whether turnpike roads or pleasure gardens. This laissez-faire mode provided common goods only inasmuch as these served private interests. It was only gradually that the state took a greater role in providing the spatial common good to safeguard publicness benefits for an emerging wider public, and eventually, with the emergence of universal suffrage, the voting public. In Hong Kong, urban public roads were built by the colonial administration mainly in service of connecting plots of land to be auctioned off, the only source of its income. These were generally useable and accessible to all.

This state protection of contiguity which took place with the advent of the British colonial administration was basic. The aim was to enable the city's operation as a trading port, providing only the most basic needs for port services and workers, through minimal regulation. The consequences of this laissez-faire approach, overseen at a high level by bureaucratic municipal regulation, is visible in the city's distinctive street scene today, including its orderly road-crossing behaviours among apparently chaotic and vibrant street markets.

The second meaning is public space governance as welfare provision by the state. Starting in the late 18th century in Europe, and accelerating in the industrialising cities in the 19th century, public space became seen as a common resource to improve the well-being of the urban population, that is, not just for circulation and access purposes, and most notably through the provision of parks and open spaces. Early in this book we describe the emergence of the state in the late 19th and early 20th centuries as guardian of the societal common good generally. Correspondingly, the role of public space expanded into the delivery of broader public welfare goals, provided and managed by the state, and this has come to define public space more in relation to its institutional provision aspect, rather than anything fundamentally spatial. Formalised state-led active provision of spaces for specific public activity and welfare – for example, parks – designated space for public use in line with socio-political norms that citizens were empowered to demand more. This formalisation clarified the terms of exclusion of the public from private property. However, while rights of access to and use of public space as a well-being resource were indeed more widely distributed, the state provision arrangement did not always succeed in addressing the changing needs of multiple publics with diverse and more articulate demands emerging in this period, nor more subtle user experience, such as comfort.

How well publicness dimensions are served by a state-led bureaucracy depends on the political priorities of the state, its attitude towards the role of different parts of society in the provision of common goods, and the powers given to the different parts of the government machinery vis-à-vis public space. As we saw in Chapters 6 and 7, in both London and Hong Kong, on the one hand, there are well-documented cases of public space governance decisions apparently working in the service of private property values but seen by the public authorities as a politically acceptable means to enable the private sector to contribute to public amenity. On the other hand, there are many episodes of bottom-up action on public space being enabled that reflect a high-level governing or even societal ethos, in which collective choice rights were exerted through interaction between public space users and government machinery. In Hong Kong, for example, the continued tolerance of the practice of waste-picking and sorting on the streets by those on the edge of poverty reflects this as providing jobs for the poorest, a solution for poverty that is 'better than welfare', and this reflects the wider East Asian norm, where universal welfare is not considered a right.

A public space whose meaning rests so much on the manner of its provision also raises the question of how well the means of provision serves publicness – in this case, the means is the bureaucratic apparatus responsible for public space governance. As state provision of public space in most of the 20th century was part of a wider offer of public services, it was organised in line with Weberian bureaucracy, which remains the organisational and legislative foundation of public space provision in practice in both London and Hong Kong today. Consequently, publicness, and especially its collective choice rights components, tends to be affected by a considerable degree of inflexibility associated with the bureaucratic logic constraints of strong hierarchy and organisational boundaries between departmental silos and, unless explicitly set out as a governing aim, the usually low political priority of the public realm. This often means that coordinated and responsive governance – necessary in a fluid public realm – is not easy to achieve. For these reasons, while a hierarchical bureaucracy can be reasonably competent in delivering on the basic routine needs such as traffic management, mowing lawns or emptying of rubbish bins that are clearly set out within the remits of specialist departments, they struggle to be effective across departmental remits.

How these two features – political priority and structure of bureaucracy – come together is illustrated in our two cities, where they are resolved differently, as Chapters 5, 6 and, especially, Chapter 7 show. The interstitial nature of public space – falling between departmental remits, and the question of which department should lead on resolving particular problems – is often nowhere addressed in policy. In any case, top-down 'policy' and organisational hierarchy alone is always too non-site-specific and too crude for dealing with the ephemeral and subtle problems and opportunities that characterise public space management. In London the bridging of top-down structural bureaucratic constraints and political needs (bottom-up or otherwise) happens in policy innovation, for example, through organisational redesign such as creating street scene departments or overarching directorates, creating partnerships or other types of agreements with the community or private entities, appointing individuals as public realm champions in the government organisation. In Hong Kong, the extreme rigidity of the bureaucratic machine and political constraints mean that the resolution happens on the street itself, through generations of practice and customs passed down through folk knowledge, and alternative and often implied management structures.

A third meaning of public space governance is as contract design and management. This arose from, on the one hand, developments in public service reform that have dramatically challenged the role of the state in public service provision, including public space, where investment, regulation, maintenance and coordination were subject of outsourcing or privatisation. This was a feature of the wider NPM movement in public administration. As the bureaucratic arrangement came under attack by policies encouraging the involvement of the private sector in diverse capacities, the meaning of public space governance as 'contract design and enforcement' emerged: a common feature of NPM involved public authorities fulfilling their responsibilities through contracting with private providers, and the management culture of public space accordingly became more contract centred and performance driven.

On the other hand, problems of public space quality and whether public space was providing what citizens needed and wanted meant the questioning of whether direct state provision was achieving its intended goals. We have seen from the preceding discussion the mismatch between the needs of a dynamic and diverse public space and the unresponsiveness of a state-led bureaucracy, and the problems of coordination and effectiveness that arose. Thus, on top of NPM as a catalyst, in the UK, the reforms to public space governance were driven by distinct concerns about urban and built environment quality, which began to be addressed in England and London from the early 2000s (CABE 2004, ODPM 2004).

We have shown in the last two chapters how London has seen a range of initiatives in public space provision that modify government's direct role. These involve various degrees of transfer of rights and responsibilities for management to private or third sector organisations. Widely seen as privatisation of public services, this, in fact, is not new in public space, as we argued in Chapter 2, either in London, where commons, voluntary and private regimes over public space never completely disappeared, or in Hong Kong, which was literally built on the back of negotiated but robust cooperation between the government and the private sector. As we saw in examples in two cities, the state, having kept regulatory oversight, tends to retain responsibility to safeguard publicness rights through contractual mechanisms and to ensure the public accountability of various non-public providers. London has a much more diverse pattern of rights transfers compared to Hong Kong, which has its own different, non-NPM tradition of cooperation between public and private sectors: as a result of history, terrain and the need to share very limited space, its regulatory structures for this are in fact, much longer established than those of London.

While ideologically driven, and especially in the case of London, these arrangements nevertheless opened the door to the potential of a different range of governance mechanisms, however limited. They also addressed some of the problems of pure bureaucracy. Are publicness rights threatened by this arrangement? On paper, it would seem so. However, publicness, or some of its key elements, remains protected by continued regulation by the state. As summarised in the examples in the previous two chapters, the extent to which publicness rights are safeguarded and the levels of sophistication in defining what those rights entail and how they can be safeguarded depend on the terms and enforcement of the contractual instruments between local authority and provider. In turn, this depends on the local authority's skills and capacities in designing, policing and enforcing those contractual instruments, its policies on issues of publicness and the power relationships of the negotiating parties. This is not necessarily an improvement on what came before. For example, pressure on local authorities and government bodies to outsource their public space services often meant the loss of local knowledge among front-line service providers no longer attached to particular localities. Neither did the problem of interstitiality go away. Lack of champions of public space inside local authorities meant funding cuts, despite the much greater understanding of the importance of public space gained in the intervening years. Varying combinations of these factors can even lead to situations in which publicness is, ironically, better protected by private property owners than by the state. For example, in Hong Kong, while there are generally far less collective choice rights over public space than in London, contractual terms regulating operational rights of public space inside private property, together with the relationship dynamics between oligarchic property owners and citizens, resulted in citizens being able to exercise freedom of speech in shopping malls during the 2019 protests without being disturbed by law enforcement, who were kept off private property.

What emerges about public space governance at this point is a picture of overlaid meanings. State provision as welfare and as protection of movement routes remained mainstream even after the advent of NPM and growing non-public sector provision. No mode of provision has a monopoly over the meaning of public space governance, just as, even during the height of state provision, alternative forms of provision, either private or community-led, existed.

The fourth and final meaning of public space governance is as placemaking, with the associated meaning of public space as co-produced place. While the concept of place is not new and pre-dates that of space when applied to the loci of our bodily inhabitation (Casey 2013), the mainstreaming of the idea that unique places can be everywhere, every day and not just in locations of historic significance, is. On paper, the implication of co-production of publicness rights promises enshrinement of collective action rights. However, in practice, co-production as a governance concept is associated with potential power capture that threatens all operational and collective action rights.

Placemaking as a distinct form of governance found in the two cities may initially seem more a collection of piecemeal responses to evolving public space problems and governance trends. We might call it co-production in response to an emergent role of public space as place. Since place is a space with meaning, it has to be governed as such. Because meaning is ascribed by groups of users or stakeholders, governance arrangements responding to the place attributes of public space require some involvement of those users and stakeholders. The governance forms described in the previous paragraphs, centred on the machinery of local authorities or on corporate private provision, are not always agile or permeable enough to address concerns of that nature. This is especially so as the importance of more everyday meanings of space has grown in the wider planning and city-making discourses and is behind the notion of sense of place.

In London, in the past 10–20 years, diverse placemaking practices have not only sprung from local communities but also been practised by developers and a diverse range of other organisations and arrangements in between, to create meaningful, and thus more valuable, places and public spaces. Local authorities have provided resources (skills, institutional capacity, money) to civil society to develop spaces such as community gardens. Often explained in terms of a response to public funding cuts, this has nevertheless become an opportunity for stakeholders to grasp collective control over their spatial common good. Chapter 7 lists a number of cases in which this has happened.

In Hong Kong, this process of taking much more account of the meaning of a space for its stakeholders has taken a different trajectory, and highlights the diametrically opposed possible flavours of placemaking, as well as the fact that placemaking is flexible enough to be moulded to state, market or community-led provision. As suggested in Chapter 7, a move in this direction by government departments seems slow, but not for the lack of a widespread desire or need for the recognition of the meaning of places. Hong Kong's wide range of NGOs have long been engaged in promoting placemaking, and there is a groundswell of volunteer support for these organisations. In all of this, government departments trapped in bureaucratic silos have mostly been seen as obstructive of these efforts to make place, as they remain restricted by formulaic, spatially homogeneous and conservative interpretations of legislation. The creation of place requires a holistic approach which is hard to achieve in Hong Kong because public space is departmentally interstitial and does not fit clearly into any single remit. The few place-led public space projects are the result of actions by organisations with a place-focused remit, such as a District Council or the hitherto unique Energising Kowloon East Office. The latter, for example, was directly empowered by DEVB, which has the power to take extra-departmental action for fulfilling objectives that are strategically important for Hong Kong. For private sector developers, the large proportion of development outlay occupied by land price means that for most, the added value of investing in places or, indeed, better design, is often not deemed to make much of a difference to the development value.

In this context, it is important to recall the continued tradition in Hong Kong of public space users making their own informal places enabled by tolerant enforcement and creating the characteristic messiness of the city's public spaces, often the result of the semi-formal livelihood activities of the economically marginal. The everyday street scene aside, the most notable of these informal public spaces was the now-closed Instagram Pier, discussed in the previous chapter, a 'place' that existed in the grey area of non-enforcement of regulation. It survived for a whole decade despite having no formal designation as a public space, a fundamental requisite in a city with a highly formalised land use regime. This may not be intentioned placemaking, but places are nevertheless made.

What is the impact on publicness of this form of public space governance, which is co-productive, in which users need to respond, to take part, to create place? It is by necessity human centred, which should at least result in context-specific governance, and it has to take into account collective choice rights. However, whether place-shaping as governance delivers on publicness attributes will still depend on the detailed design of the structures and mechanisms through which user and stakeholder needs are incorporated, and on the mechanisms for balancing different interests and the capacity for action and power that exist among stakeholders. As we saw in examples in Chapters 6 and 7, in most cases in which governance is devolved to stakeholders there are clearly dominant interests which might or might not coincide with those of other stakeholders, or with the interests of the wider community. Even when they do coincide, this might be temporary, and mechanisms need to be in place to recreate degrees of consensus and commonality of purpose.

To conclude this section, we sketch the overall trajectories of public space governance in our two cities to provide an overarching conclusion from the empirical material. In London, the picture is of the meanings of public space governance tending to have gone with the flow of wider trends in state–society relations, whether it was the shift from commons management and turnpike roads, to Victorian philanthropic largesse and the beginnings of state provision and the public as government-managing-on-behalf-of-the-people, and thence to privatisation, outsourcing and governance associated with NPM, and finally to a more locally focused placemaking. These last two phases have been strongly driven by narratives of efficiency, economy and public accountability. London's public space management has kept up with these patterns of urban governance, with associated systemic structural governance changes. In Hong Kong, it is not so much history but tradition – how things have always (apparently) been – that looms large, built on starting points rooted in a mercantilist history, the colonial land management model, an extreme terrain requiring a great deal of infrastructure to produce land at all, and inventive ways to manage space sharing. Even more than in London, public space is often seen as service space for private property values and, thus, owners. Hong Kong's conservative culture has set these traditions in stone, while strategic leadership has in recent times barely focused on public realm issues. While the basics of publicness are there, including increasingly sophisticated mechanisms that shape how the private sector produces such spaces, there has been no strategic review for an enhanced publicness for contemporary needs. Public space's role remains strongly residual in policy terms, a situation not dissimilar to the UK in the late 1980s. In both cities, however, the policy relevance of public space is changing, as a placemaking trend has finally put public space at the heart of a post-industrial city of leisure.

The public nature of governance requires explicit concepts and meanings, including those applying to high-level overall meaningfulness of the enterprise, and not just those about technicalities of management. The four meanings also have direct and less direct implications for publicness. All four are always in play, so a practical theory of public space governance needs to be general enough to deal with any of them.

A practical theory of public space governance

Why a theory?

Theory is 'a form of generalization [which] allows us to move between instances within the same study and between studies as well as to expect certain things to happen and explain how and why certain events have happened' (Timmermans and Tavory 2012: 174). If we are to contribute to the academic discourse and practice of public space governance, then we need to be able to make the findings of our research transferable, if not generalisable. The more widely a theory is useful in describing and explaining, the more useful it will be to both discourse and practice.

This is a definitional theory; it proposes how we should structure our explorations of public space governance, and should ideally be applicable in as many places as possible – it should be transferable (Lincoln and Guba 1986), if not generalisable. This is also a practical theory. These conceptualisations should also inform decisions in practice.

A theory of public space governance articulates the conceptualisation of public space governance and of public space in it. In the following section, five key features of the theory are discussed. First, we suggest that a practical theory of public space governance posits that public space is a complex common good which is spatial as well as social and is spatially contiguous. Second, we argue that public space is necessarily socially constructed, and cannot exist if it lacks sufficient social agreement either for its existence or for dealing with the brute facticity of its spatiality. Third, we set out that cities govern public space so that it can fulfil its role as a resource for wider urban governance by securing the delivery of the fundamental functions of circulation and use of space as a locus for various activities, both collective and individual, while delivering well-being and sustainability for the city. Fourth, maximising public value, given constraints, is a principle of governing public space: city governments seek to enhance the value of the various attributes of public space as they are part of the infrastructure that allows the city to work. Determining how this value is distributed, to whom it is allocated and in what proportion is the aim of public space governance. Fifth and finally, we argue that the allocation of publicness rights (operational rights and collective choice rights) is the basic mechanism through which the value of public space attributes is distributed to stakeholders and the overall value of public space is materialised. Operational decisions require contextual local interpretation, and it is through them that materialisation of that value occurs in each public space.

The theory discussed

For the purposes of public space governance, public space is a resource that delivers valuable benefits to the city and its citizens via their direct or indirect interactions with the space itself. The most fundamental function of public space is that of circulation, movement through the city for all. Public space is a means through which people can navigate around private, non-accessible parts of the space. This is why the basic defining feature of the public space resource is spatial contiguity, which is further enhanced through the design and provision of such movement technologies as canals, railways and roads. A second group of functions that the public space resource enables relate to interactions between people and for various activities that contribute to individual and societal benefits such as leisure, health and symbolic meanings. These functions are socio-spatially diverse, and are specific to a culture, city or even neighbourhood. They include solo or group activity, work, leisure or even domestic activity. The functions of access and of use benefit both citizens individually and the city as a whole, and are fundamental for the city to work, and even to exist. This is why we have argued that what we call 'public space' is actually a common good, a shared resource that society recognises as needing to actively provide, due to its essential urban role. Societies therefore designate public space as a common resource.

The term 'public space' is the source of much of the confused debate around publicness. In the book, we have clarified that concept of 'public' when applied to public space is not identical to that in economics which defines a public good as one that is non-excludable and non-subtractable. However, the term 'public' does imply non-exclusiveness as a normative aim for anything public, and it is this that informs the everyday understanding of what is public about public space. We have also contended that the concept of public in public space is not identical to the meaning of public as owned or provided by the state, a meaning that is often behind discussions about privatisation of public space. Instead, we have posited that the notion of public in public space should be understood essentially as a result of its common good character rather than its circumstantial attributes of either non-excludability, non-exclusiveness or of state ownership. However, these circumstantial factors – in the sense that individual public spaces might exhibit some of them some of the time in a larger or smaller degree – infuse our cultural understanding of public space and relate to the aspirations of society for them and, hence, governance and management choices.

Since maintaining the status of common good requires the agreement of the members of society, public space is a social construct, existing only by sufficient societal agreement. In even the smallest, simplest space with few people, such agreement requires orchestration. Such an agreement sets out arrangements for shared use of the space, usually by defining rights, responsibilities and conditions of use. The specifics of those arrangements will be context and situation specific, as each society has its particular cultural norms, and each space its particular characteristics. Institutional economics has given us some typical arrangements of rights for shared resources – public, common pool, club and private goods – but public space is complex and actually made up of a hybrid package of interacting economic facilities and attributes, delivered via a wide range of semi-discrete and less discrete spaces – the individual public spaces – and serving diverse publics. At the same time, public space as a whole should be seen as a common good, a notion which guides how trade-offs between demands on public space resources should proceed. If the common good nature of public space is to be maintained, these trade-offs at an operational level should be informed by the balance of publicness rights allocated to different stakeholders and how this ultimately shapes that common-ness.

The allocation of rights is what public space governance involves, and cities govern public space so that it can fulfil its role as resource for fundamental functions of circulation and use of space as the locus of various activities, both collective and individual, while delivering well-being and sustainability for the city. Governance means keeping that societal agreement in place, updated and functioning, so that public space can fulfil role is as a common resource for wider urban benefit, via the governance of complex spatial environments and diverse stakeholders with a range of rights and interests.

Governance includes all patterns of rule to solve societal problems and realise societal opportunities. Urban governance means dealing with urban problems or opportunities. Public space is one resource that can be utilised to help solve these societal problems and grasp societal opportunities in the city. Rather than simply the governing of public space, where public space is an end in itself and the object of governance, public space governance therefore involves governance of public space to enable governance by it.

Put differently, public space governance entails governance of public space as a way to contribute to the governance of the city by public space, or by using it as a resource for city governance.

Public space governance aims to deliver access and use functions, well-being and sustainability in a manner that is high in 'publicness' qualities, as defined earlier. Public space governance objectives should be framed as delivering valuable access, use, well-being and sustainability outcomes to relevant stakeholders and to the city as a whole. Valuable outcomes must be defined not just by what it is they deliver, but also by how and how well they are delivered. For example, a street should not just be generally accessible, but should ideally be non-congested: not simply useable, but also enjoyable, not just a way to simply meet each other's interests but to realise the potentials of collaboration and co-production. Similarly, a park or green area should not be there just to meet a statistically demonstrated need for green spaces in a particular neighbourhood, but it should be designed and managed in ways that allow most users and stakeholders to make the most of the attributes they demand, that in fact create the opportunities for those and other attributes.

Public space governance also safeguards publicness of processes. Four processes of public space provision were discussed in Chapter 4: investment, maintenance, regulation and coordination. The manner in which these processes proceed matter as much as their outcomes. Whether the processes are transparent and accountable, technically competent, efficient and effective, and fair, contributes to delivering publicness, the optimum degree of the common good attributes that make a space public. Since benefitting from public space attributes often requires active participation, whether the users or stakeholders of public space are enabled to enjoy the attributes and benefits they seek, such co-productive processes not typically thought of as space provision should also be a governance consideration, but have historically rarely been in the remit of public space management, although this is changing with the rise of placemaking. This is for instance the case of valuable attributes such as the character of a public space or its symbolic meaning, which often cannot be designed beforehand, and it is actually defined through use. The already mentioned Instagram Pier in Hong Kong is an example of meaning and forms of use shaped through co-production. Variables such as user capacity, legitimacy, interest and power should be taken into account in shaping governance mechanisms. The point is not just whether stakeholders have the operation and collective choice rights that they require to fully benefit from public space, but whether they are able to, and do, exercise those rights.

Securing socially desired levels of publicness of individual public space is a principle and aim of public space governance. The principle of optimised publicness, the aim of distributing value to best realise the common good dimension of public space and the allocation of publicness rights that best suits those aims, provides overarching normative direction for all public space governance activity, provides guidance to public space governors in securing publicness along the lines we defined in Chapter 3. In that chapter we proposed a conceptualisation of publicness that is distinct from publicness as state-owned or provided, and that the public character of public spaces and their attributes arises from societal arrangements based on the allocation of some basic rights rather the economics understanding of publicness as non-excludability and non-subtractability. That view of publicness is closely aligned with the common good understanding of public space, as it seeks to capture the common good qualities of public space. As we have argued earlier, since public space serves diverse publics, and since publicness is meaningful only if defined in relation to its societal context and to the needs and demands of stakeholders, publicness is simply the extent to which different interests in public space are contemplated and met in relation to others' interests and needs. When interests are contemplated and met, functions of public space are said to be performed, and value derived by stakeholders, as a result.

Public space should benefit citizens as non-exclusively as possible in its particular context, and the state should act as the guarantor of the basic rights associated with publicness, even if the state does not provide or manage the space directly. The specifics of what publicness means will be articulated through local interpretation in each instance of governance, reflecting public space's socially constructed nature. Local interpretation increases the responsiveness of management decision making. All this may mean that, as we saw in many of the examples in Chapters 6 and 7, a public space may be subject to limitation of access at certain times for operational purposes dictated locally, or for crowd-control reasons (a wider public good that may not be perceivable locally), or access to some attributes might be regulated and rationed. Asserting publicness through public space governance may mean more open and fair access to the attributes valued by users and stakeholders, less congestion in use through forms of access control, and fairer and greater effectiveness in the assertion of collective choice rights.

It follows that maximising public value, given constraints, is a principle and aim of governing public space. When the resource of public space is put to use, it creates value. Therefore, public space governance can be conceptualised through a value-based approach. This posits that value, what people and societies seek – all internal conflicts and contradictions notwithstanding – is delivered by the utilisation (or consumption, or enjoyment) of the resource public space. This concept of value is an instrumentalised way of understanding what public space governance produces as it addresses and tries to bring together the multiple and conflicting demands for public space attributes. In these terms, the aim of public space governance is to achieve public value, roughly defined as the best use of the common good public space within the constraints posed by the particular societal agreement defining that common good character. This will include the prioritisation of some views over others and will reflect the relative power of different stakeholders, which determines the nature of that societal agreement. Such a public-value rationality with all its caveats is what does and must inform public space governance. City governments seek to enhance the value of the various attributes of public space as they are part of the infrastructure that allows the city to work. Determining how this value is distributed, to whom it is allocated and in what proportion is the aim of public space governance.

What are, then, the aims of public space governance in terms of value? The aims of public space governance can be set out in terms of the value configuration it should achieve. Public space governance is therefore about managing public space resources to create a more acceptable value configurations between, first, interests held in common by all citizens – that is, public value – and second, private or sectional interests of stakeholders. The process of creating value in public space is a process of socio-spatial construction which produces an outcome that is context specific in nature and should therefore be contextually judged for goodness or badness. Thus, the aim of public space governance is a better configuration of values between interests in common and individual interests, given constraints. It is to maximise publicness from that common good by better distributing constructed value to as many interests as possible, including to the city as a whole.

Fifth and finally, the allocation of publicness rights (operational rights and collective choice rights) is the basic mechanism through which the value of public space attributes is distributed to stakeholders and the overall value of public space is materialised. Operational decisions require contextual local interpretation, and it is through them that materialisation of that value occurs in each public space. The fundamental mechanism for governance is the allocation to stakeholders of rights and responsibilities regarding access to, use of and collective choice on public space. These sets of rights and responsibilities define the essence of publicness and determine exclusiveness, congestion and other experiential qualities of use, and the legitimacy and power of stakeholders to shape and benefit from the space.

However, the existence of rights by themselves does not suffice as a means to deliver on the publicness aim, which is a key purpose of public space governance. The ability to do so would depend on the design and operation of governance institutions such as funding arrangements, rules and regulations, contracts and agreements, and customs.

The design of rights allocation instruments is also influential. Since the publicness of public space is a reflection of its ability to deliver on its common good qualities while meeting the sectional or private needs and desires of citizens, we need to articulate what this delivery is. The empirical examples in Chapters 5, 6 and 7 showed us some of the publicness rights and their interpretation and exercise, via institutions and processes of governance. They showed us that while rights allocation is the essential foundation, they are not sufficient to explain the eventual level of publicness achieved. For this we need to examine the design of institutions and practices of governance that directly affect the everyday operation of public space governance.

Wrapping up the theorisation of governance practice

We started this book by theorising public space governance as the allocation of publicness rights around the provision of public space as a 'common good'. Throughout the book we have elaborated this position further by pointing to the contiguous and spatial nature of public space and the facilitating nature of public space that needs to underpin the broader meaning of public space governance.

To wrap up this theorisation which has so far focused on stitching together operational- and strategic-level concepts from the literature and empirical cases described in previous chapters, we propose five theoretical extensions that could take forward research and theoretical development of public space governance. These can be explored individually but are potentially mutually enriching.

Theorising public space governance in value terms sets value up as a foundation for explaining why governance situations play out as they do. Since value is 'that which is of worth', it is possible to couch everything from governance objectives to governance mechanisms in value terms. Sense-making is the process of assigning meaning, or value, to our experiences (Weick 1995, Kramer 2017), and gives us our second theoretical extension. Sense-making is a social psychology-based theoretical perspective that can explain the dynamics of people's search for value. This can explain many decisions and actions in public space governance and generally, in many situations of multi-actor interactions. Third, both value and sense-making can operationalise Hoppe's (2011) idea that in governance situations that are unstructured, governance actions need to be conceptualised not as solving but as structuring societal problems. Public space governance situations are often of the unstructured kind: the socially constructed and contingent nature of the common good public space means that the knowledge of outcomes of governance actions is not certain and there is not a widely agreed set of value, norms and goals, as they will vary from case to case (Hoppe 2011). Thus, value is operationalised by sense-making, and both can help with structuring public space governance problems so that they can be acted upon. The fourth and fifth theoretical extensions draw on practice-leaning knowledge: the concept of service and how public space governance needs to be packaged in service terms, and that a design-thinking approach needs to power any approach to this or, indeed, any approach to dealing with structuring and governing public space's complexities.

First, as we have suggested, we propose that a concept of value underpins this new public space governance theorisation. Public space governance can be conceptualised as the better distributive configuration of value among different stakeholders, interests and priorities. Specifically, it has been reframed as the configuration of rights, or rights regimes, and benefit-distribution mechanisms to optimise value for all. This idea of 'configuring' resonates strongly with design, as we see later. In terms of value, the aim of public space governance is to achieve a better distribution of values that helps in optimising that common good. Since value is itself valueless, it is up to the governing actors, in negotiation, to agree the substantive content of the values to be achieved, as an aim.

Value or, more precisely, people's psychological value-seeking tendencies, can explain a great deal of decisions and behaviour. Value is therefore powerful in explaining those, even outside of what legislation, policy, contracts and even customs might be able to explain. Value allows us to take into account the everyday politics of public space governance that are in play, and therefore to take a view as governance participants themselves might as they weigh up trade-offs holistically. As we will see later, sense-making provides a coherent set of theories to operationalise the study of this value-seeking behaviour.

Value is also the concept that links resource and benefits; thus, we are also able to think of public space itself in terms of value. It is a common value-carrying resource from which benefits (for individuals or for wider urban governance) may be derived. Value has also strong links to design as value configuration, and thus we can think of particular configurations producing certain types or degrees of value. Value also underpins the concept of service, which is an interaction that generates value. Public space governance in terms of design and in terms of 'service' will be explored later. While the concept of value is sufficiently abstract to frame the diverse functions, stakeholders and dynamics of public space, yet it is supported by a wide range of tools that apply this concept performatively, to solve problems. Thus, we can conceptualise the whole of public space governance, its aims, mechanisms, dynamics, in terms of value and the management of its construction.

Second, sense-making is about assigning meaning, or value, to our experiences. Sense-making is a useful theoretical perspective and provides the socio-technical apparatus to operationalise the study of public space governance in terms of value (Sieh 2014). Sense-making is particularly useful when experiences are equivocal and ambiguous meanings are involved, as it can explain the relationships between the experiences and the actions we take. Sense-making therefore could explain, in terms of people's value-seeking patterns, how problem structuring proceeds in terms of value construction in fluid multi-actor situations such as public space governance.

Third, public space governance situations can range from being unstructured to the highly structured, but most are in between and require the application of local rationalities (informed by context-specific knowledge) to city-wide principles (such as laws and policies), since all public space governance problems play out in specific localities, which are unique. To extract benefits afforded by public space in fact involves dealing with a complex mix of the structured and unstructured governance problems. When dealing with the latter, we need to be prepared to structure those problems, not simply solve them (Hoppe 2011). This means we need to deal with the politics of public space governance to arrive at sufficient structuredness, something that sense-making can explain and address. A problem-structuring conceptualisation is resonant with the double-diamond model of design discussed later, and effectively draws our attention to the importance of formulating the most appropriate set of issues for governance to act upon. This need to structure instead of solving problems became truly clear when looking at public space governance in Hong Kong, where looking only at the formal mechanisms for governance is inadequate for explaining what happens and what is observed on the ground. Governance as problem structuring is thus a strategic-level theoretical approach to explaining the wide range of observations about the publicness of public space, how it is defined and how it is delivered.

Fourth, since we are developing a practical theory, and practical wisdom is to be found in tools and techniques from practice, we draw on two practice-oriented and technique-rich ways of thinking to actively deal with public space governance's problem-structuring sense-making: service and design. Service, broadly defined, involves an interaction which generates value for the interacting parties. In the past three decades, the theorisation of services as a major sector of advanced economies and their management has grown substantially (see, for example, Vargo and Lusch 2016). However, here service-dominant thinking is useful because it points to a customer/user focus, as services are co-produced. This is resonant with the human-centred approach of design (see, for example, Penin 2018). Since a service approach is alert to co-production, service-quality models also point to the demand, not just the supply side of a service. The link to value is this: value is understood to arise from the match between expectation (demand-related concept) and experience (of the supplied service).

A service-dominant approach also reframes public space governance as relationships between tangible and intangible elements of the public realm, and points to how their interactions and design create meaning or value. A service-focused view suggests that value can arise when tangible/intangible elements interact in a way to deliver what the user/customer expects and wants. Tools and techniques from service management studies provide a rich seam of ideas that bridge tangible and intangible elements for dealing with public space, which similarly sees value, whether positively or negatively, being extremely sensitive to tangible/intangible configurations.

Importantly, if we are to couch public space governance as a major urban service in itself with explicit objectives, budgets and so on – and some municipal authorities have tried to do this – then this will reshape the way that public space is provided, regardless of who does it, whether public bodies or private or community actors. The notions related to a service, service itself, the scope, its aims and objectives, are something that local governments everywhere understand and can cope with as organisations, provided they are given the remit and resources and are structured to do so. Service, as discussed, is intricately and richly related to the concepts of value (service is a value-generating interaction, servicing creates value) and design (we can design services, by configuring their tangible and intangible elements).

Fifth and finally, design or actions to create preferred situations involve the configuring of things, spaces, institutions, ideas. This is resonant with governance in the sense that they both are strongly intentional and seek to improve existing situations. Design, however, suggests manipulating detailed interactions between components. Earlier, we referred to the need for further context-specific detail – essentially, a better, more detailed control and understanding of socio-technical configurations to achieve better value configurations. Design is linked to the idea of service, since services can be designed. Like services, design is human-centred, and should be user-focused. Design and service and public space governance are linked by the idea of value, as design can change or create value. In relation to the complexities of public space governance, design is a well-known approach for addressing the wicked problems of the social sciences (Rittel and Webber 1973), problems which are complex, unstructured and for which no single or best solution exists. The attitude inbuilt into design thinking makes it an ideal approach to formulate governance actions as problem structuring, as we discussed earlier. Design thinking, therefore, can provide an approach and a set of techniques to govern in such instances. Finally, design implies performative action. This means not just understanding the problem and devising courses of action to solve it but acting on it. In dealing with publicness rights, a design attitude will go further to enable the exercise of those rights. It is an attitude that is empowering (and infuses a lot of tactical urbanism episodes in placemaking around the world) and that is much needed in public space governance.

Public space governance in terms of value could therefore be conceptualised as a service which involves the constant designing of tangible and intangible configurations as benefit-distribution mechanisms, with the aim of maximising both individual and collective value, given constraints. This whole process can be analysed using a sense-making lens, which assumes a value-seeking dynamic among actors.

Conclusion

We have now gone full circle in our discussion of public space provision and management. We started the book by defining how we understood public space, publicness and public space governance, with the aim of setting the ground for looking at the recent experience of London and Hong Kong and how they have faced their own public space challenges. Having done that, and with the purpose of contributing towards the practice of public space governance, we have concluded the book by suggesting the contours of a practical theory of governance that could help with conceptualising public space provision and management and instrumentalising it for practice. If we accept the view of public space as a common good whose roles and functions are socially determined and context specific, and that publicness is about the allocation and exercise of rights to the attributes and benefits that public space creates to multiple stakeholders, then we need a way of articulating how the challenges to provision and management we discussed in Chapters 6 and 7 can be tackled by the governance machinery that in both cities, and in many others like them, are in charge of that. Doing that is how we have concluded our narrative.

We have seen how both cities have devolved the responsibility for the provision of public spaces – and in London also for the management of existing spaces – to actors outside the public sector, and have discussed the mechanisms that have been put in place to secure that publicness is maintained, albeit in different forms. These mechanisms assume a wide range of forms, but mostly they depend on contractual instruments, backed up by legislation and relying on complex and not always responsive measures for compliance and enforcement. How effective they are or can be is ultimately a function of the institutional context in which they operate. As the cases in both cities suggest, even when they work as intended, those mechanisms seem more effective in securing some form of operational rights of access and use for the relevant stakeholders than they do as regards the collective choice rights of those not directly involved in the devolution arrangements, and that may include the general public. Whereas in London there is an institutional environment that guarantees a wider distribution of those rights, the much more rigid system in Hong Kong means that collective choice rights are all primarily vested within an established understanding that exists between the government machinery and major corporate interests, and are rarely transferred to those outside it, such as community organisations. Exceptions to this are very much that: real exceptions that are mostly temporary.

All the foregoing suggests that both cities try to address the challenges of providing and managing public spaces by relying on a varying mix of private investment, community social capital and stakeholder commitment. The unavoidable consequence is a greater fragmentation of public space, in the sense of a collection of spaces with increasingly varying sets of management responsibilities by different stakeholders, varying allocation of publicness rights and therefore varying publicness regimes. We have argued that this was to some extent always the case, but the contraction of the public-as-state-provided type of public space exacerbates the problems of coordination of governance and management activities and of implementing the policy objectives for public spaces in the wider context of the city. The paradox here is that public space provision and management with more active engagement of stakeholders tends to result in a higher degree of collective choice rights and agency allocated locally, but a reduced degree and agency at the aggregate level of the city. This is certainly visible in London: as the cases in the previous two chapters suggest, the dependence on real estate development for the provision of new or refurbished public space, together with an increasing transfer of management rights over existing spaces, results in a patchwork of contiguous public spaces with different rules for access, different management responsibilities and routines, different accountability mechanisms, but which still need to be functional and integrated parts of the whole physical public realm and to fulfil functions and respond to demands that go beyond those of their immediate stakeholders. In Hong Kong this issue is manifested in the complexities of bringing together state-provided and often undifferentiated public space with privately provided spaces and with informal forms of usage of public space that emerge in response to the need to adapt spaces to actual user demand, with rigid and inflexible instruments and institutional structures.

What those considerations point to is that the complexity of dealing with the physical public realm in both cities and of managing diverse 'publicnesses' as a coherent whole requires us to explore further the ideas about public space governance formulated in Chapter 4. In this chapter we have refined those ideas to put forward an approach that can address the kinds of issues suggested in our case study chapters. We suggest this requires a clear conceptualisation of public space functions, the understanding of provision and service as provision of value and the formulation of the key concept of publicness as a function of the allocation of publicness rights to benefit from those values. It also requires an understanding of the relationship between the wider societal demands for the complex common good that is public space and the local, context-specific manifestations of this common good.

As we have tried to argue in this book, as public space governance starts to diverge from the state-provided-and-managed model, bringing together an increasingly fragmented physical public ream into a holistic common good that ensures diverse public spaces fulfil the expectations society has of them becomes a key governance objective. This has to happen while at the same time recognising the right to and the power of local specificity through which most of the meaning of public spaces is constituted for their users and stakeholders. London and Hong Kong, in their own ways – as do most cities – are trying to grapple with those issues and, in this process, they show us the real nature of the remit, difficulties and potential for public space governance to ensure that public space continues to be a vital component of urban life. In doing so, they show us that the death of public spaces occasionally referred to in the literature will never be more than an exaggerated figure of speech, useful to alert us of the contemporary challenges facing public space, but far from adequate to describe the inventiveness with which cities and societies tackle and solve those challenges.

References

Akkar, M. (2005) The changing 'publicness' of contemporary public spaces: a case study of the Grey's Monument area, Newcastle Upon Tyne, *Urban Design International*, vol 10 (2), pp 95–113.

Amin, A. (2008) Collective culture and urban public space, *City*, vol 12 (1), pp 5–24.

Andersen, H. and van Kempen, R. (eds) (2001) *Governing European Cities: Social Fragmentation, Social Exclusion and Urban Governance*. Aldershot: Ashgate.

Arendt, H. (1998) *The Human Condition* (2nd edition). Chicago: University of Chicago Press.

Audit Commission (2002) *Street Scene*. London: The Audit Commission.

Bailey, N. (1995) *Partnership Agencies in British Urban Policy*. London: UCL Press.

Ballas, D. (2013) What makes a 'happy city'? *Cities*, vol 32, pp 39–50.

Banerjee, T. (2001) The future of public space: beyond invented streets and reinvented places, *APA Journal*, vol 67 (1), pp 9–24.

BD – Buildings Department (2008) *Background Information on Provision of Public Facilities within Private Developments*. Hong Kong: HKSAR Government

BD – Buildings Department (2022) *Areas within Private Properties Dedicated for Public Use*. Hong Kong: HKSAR Government.

Benn, S. and Gauss, G. (eds) (1983) *Public and Private in Social Life*. London: Croom Helm.

Bevir, M. (2009) *Key Concepts in Governance*. London: SAGE.

Bishop, P. and Williams, L. (2019) *Planning, Politics and City-making: A Case Study of King's Cross*. London: Routledge.

Blomley, N. (2004) Un-real estate: proprietary space and public gardening, *Antipode* vol 36 (4): 614–641.

Blomley, N. (2013) Performing property: making the world, *Canadian Journal of Law & Jurisprudence*, vol 26 (1), pp 23–48.

Box, R., Marshall, G., Reed, B. and Reed, C. (2001) New public management and substantive democracy, *Public Administration Review*, vol 61 (5), pp 608–619.

Bundred, S. (2006) Solutions to silos: joining up knowledge, *Public Money and Management*, vol 26 (2), pp 125–130.

Burch, S. (2002) Shaping symbolic space: Parliament Square, London as sacred site, in Ashworth, G. and Phelps, A. (eds) *The Construction of Built Heritage*. London: Routledge, pp 223–236.

CABE – Commission for Architecture and the Built Environment (2004) *Is the Grass Greener …? Learning from International Innovations in Urban Green Space Management*. London: CABE.

Carmona, M. (2015) Re-theorising contemporary public space: a new narrative and a new normative. *Journal of Urbanism*, vol 8 (4), pp 373–405.

Carmona, M. (2022) The 'public-isation' of private space – towards a charter of public space rights and responsibilities, *Journal of Urbanism* vol 15 (2), pp 133–164.

Carmona, M. and Wunderlich, F. (2012) *Capital Spaces: The Multiple Complex Public Spaces of a Global City*. London: Routledge.

Carmona, M., De Magalhães, C. and Hammond, L. (2008) *Public Space: The Management Dimension*. Abingdon: Routledge.

Carr, E., Dunlap, G., Horner, R., Koegel, R., Turnbull, A., Sailor, W., Anderson, J., Albin, R., Koegel, L. and Fox, L. (2002) Positive behavior support: evolution of an applied science, *Journal of Positive Behavior Intervention*, vol 4 (1), pp 4–16.

Carroll, J. (2007) *A Concise History of Hong Kong*. Washington, DC: Rowman & Littlefield Publishers.

Casey, E. (2013) *The Fate of Place: A Philosophical History*. Berkeley: University of California Press.

Cheng, A.K.C.W. (2012) The blame game: how colonial legacies in Hong Kong shape street vendor and public space policies, PhD Thesis, Massachusetts Institute of Technology.

Cheung, L. (2019) Housing estates' shopping malls banned the police from entering, suspected of breaking the law. HKCD. Available in https://www.hkcd.com/content/2019-08/12/content_1151674.html.

Chu, C.L. (2012) Speculative modern: urban forms and the politics of property in colonial Hong Kong. PhD Thesis, UC Berkeley.

Clark, F. (1973) Nineteenth-century public parks from 1830, *Garden History*, vol 1 (3), pp 31–41.

Crang, M. and Thrift, N. (2000) Introduction, in Crang, M. and Thrift, N. (eds) *Thinking Space* (vol 9). London: Routledge, pp 1–30.

Crouch, C. (2010) Competitive cities and problems of democracy, in Pike, A., Rodriguez-Pose, A. and Tomaney, J. (eds) *Handbook of Local and Regional Development*. London: Routledge, pp 295–305.

Cuthbert, A.R. and McKinnell, K.G. (1997) Ambiguous space, ambiguous rights—corporate power and social control in Hong Kong, *Cities*, vol 14 (5), pp 295–311.

Dapiran, A. (2019) Be water! Seven tactics that are winning Hong Kong's democracy revolution, *New Statesman*, 1.

De La Latta, S. (2021) Spaces of becoming: lessons for planners from the square movements, *Planning Theory & Practice*, vol 22 (1), pp 90–107.

De Magalhães, C. (2010) Public space and the contracting-out of publicness: a framework for analysis, *Journal of Urban Design*, vol 15 (4), pp 559–574.

De Magalhães, C. and Carmona, M. (2006) Innovations in the management of public space: reshaping and refocusing governance, *Planning Theory and Practice*, vol 7 (3), pp 289–303.

De Magalhães, C. and Carmona, M. (2009) Dimensions and models of contemporary public space management in England, *Journal of Environmental Planning and Management*, vol 52 (1), pp 111–129.

De Magalhães, C. and Freire Trigo, S. (2017a) Contracting out publicness: the private management of the urban public realm and its implications, *Progress in Planning*, vol 115 (2017), pp 1–28.

De Magalhães, C. and Freire Trigo, S. (2017b) 'Clubification' or urban public Spaces? The withdrawal or the re-definition of the roles of local government in the management of public spaces, *Journal of Urban Design*, vol 22 (6), pp 738–756.

Dempsey, N. and Burton, M. (2012) Defining place-keeping: the long-term management of public spaces, *Urban Forestry & Urban Greening*, vol 11, pp 11–20.

Dempsey, N., Burton, M. and Selin, J. (2016) Contracting out parks and roads maintenance in England, *International Journal of Public Sector Management*, vol 29 (5), pp 441–456.

DETR – Department for the Environment, Transport and the Regions (2000) Our Towns and Cities: The Future. Delivering an Urban Renaissance. The White Paper on Urban Policy. London: DETR.

DEVB – Development Bureau (2011) *Public Open Space in Private Developments Design and Management Guidelines*. Hong Kong: HKSAR Government.

Di Masso, A. (2012) Grounding citizenship: toward a political psychology of public space, *Political Psychology*, vol 33 (1), pp 123–143.

Dovey, K. and King, R. (2011) Forms of informality: morphology and visibility of informal settlements, *Built Environment*, vol 37 (1), pp 11–29.

DTLR – Department for Transport, Local Government and the Regions (2001) *Strong Local Leadership – Quality Public Services*. London: DETR.

DTLR – Department for Transport, Local Government and the Regions (2002) *Green Spaces, Better Places: Final Report of the Urban Green Spaces Taskforce*. London: DETR.

Edwards, N. (1992) The colonial suburb: public space as private space, in Chua, B.H. and Edwards, N. (eds) *Public Space: Design, Use and Management*. Singapore: Singapore University Press, pp 24–39.

Electoral Affairs Commission (2020) *2019 District Council Ordinary Election Constituency Boundaries*. Hong Kong: HKSAR Government.

Ellin, N. (1996) *Postmodern Urbanism*. Oxford: Blackwell.

Endacott, G. (1958) *A History of Hong Kong*. Oxford: Oxford University Press.

Ettlinger, N. and Bosco, F. (2004) Thinking through networks and their spatiality: a critique of the US (public) war on terrorism and its geographic discourse, *Antipode*, vol 36 (2), pp 249–271.

Farris, J. (2018) Contingency and opportunity: the first century of Hong Kong's public parks, *International Planning History Society Proceedings*, vol 18, pp 88–96.

Forrest, R., La Grange, A. and Yip, N.-M. (2004) Hong Kong as a global city? Social distance and spatial differentiation, *Urban Studies*, vol 41 (1), pp 207–227.

Foster, S. (2011) Collective action and the urban commons, *Notre Dame Law Review* vol 87 (1), pp 57–134.

Fraser, E.D., Dougill, A.J., Mabee, W.E., Reed, M. and McAlpine, P. (2006) Bottom up and top down: analysis of participatory processes for sustainability indicator identification as a pathway to community empowerment and sustainable environmental management, *Journal of Environmental Management*, vol 78 (2), pp 114–127.

Guardian (2017) 'Revealed: the insidious creep of pseudo-public space in London', London: *Guardian*, 24 July 2017.

GLA – Greater London Authority (2021) *London Plan Guidance: Public London Charter*. London: Greater London Authority.

Glaeser, E. (2011) *Triumph of the City: How Our Greatest Invention Makes Us Richer, Smarter, Greener, Healthier, and Happier*. New York: Penguin Press.

Goss, S. (2001) *Making Local Governance Work: Networks, Relationships and the Management of Change*. Basingstoke: Palgrave Macmillan.

Govada, S.S., Spruijt, W., Rodgers, T., Cheng, L., Chung, H. and Huang, Q. (2020) Smart Living for Smart Hong Kong. Smart Living for Smart Cities: Case Studies, pp 75–135.

Guadarrama Sánchez, G.J. and Pichardo Martínez, P.M. (2021) Appropriation types and use of the urban public space. The commons in the urban park, *Economía, sociedad y territorio*, vol 21 (65), pp 57–85.

Habermas, J. (2001) *The Structural Transformation of the Public Sphere: An Inquiry into a Category of the Bourgeois Society* (Cambridge MA: MIT Press). Cited in S. Low and N. Smith (2006) *The Politics of Public Space* (London: Routledge).

HAD – Home Affairs Department (2021) *Hong Kong: The Facts – District Administration*. Hong Kong: HKSAR Government.

Haila, A. (2000) Real estate in global cities: Singapore and Hong Kong as property states, *Urban studies*, vol 37 (12), pp 2241–2256.

Hajer, M. and Wagenaar, H. (2003) *Deliberative Policy Analysis: Understanding Governance in the Network Society*. Cambridge: Cambridge University Press.

Hambro, E. (1957) Chinese refugees in Hong Kong, *The Phylon Quarterly*, vol 18, pp 69–81.

Hannikainen, M. (2016) *The Greening of London, 1920–2000*. London: Routledge.

Haque, M. (2001) The diminishing publicness of public service under the current mode of governance, *Public Administration Review*, vol 61 (1), pp 65–82.

Hardin, G. (1968) The tragedy of the commons: the population problem has no technical solution; it requires a fundamental extension in morality, *Science*, vol 162 (3859), pp 1243–1248.

Harvey, D. (2012) *Rebel Cities: From the Right to the City to the Urban Revolution*. London: Verso.

Hasluck, E. (1948) *Local Government in England*. Cambridge: Cambridge University Press.

Hastings, A., Bailey, N., Gannon, M., Besemer, K. and Bramley, G. (2015) Coping with the cuts? The management of the worst financial settlement in living memory, *Local Government Studies*, vol 41 (4), pp 601–621.

Hayllar, M. (2010) Public-private partnerships in Hong Kong: good governance, the essential missing ingredient? *Australian Journal of Public Administration*, vol 69, pp 99–119.

Healey, P. (1997) *Collaborative Planning: Shaping Places in Fragmented Societies*. London: Macmillan.

Healey, P. (1998) Building institutional capacity through collaborative approaches to urban planning, *Environment and Planning A: Economy and Space*, vol 30 (9), pp 1531–1546.

Healey, P. (2020) Citizen innovation in place governance, in Edelenbos, J., Molenveld, A. and van Meerkerk, I. (eds) *Civic Engagement, Community-Based Initiatives and Governance Capacity: An International Perspective*. New York: Routledge, pp 43–69.

Heng, C.K. (2007) Chinese public space: a brief account, in Douglass, M., Ho, K.C. and Ooi, G.L. (eds). *Globalization, the City and Civil Society in Pacific Asia: The Social Production of Civic Spaces*. London: Routledge, pp 80–103.

Hirschman, A. (1970) *Exit, Voice and Loyalty: Responses to Decline in Firms, Organisations and States*. Cambridge, MA: Harvard University Press.

HKPSI (Hong Kong Public Space Initiative) (2018) Privately owned public space: Audit report, Hong Kong: HKPSI

Ho, K.C. and Lim, N.E. (1992) Back lanes as contested regions: construction and control of physical space, in Chua, B.H. and Edwards, N. (eds) *Public Space: Design, Use and Management*. Singapore: Singapore University Press, pp 40–54.

Ho, M.S. and Wan, W.K. (2021) Universities as an Arena of Contentious politics: mobilization and control in Hong Kong's Anti-Extradition movement of 2019. *International Studies in Sociology of Education*, pp 1–24.

Ho, P.-Y. (2018) *Making Hong Kong*. Cheltenham: Edward Elgar Publishing.

Hodkinson, S. (2011) The Private Finance Initiative in English council housing regeneration: a privatisation too far? *Housing Studies*, vol 26 (6), pp 911–932.

Honey-Rosés, J., Anguelovski, I., Chireh, V., Daher, C., Konijnendijk van den Bosch, C., Litt, J., Mawani, V., McCall, M., Orellana, A., Oscilowicz, E. and Sánchez, U. (2021) The impact of COVID-19 on public space: an early review of the emerging questions–design, perceptions and inequities, *Cities and Health*, vol 5 (sup 1), pp 263– 279.

Hoppe, R. (2011) *The Governance of Problems: Puzzling, Powering, Participation*. Bristol: The Policy Press.

Hylen, S. (2020) Public and private space and action in the early Roman period, *New Testament Studies*, vol 66, pp 534–553.

Ikegami, E. (2000) A sociological theory of publics: identity and culture as emergent properties in networks, *Social Research*, vol 67 (4), pp 989–1029.

Ingham, M. (2007) *Hong Kong: A Cultural History*. Hong Kong: Hong Kong University Press.

Iveson, K. (2008) *Publics and the City*. Oxford: Blackwell.

Jones, P., Boujenko, N. and Marshall, S. (2007) *Link and Place: A Guide to Street Planning and Design*. Washington, DC: Local Transport Today.

Jordan, H. (1994) Public parks, 1885–1914, *Garden History*, vol 22 (1), pp 85–113.

Kayden, J. (2000) *New York City Department of Planning and Municipal Art Society, Privately Owned Public Space: The New York City Experience*. New York: John Wiley and Sons.

Kinoshita, H. (2001) The street market as an urban facility in Hong Kong, in Miao, P. (ed) *Public Places in Asia Pacific Cities: Current Issues and Strategies*. Dordrecht: Kluwer, pp 71–86.

Kohn, M. (2004) *Brave New Neighbourhoods: The Privatisation of Public Spaces*. London: Routledge.

Kooiman, J. (ed) (1993) *Modern Governance: New Government-Society Interactions*. London: Sage.

Kooiman, J. (2003) *Governing as Governance*. London: SAGE.

Kramer, M. (2017) Sensemaking, in Scott, C. and Lewis, L. (eds) *The International Encyclopaedia of Organizational Communication*. New York: John Wiley & Sons, pp 1–10.

Kwok, Y.-C. (ed) (1998) *The Production of Space in Hong Kong*. Hong Kong: Crabs.

Lai, C. (2021) *Private Development and the Management of Public Open Spaces on the Victoria Harbour Waterfront*. Hong Kong: Civic Exchange.

Lai, C. and Da Roza, A. (2018) *Managing Vibrant Streets*. Hong Kong: Civic Exchange.

Lai, K. (2012) Differentiated markets: Shanghai, Beijing and Hong Kong in China's financial centre network, *Urban Studies*, vol 49 (6), pp 1275–1296.

Lam, W.-M. (2012) District councils, advisory bodies, and statutory bodies, in Lam, W.-M., Lui, P.L.-T. and Wong, W. (eds) *Contemporary Hong Kong Government and Politics*. Hong Kong: Hong Kong University Press, pp 111–132.

LandsD – Lands Department (2011) *Provision of Public Facilities within Private Developments*. Hong Kong: HKSAR government.

Lau, S.S.Y., Giridharan, R. and Ganesan, S. (2005) Multiple and intensive land use: case studies in Hong Kong, *Habitat International*, vol 29 (3), pp 527–546.

Lau, Y.W. (2002) *A History of the Municipal Councils of Hong Kong: 1883–1999: From the Sanitary Board to the Urban Council and the Regional Council*. Hong Kong: Leisure and Cultural Services Department.

Law, L. (2001) Home cooking: Filipino women and geographies of the senses in Hong Kong, *Ecumene*, vol 8 (3), pp 264–283.

Law, L. (2002) Defying disappearance: cosmopolitan public spaces in Hong Kong, *Urban Studies*, vol 39 (9), pp 1625–1645.

Leach, R. and Percy-Smith, J. (2001) *Local Governance in Britain*. Basingstoke: Palgrave Macmillan.

Lee, E.W.Y. and Haque, M. (2006) The New Public Management reform and governance in Asian NICs: a comparison of Hong Kong and Singapore, *Governance*, vol 19 (4), pp 605–626.

Lee, E.W., Chan, E.Y., Chan, J.C., Cheung, P.T. and Lam, W.F. (2013) *Public Policymaking in Hong Kong: Civic Engagement and State–Society Relations in a Semi-democracy*. London: Routledge.

Lee, L.O.-F. (2008) *City between Worlds: My Hong Kong*. Cambridge, MA: The Belknap Press.

Lefebvre, H. (1991) *The Production of Space*. Oxford: Blackwell.

Leong, L. (2016) The 'Rail plus Property' model: Hong Kong's successful self-financing formula. *McKinsey Insights*. McKinsey & Company, Washington, DC.

Lincoln, Y. and Guba, E. (1986) But is it rigorous? Trustworthiness and authenticity in naturalistic evaluation, *New Directions for Program Evaluation*, 1986 (30), pp 73–84.

Locke, J. (1988) Locke: Two Treatises of Government, in Laslett, P. (ed) *Cambridge Texts in the History of Political Thought*. Cambridge: Cambridge University Press, pp 137–428.

Low, S. and Smith, N. (eds) (2006) *The Politics of Public Space*. London: Routledge.

Low, S., Taplin, D. and Scheld, S. (2009) *Rethinking Urban Parks: Public Space and Cultural Diversity*. Austin: University of Texas Press.

Luk, W.L. (2009) November. Privately owned public space in Hong Kong and New York: The urban and spatial influence of the policy. In The 4th International Conference of the International Forum on Urbanism (IFoU) (pp 697–706).

Madanipour, A. (2003) *Public and Private Spaces of the City*. London: Routledge.

Madanipour, A., Knierbein, S. and Degros, A. (eds) (2014) *Public Space and the Challenges of Urban Transformation in Europe*. Abingdon: Routledge.

Mayhew, S. (2009) Spatiality, in *A Dictionary of Geography* (4th edition), Oxford: Oxford University Press, p 273.

Mayor of London (2016) The London Plan. *The Spatial Development Strategy for London Consolidated with Alterations since 2011*. London: Greater London Authority.

Mayor of London (2021) *Public London Charter – London Plan Guidance*. London: Mayor of London and London Assembly.

Miao, P. (2001) *Public Places in Asia-Pacific Cities: Current Issues and Strategies*. Dordrecht: Kluwer Academic Publishers.

Minton, A. (2006) *What Kind of World Are We Building? The Privatisation of Public Space*. London: RICS – The Royal Institution of Chartered Surveyors.

Mitchell, D. and Staeheli, L. (2006) Clean and safe? Property redevelopment, public space and homelessness in Downtown San Diego, in Low, S. and Smith, N. (eds) *The Politics of Public Space*. London: Routledge, pp 143–175.

Neal, P. (2013) *Rethinking Parks: Exploring New Business Models for Parks in the 21st Century*. London: Nesta.

Németh, J. (2009) Defining a public: the management of privately owned public space, *Urban Studies*, vol 46 (11), pp 2463–2490.

Németh, J. and Schmidt, S. (2011) The privatization of public space: modelling and measuring publicness, *Environment and Planning B: Planning and Design*, vol 38 (1), 5–23.

ODPM – Office of the Deputy Prime Minister (2004) *Living Places: Caring for Quality*. London: RIBA Enterprises.

Oldenburg, R. (1999) *The Great Good Place: Cafe's, Coffee Shops, Bookstores, Bars, Hair Salons and the Other Hangouts at the Heart of a Community*. New York: Marlowe.

Osborne, D. and Gabler, T. (1992) *Reinventing Government*. New York: Penguin Press.

Ostrom, E. (1990) *Governing the Commons: The Evolution of Institutions for Collective Action*. Cambridge: Cambridge University Press.

Ostrom, E. (2003) How types of goods and property rights jointly affect collective action, *Journal of Theoretical Politics*, vol 15 (3), pp 239–270.

Ostrom, E. (2010) Beyond markets and states: polycentric governance of complex economic systems, *American Economic Review*, vol 100 (3): 641–672.

Ostrom, E. and Hess, C. (2010) Private and common property rights, in Bouckaert, B. (ed) *Property Law and Economics*. Cheltenham: Edgar Elgar, pp 53–106.

Ostrom, V. and Ostrom, E. (1977) Public goods and public choices, in Savas, E.S. (ed) *Alternatives for Delivering Public Services: Towards Improved Performance*. Boulder, CO: Westview Press, pp 7–49.

Parr, J. (2020) Local government in England: evolution and long-term trends, *Commonwealth Journal of Local Governance*, vol 23, pp 1–15.

Peck, J. (2012) Austerity urbanism, *City*, vol 16 (6), pp 626–655.

Peel, D., Lloyd, G. and Lord, A. (2009) Business Improvement Districts and the discourse of contractualism, *European Planning Studies*, vol 17 (3), pp 401–422.

Penin, L. (2018) *An Introduction to Service Design: Designing the Invisible*. London: Bloomsbury Publishing.

Pierre, J. and Peters, B. (2000) *Governance, Politics and the State*. London: Macmillan.

Plato (1968) *The Republic*. Translated by Cornford, F.M. London: Oxford University Press.

Plumb, J. (1982) The commercialization of leisure in eighteenth-century England, in McKendrick, N., Brewer, J. and Plumb, J. (eds) *The Birth of a Consumer Society: The Commercialization of Eighteenth-Century England*. Bloomington: Indiana University Press, pp 265–285.

Punter, J. (1990) The privatisation of the public realm, *Planning Practice and Research*, vol 5 (3), pp 9–16.

Qian, J. (2014) Public space in non-Western contexts: practices of publicness and the socio-spatial entanglement, *Geography Compass*, vol 8 (11), pp 834–847.

Raco, M. (2013) *State-led Privatisation and the Demise of the Democratic State*. Farnham: Ashgate.

Radovic, D. (2020) The strange idea of the public – no, hiroba is not public space; so, what?!, in Mehta, V. and Pallazo, D. (eds) *Companion to Public Space*. Abingdon: Routledge, pp 191–203.

Rasmussen, S. (1948) *London: The Unique City*. London: Jonathan Cape.

Rawls, J., (1999), *A Theory of Justice*. Cambridge, MA: Harvard University Press.

Richards, S., Barnes, M., Coulson, A., Gaster, L. Leach, B. and Sullivan, H. (1999) *Cross-Cutting Issues in Public Policy and Public Services*. London: DETR – Department for the Environment, Transport and the Regions.

Rimmer, P. and Dick, H. (2009) *The City in Southeast Asia: Patterns, Processes and Policy*. Singapore: Singapore University Press.

Rishbeth, C., Ganji, F. and Vodicka, G. (2018) Ethnographic understandings of ethnically diverse neighbourhoods to inform urban design practice, *Local Environment*, vol 23 (1), pp 36–53.

Rittel, H. and Webber, M. (1973) Dilemmas in a general theory of planning, *Policy sciences*, vol 4 (2), pp 155–169.

Roberts, M. and Turner, C. (2005) Conflicts of liveability in the 24-hour city: learning from 48 hours in the life of London's Soho, *Journal of Urban Design*, vol 10 (2), pp 171–193.

Rose, C. (1994) *Property and Persuasion: Essays on the History, Theory, and Rhetoric of Ownership*. Boulder, CO: Westview, cited in Blomley, N., 2008, Enclosure, common right and the property of the poor, *Social & Legal Studies*, vol 17 (3), pp 311–331.

Rossini, F. (2019) Temporary urban intervention in the vertical city: a place-making project to re-activate the public spaces in Hong Kong, *Journal of Urban Design*, vol 24 (2), pp 305–323.

Rossini, F. (2022) Public open space in high density cities: the case of Hong Kong, *Journal of Urbanism*, https://doi.org/10.1080/17549175.2022.2123380.

Rossini, F. and Yiu, M. (2021) Public open spaces in private developments in Hong Kong: new spaces for social activities? *Journal of Urbanism*, vol 14 (2), pp 237–261.

Royal Commission (1928) *Report of the Royal Commission on London Squares*. London: H.M. Stationery Office.

Ruddick, S. (1996) Constructing difference in public spaces: race, class, and gender as interlocking systems, *Urban Geography*, vol 17 (2), pp 132–151.

Russell, A. (2016) *The Politics of Public Space in Republican Rome*. Cambridge University Press.

Savage, V. (1992) Street culture in colonial Singapore, in Chua, B.H. and Edwards, N. (eds) *Public Space: Design, Use and Management*. Singapore: Singapore University Press, pp 11–23.

Schlager, E. and Ostrom, E. (1992) Property-rights regime and natural resources: a conceptual analysis, *Land Economics*, vol 68 (3), pp 249–262.

Sexby, J. (2014) *Municipal Parks, Gardens, and Open Spaces of London*. Cambridge: Cambridge University Press.

Shelton, B., Karakiewicz, J. and Kvan, T. (2011) *The Making of Hong Kong: From Vertical to Volumetric*. London: Routledge.

Shen, L.Y., Platten, A. and Deng, X.P. (2006) Role of public private partnerships to manage risks in public sector projects in Hong Kong, *International Journal of Project management*, vol 24 (7), pp 587–594.

Sheppard, E. (2004) The spatiality of the limits to capital, *Antipode*, vol 36 (3), pp 470–479.

Shi, M. (1998) From imperial gardens to public parks: the transformation of urban space in early twentieth-century Beijing, *Modern China*, vol 24 (3), pp 219–254.

Sieh, L. (2014) Public space governing as the management of meaning-making. PhD Thesis, University College London.

Sieh, L., Chiaradia, A., Jones, S., Waters, F. (2021) The value gradient map, *Urban Design Journal*, vol 157, pp 36–39.

Smart, A. (2006) *The Shek Kip Mei Myth: Squatters, Fires and Colonial Rule in Hong Kong, 1950–1963*. Hong Kong: Hong Kong University Press.

Southworth, M. and Ben-Joseph, E. (1997) *Streets and the Shaping of Cities and Towns*. New York: McGraw-Hill.

Sullivan, H. and Skelcher, C. (2002) *Working across Boundaries: Collaboration in Public Services*. Basingstoke: Palgrave Macmillan.

Tan, Z. and Xue, C.Q.L. (2015) The evolution of an urban vision: the multilevel pedestrian networks in Hong Kong, 1965–1997, *Journal of Urban History*, vol 42, pp 688–708.

Taylor, C. (1995) Liberal politics and the public sphere, in Etzioni, A. (ed) *New Communitarian Thinking: Persons, Virtues, Institutions and Communities*. Charlottesville: University of Virginia Press, pp 196–217.

TfL – Transport for London (2017) *Healthy Streets for London*. London: Transport for London.

Thompson, C., Aspinall, P., Bell, S. and Findlay, C. (2005) 'It gets you away from everyday life': local woodlands and community use – what makes a difference? *Landscape Research*, vol 30 (1), pp 109–146.

Timmermans, S. and Tavory, I. (2012) Theory construction in qualitative research: from grounded theory to abductive analysis, *Sociological Theory*, vol 30 (3), pp 167–186.

Too, W.K. (2007) A study of private/public space in Hong Kong. (Thesis). University of Hong Kong, Pokfulam, Hong Kong SAR.

UK Government (1874) Leicester Square Act 1874. London: The Government of the United Kingdom.

UK Government (1965) Commons Registration Act. London: The Government of the United Kingdom.

UK Government (1999) Greater London Authority Act 1999. London: The Government of the United Kingdom.

UK Government (2011) The Localism Act 2011. London: The Government of the United Kingdom.

Urban Task Force (1999) *Towards an Urban Renaissance*. London: E&F Spon.

Van Kempen, R., Dekker, K., Hall, S. and Tosics, I. (eds) (2005) *Restructuring Large Housing Estates in Europe: Restructuring and Resistance inside the Welfare Industry*. Bristol: Policy Press.

Vargo, S. and Lusch, R. (2016) Institutions and axioms: an extension and update of service-dominant logic, *Journal of the Academy of marketing Science*, vol 44, pp 5–23.

Varna, G. (2014) *Measuring Public Space: The Star Model*. Farnham: Ashgate.

Villani, C. and Talamini, G. (2021) Pedestrianised streets in the global neoliberal city: a battleground between hegemonic strategies of commodification and informal tactics of communing, *Cities*, vol 108, 102983.

Vincent-Jones, P. (2000) Contractual governance: institutional and organisational analysis, *Oxford Journal of Legal Studies*, vol 20 (3), pp 317–351.

Watson, S. (2006) *City Publics: The (Dis)Enchantments of Urban Encounters*. London: Routledge.

Webster, C. (2002) Property rights and the public realm: gates, green belts and Gemeinschaft, *Environment and Planning B*, vol 29, pp 397–412.

Webster, C. (2007) Property rights, public space and urban design, *Town Planning Review*, vol 78 (1), pp 81–101.

Webster, C. and Lai, L.W.C. (2003) *Property Rights, Planning and Markets: Managing Spontaneous Cities*. Cheltenham: Edward Elgar Publishing.

Weick, K. (1995) *Sensemaking in Organizations*. London: Sage.

Whitney, R., Hess, P. and Sarmiento-Casas, C. (2020) Livable streets and global competitiveness: a survey of Mexico City, *Journal of Planning Education and Research*, https://doi.org/10.1177/0739456X20904428.

Whitten, M. (2019) Blame it on austerity? Examining the impetus behind London's changing green space governance, *People Place and Policy*, vol 12 (3), pp 204–224.

Wilson, O. and Hughes, O. (2011) Urban green space policy and discourse in England under New Labour from 1997 to 2010, *Planning Practice and Research*, vol 26 (2), pp 207–228.

Wong, R. (2016) *How Hong Kong Came to Be Governed by an Oligarchy*. Hong Kong: South China Morning Posti6.

Wong, W. (2013) The search for a model of public administration reform in Hong Kong: Weberian bureaucracy, new public management or something else? *Public Administration and Development*, vol 33 (4), pp 297–310.

Worpole, K. and Knox, K. (2007) *The Social Value of Public Space*. York: Joseph Rowntree Foundation.

Wunder, H. (2022) Considering 'privacy' and gender in early modern German-speaking countries, in Green, M., Norgaard, L.C. and Bruun, M.B. (eds) *Early Modern Privacy: Sources and Approaches*. Leiden: Brill, pp 63–78.

Xue, C.Q. (2016) *Rail Village and Mega-Structure. Hong Kong Architecture 1945–2015*. Singapore: Springer.

Xue, C.Q. and Manuel, K. (2001) The quest for better public space: a critical review of urban Hong Kong, in Miao, P. (ed) *Public Places in Asia Pacific Cities: Current Issues and Strategies*. Dordrecht: Kluwer, pp 171–190.

Xue, C.Q., Manuel, K. and Chung, R.H. (2001) Public space in the old derelict city area – a case study of Mong Kok, Hong Kong, *Urban Design International*, vol 6, pp 15–31.

Xue, C.Q., Ma, L. and Hui, K.C. (2012) Indoor 'public' space: a study of atria in mass transit railway (MTR) complexes of Hong Kong, *Urban Design International*, vol 17, pp 87–105.

Yeung, H.-Y. (2001) Property rights to views: a study of the history of reclamation in Victoria Harbour. PhD thesis, Hong Kong University.

Yoshida, S. (1999) Rethinking the public interest in Japan: civil society in the making, in Tadashi, Y. (ed) *Deciding the Public Good: Governance and Civil Society in Japan*. Tokyo: Japan Centre for International Exchange, pp 13–49.

Yu, Y. (2013) *Urban Regime and POSPD Development in Hong Kong*. PhD Thesis, University of Illinois at Chicago.

Yu, Y. (2018) The changing urban political order and politics of space: a study of Hong Kong's POSPD policy, *Urban Affairs Review*, vol 54 (4), pp 732–760.

Zakus, J.D.L. and Lysack, C.L. (1998) Revisiting community participation, *Health Policy and Planning*, vol 13 (1), pp 1–12.

Zandi-Sayek, S. (2001) Public space and urban citizens: Ottoman Izmir in the remaking, 1840–1890. PhD Thesis, University of California Berkeley.

Index

References to figures appear in *italic* type; those in **bold** type refer to tables.

A

access *see* operational rights of access
accessibility
  barriers to 36–7, 130
  public spaces and 7, 8, 14–15, 34, 126–7, 175–6
  regulation of 8–9, 105, 121–2
  unequal access 1, 41
agency rights *see* collective choice rights
Akkar, M. 34
Amin, A. 35
Arendt, H. 16, 38
attributes
  of goods 24–5
  measuring of 37
  openness as an 40, 66–7
  of publicness 5, 9, 32, 33–4, 38, 181
  of public space 4, 8–9, 21, 26–8, 29–30, 39–40
  rights over, allocation of 44–8, 50–1, 64–5, 69, 110
  valuing of by users 40, 45–6, 51, 64–5
authorities
  management of public space by **80**, 81–3, 85–6, 107, 136, 164
  roles of 53–4, 56, 75–6, 77–8
  users, responding to needs of 149
Avenue of Stars (Hong Kong) 117, 123, *124*

B

Bankside Open Spaces Trust *see* BOST (Bankside Open Spaces Trust)
Battersea (London) 74, 133
Benn, S. 34
BIDs (Business Improvement Districts) 63, 66–8, 74, 78, 135, 139–40
  boards 74, 84, 136–7, 138, 139, 140, 141, 163–4
BOST (Bankside Open Spaces Trust) 137–8, 164
bottom-up
  about 149
  action / input on public space 156, 158–9, 165–9, 176–7
  public space, spontaneous 152, 153–7, 170
Broadgate (London) 73, *74*, 129–30, 131
build-operate-transfer contracts 116, 135, 142
  see also contracts / contractual agreements

bureaucracy 57–60, 79, 108–9
Business Improvement Districts *see* BIDs (Business Improvement Districts)
busking 42, 126

C

Camden Council (London) 161, 167
Canary Wharf (London) 73, 84, 130, *130*, 131, 166–7
capitalism 3, 17, 125
  see also Occupy movement
cardboard sorting 101, *106*, 106–7
centres *see* shopping malls
challenges
  with governance/management of public space 1–3, 53–4, 61–2, 95–6, 108–10
  with leases 145–6
  with public space 10–12, 61, 62, 95–6, 134–5
  see also qualitative challenges; quantitative challenges
Charter *see* London; Public London Charter
Cheng, A.K.C.W. 102
China 17–18, 60, 61
cities
  government structures of 74–8
  management of public space 1–3, 21, 111–12
  see also government; Hong Kong; London; public sector
club/toll goods 23, 24, 25, 27, 28, 37, 40, 44, 65–6, 184
collective choice rights
  about 47–8, 163–4
  allocation of 150, 151–2, 160, 165, 168–9, 170, 174, 192–3
  bottom-up 155–6, 161–2, 168
  lack of 130, 134, 177, 179
  publicness and 44, 109, 148, 186–7
  public space and 64–5, 68–9, 133
colonialism 55–7, 87–90, 91, 97, 102, 112, 175–6
commodification 2–3, 61
common good
  about 16, 22–3, 173
  provision of 7–8, 13, 55, 75, 97, 133–4
  public space as 7, 20–1, 22, 26–7, 38–9, 148, 173–4, 184
  shared ownership and 16–17

common pool goods / resources
  about 23–4, 28, 32
  management of 25, 43–4
  public space as 40, 175, 183
  rights to 5, 9, 46–7
commons, tragedy of the 17
community gardens *see* gardens
community involvement *see* bottom-up; stakeholders; users of public space
congestion of public space 24–5, 27–8, 40, 65, 69, 91, 128, 175, 186, 187
consumption 23–4, 27–8, 36, 40, 41, 44, 130, 187
contracts / contractual agreements
  about 48, 59–60
  experiences with 60
  leases (*see* leases)
  PFI (build-operate-transfer) 116, 135, 142, 145, 165–6
  for private management 78, **80**, 80–1, 83–5, 104–5, 165–6, 177–9
  publicness rights through 63–8, 73
  for user management 85–6, 141–2
coordination of public space
  about 53–4, 81–2, 174
  contractual agreements and 67–8, 86
  examples of **100**, 102–3
  lack of 62
  in POPS 105–6
  see also governance of public space; management of public space
COVID-19 pandemic 1, 108

D

deeds of dedication **100**, 105, **114**, 115–16, 123–6, 128, 144, 146
  see also contracts / contractual agreements
design of public space 4, 14, 190, 191
differential space 38
diversification 147, 148–9, 165
domestic helpers 122, 124–5, 155–6, *156*

E

economy 17, 58, 60–1, 73, 181
exit option (exit voice duality) 46, 64

F

financial crisis 1, 58–60, 83, 135
for-profit entities *see* POPS (Privately Owned Public Spaces)

G

Gabler, T. 60
gardens
  community 150, 160–2, *161*, *162*, 180
  private 71, 89–90
  public 117–19, 137–40, *138*, *139*, 162–4, *163*
  restricted access 127, 130

Gauss, G. 34
GLA (Greater London Authority) 76, 134, 136, 140
GLC (Greater London Council) 76, 138
Glendale 142, 165–6
gong gong (public) 17–18
goods
  attributes of 24–5
  consumption of 23–4, 27–8, 36, 40, 44, 130, 187
  non-excludable 23–4, 27, 183, 186
  non-rivalrous 23–4, 65
  non-subtractable 23–4, 28, 65, 183, 186
  public spaces, offered by 26–8
  types of (*see* club/toll goods; common pool goods; private goods; public goods)
governance of public space
  about 30–1, 50, 51–2
  challenges 61–2, 95–6, 108–10
  changes in 5, 58–9
  contracts / contractual agreements (*see* contracts / contractual agreements)
  history of 54–6, 64–5
  meanings of 175–80
  processes involved with 52–4, 67–8
  rights and 9, 51, 112, 174, 184
  theory of 182–8, 188–91
  see also coordination of public space; investment in public space; maintenance of public space; management of public space; regulation of public space
government
  funding cuts 58
  public space, as provider of 18, 20–2, 54–6
  see also Hong Kong; London; public sector
Granary Square (London) 130–1, *131*
Greater London Authority *see* GLA (Greater London Authority)
Greater London Council *see* GLC (Greater London Council)
green space *see* gardens
Guadarrama Sánchez, G.J. 15

H

Haque, M. 60
Hardin, G. 17
Hess, C. 30
Hirschman, A. 46, 64
HKPSI (Hong Kong Public Space Initiative) 145, 159
HKSAR (Hong Kong Special Administrative Region of the People's Republic of China) 87, 150
Hong Kong
  about 6–7, 87, 88
  bottom-up public spaces 152–9, 170, 176–7

Index

challenges, public space 10–12, 62, 95–6, 108–10
deeds of dedication 123–6, 128
government structure 96–7, *97*, 115–16, 150
history of public space 87–91, 91–3, 94–5, 102
Instagram Pier 107, 152, *152*, *153*, 154, 181, 185
management of public space 92–4, 98–101, **99–100**, 101–3, 103–5, 106–7, 151
NPM (New Public Management) 59–60
open space, provision of 126–7
placemaking 180–2
PPPs (public private partnerships) 60, 116–17, 123, *124*, 143–4, 151
protests 1, 120–1, 123, 125, 149, 155–6, 179
provision of public space 113–17, **114**, 117–23, 150–1
public, concept of 17–18
SAR (Special Administrative Region) 57, 62, 94, 96, 97
Statue Square 90, 155
Hoppe, R. 188

I

inaccessibility *see* accessibility
Instagram Pier (Hong Kong) 107, 152, *152*, *153*, 154, 181, 185
investment in public space
 about 52, 53, 54, 83, 174
 contractual agreements and 63, 67–8, 73, 86
 examples of **100**, 102–3
 private 111–12
 from users 46, 86
 see also governance of public space; management of public space

J

Japan 17–18
Jubilee Gardens (London) 138–40, *139*, 162–4, *163*
Jubilee Garden Trust 139

K

Kayden, J. 115
King's Cross (London) 73–4, 84, 130–1, *131*, 132, 166–7
Kingston International Centre (Hong Kong) *118*, 119
Knox, K. 34
Kohn, M. 34
ko kyo (public) 17–18
Kwun Tong (Hong Kong) 97, 117, *118*, 119

L

Lai, K. 105, 117
Lai, L.W.C. 24, 44
Landmark East (Hong Kong) 119, *119*
LandsD (Lands Department) (Hong Kong) 96, **100**, 101, **114**, 115–16, 122–3, 144, 151, 154
Law, L. 155
leases
 about 63
 challenges with 145–6
 long 78, 87, 135, 137, 138, 139
 NGOs (non-governmental organisations) 98
 for not-for-profit trusts 78, 85–6, 135–40, 145, 162–4
 to private developers 73, 74, 90, 105, 113–17, **114**, 121–3, 143–4
 See also contracts / contractual agreements
Leathermarket neighbourhood (London) 140–1, *141*
Lee, E.W.Y. 60
Lefebvre, H. 38
Lewisham (London) 75, 78, 82, 142, 165
Lloyd, G. 59
London
 about 6–7
 bottom-up public space 159–68, 170
 challenges, public space 10–12, 61, 62, 108–10, 134–5
 government structure 74–5, *75*, 79
 history of public space 21, 70–4, 128–9
 management of public space 75–8, 79–80, **80**, 81–3, 84–6, 131–2
 management transfers 134–42, 143, 165–6
 new (large) public spaces, provision of *133*, 133–4
 placemaking 180, 181
 POPS (Privately Owned Public Spaces) 129–32, 144–5
 protests 1, 149–50
 Public London Charter 84, 166–7, 168
 Queen Elizabeth Olympic Park 74, 76, 129
London Legacy Development Corporation 74, 129
Lord, A. 59
Low, S. 34

M

Madanipour, A. 15, 64
maintenance of public space
 about 52–4, 174
 contractual agreements for 59, 63, 64–5, 67–8, 78, **80**, 82–3
 cost of 111–12
 examples of **99**, 102, 103

209

of POPS 105–6, 131–2, 139–40
by users 46, 86
see also governance of public space; management of public space
malls *see* shopping malls
management of public space
  about 51–2
  by authorities (*see* authorities)
  bureaucracy of 57–60, 79, 108–9
  challenges 1–3, 53–4, 108–10
    (*see also* qualitative challenges; quantitative challenges)
  contracts / contractual agreements (*see* contracts)
  diversification of 148–9, 165
  NPM (New Public Management) 58, 59–61, 101–2, 178, 179, 181
  private (*see* POPS (Privately Owned Public Spaces))
  reality of 20–1
  transfer of responsibilities 24–5, 46, 76–8, 80, 81–3, 135, 165–6
  by trusts (*see* trusts)
  by users 66, 85–6, 101, 106–7
  see also coordination of public space; governance of public space; investment in public space; maintenance of public space; regulation of public space
Manulife Place (Hong Kong) 117, *118*
Marchmont Community Garden (London) 161, *161*
mass protests *see* protests
meaning *see* placemaking
More London 136–7
municipalities *see* cities
Myatts Field North (London) 142

N

Németh, J. 34, 37
New Public Management *see* NPM (New Public Management)
NGOs (non-governmental organisations)
  activities by 154, 155, 158–9, 180
  management of public space 24–5, 95, *95*, 98, 170
Nine Elms Park (London) 74, 84, 133, 166–7
non-excludable goods 23–4, 27, 183, 186
non-rivalrous goods 23–4, 65
non-subtractable goods 23–4, 28, 65, 183, 186
not-for-profit trusts *see* trusts
NPM (New Public Management) 58, 59–61, 101–2, 178, 179, 181
Nullahplace (Hong Kong) 158, *158*

O

Occupy movement 1, 3, 125, 149–50, 156
openness
  about 14–15, 26, 36–7

attribute, as an 40, 66–7
publicness and 7, 8, 32, 33, 42–3, 45, 47
rules of 42–3, 78, 84, 164–5
open space 165–6
  access to 108, 120–2, 123, 126–7
  allocation of 101, 102–4, 115
  community-run 2
  history of 70–1, 73, 90–1, 112–13
  management of 20, 75–6, 93–4, 127–8, 139–42, 165–6
  private 21, 25
operational rights of access
  about 14–5, 44–5, 130, 133, 174, 179
  allocation of 47–8, 49, 64–5, 145–6, 168–9, 187–8
  publicness and 187
Osborne, D. 60
Ostrom, Elinor 5, 9, 25, 30, 43–4, 46–7, 50
ownership
  private 21
  of public spaces 34, 71, 166–7
  shared 16–17
  by trusts 21, 63

P

Pacific Place 119–20, *120*, 123
pandemic *see* COVID-19 pandemic
parking 24, 40, 41, 99, 156
Peel, D. 59
People's Republic of China 87, 91, 94
PFI (private finance initiative) 116, 135, 142, 145, 165–6
PFPD (public facilities in private developments) 10, 111, 117–23, *119*, *120*, *122*
Pichardo Martínez, P.M. 15
placemaking 1, 61–2, 74, 108, 149, 159, 179–82
  see also urban regeneration
plurality 38
POPS (Privately Owned Public Spaces)
  about 21, 151, 155–6
  contractual agreements and 68, 84–5
  examples of 71, 90–1, 113–15, 129–30
  governance and 63
  management of 105–6, 131–2
  revitalisation and 61
POSPDs (Public Open Spaces in Private Developments) 21, 97, 98, **100**, 101, 104–5, 113, **114**, 117–22, 144
Potters Fields Park (London) 135–7, *136*, 162, 163, 164
PPPs (public private partnerships) 60, 63, 105, **114**, 116–17, 123, *124*, 128, 143–4, 151
private 15–18, 38–9
private finance initiative *see* PFI (private finance initiative)
private goods 23–5, 27, 28, 39, 184

Index

Privately Owned Public Spaces *see* POPS (Privately Owned Public Spaces)
private space 14, 20, 34, 88, 113, 117
privatisation 2–3, 19, 39, 84, 102, 128–34, 178, 181
property rights *see* rights
protests 1, 22, 120–1, 123, 125, 149–50, 156, 179
provision
 of common goods 7–8, 13, 39, 55, 75, 97, 176–7
 contractualised 63, 65–8
 direct 59, 60, 79, 98, **99**
 diversification of 148–9
 of goods 23–4
 history of 54–6, 59–60, 70–4, 87–95
 indirect private sector 60, 79–80, 96–7, 98, 101, 103–5, **114**
 modes of 79–80, 81–3, 83–5, 96, 97–8, 101–5
 of new (large) public spaces 133–4, *134*
 of open space 126–7
 publicness and 34, 174
 of public space 18–21, 26, 30, 75–6, 77–8, 113–17, 117–23, 129–34
 of services 17, 51–2, 54–5, 57–9, 79, 86
public
 about 15–18, 183–4
 private, compared to 38–9
public facilities in private developments *see* PFPD (public facilities in private developments)
public goods 23–4, 27–8, 36, 39, 65, 97, 116, 183–4
public health 1, 19, 56, 88, 98, **99**, **100**, 102
Public London Charter 84, 166–7, 168
publicness
 about 5, 8–9, 30, 32, 48, 148, 174
 attributes of 5, 9, 32, 33–4, 38, 181
 as context specific 41–3, 66–7, 185–6
 defining 33–7
 private space and 112, 113–17, **114**, 145–6
 restrictions to enable 42–3
 rights and 4, 5, 9, 32–3, 44–8, 50, 64–5, 132, 178–9
 of a space 33–4
 value of 41
Public Open Spaces in Private Developments *see* POSPDs (Public Open Spaces in Private Developments)
public private partnerships *see* PPPs (public private partnerships)
public sector 16, 39, 58, 58–9
public space
 about 1, 13–15, 18–19, 28–9, 173, 183
 access (*see* access)
 attributes (*see* attributes)
 common good, as a (*see* common good)
 design of (*see* design of public space)
 governance (*see* governance of public space)
 management of (*see* management of public space)
 open space (*see* open space)
 provision (*see* provision)
 public health and (*see* public health)
 publicness (*see* publicness)
 spatiality (*see* spatiality)
 stakeholders (*see* stakeholders)
 users of (*see* users of public space)

Q

Qian, J. 144
qualitative challenges
 about 10, 11, 109, 147–50
 in Hong Kong 150–9
 in London 159–68
quantitative challenges
 about 10, 108, 111
 in Hong Kong 113, 115–17, 117–23, 124–6, 127–8
 in London 128–33, 134–42
Queen Elizabeth Olympic Park 74, 76, 129

R

regeneration *see* urban regeneration
regulation of public space
 about 48, 53, 54, 82, 174
 contractual agreements for 67–8, 84–5, 86
 examples of **99**, 101–2, 103
 private sector-provided 105, 115, 121–2
 see also governance of public space; management of public space
resourcing *see* investment in public space
responsibilities
 goods, management/provision of 17, 97
 public space management 81–3, 145–6
 space, over 45
restrictions
 to access, no restrictions 27, 36, 139–40
 to openness / access 36–7, 39, 42–3, 47, 53, 82, 144, 163
rights
 of access (*see* operational rights of access)
 allocation of 44–8, 50–1, 64–5, 69, 150–2, 160, 165, 168–9, 170, 174, 184, 192–3
 collective choice (*see* collective choice rights)
 contractual agreements and 63–8, 73
 operational (*see* operational rights of access)
 to political action 144–5
 property 24

publicness and 4, 5, 9, 32–3, 44–8, 50, 64–5, 132, 178–9
  of stakeholders 4, 5, 66–7, 112
  transfer of 46, 112, 151–2, 163–5
Royal Parks (London) 76–7, 140

S

SAR (Special Administration Region of the People's Republic of China) 57, 62, 94, 96, 97
Sawley Road gardens (London) 150, 161–2, *162*
Schlager, E. 44, 46–7
Schmidt, S. 34, 37
sense-making 188–91
services
  provision of 17, 51–2, 54–5, 57–9, 79, 86
  public space 13, 14, 15, 18
Sham Shui Po reservoir (Hong Kong) 154–5
shared goods / resources *see* common good; common pool goods / resources
Sha Tin New Town Plaza (Hong Kong) 122, *122*, 123
shopping malls 116, 119, 120–2, 125–6, 129–30, 132, 179
si (private) 17
Smith, N. 34
social protests *see* protests
society
  about 16
  common good and 22–3, 28–9, 38–9
  space *see* private space; publicness; public space
  spatiality 25–8, 29, 47
Special Administration Region *see* SAR (Special Administration Region of the People's Republic of China)
stakeholders
  bottom-up input (*see* bottom-up)
  engagement of 11, 148–50, 160–2, 163–6
  of public spaces 26
  rights of 4, 5, 66–7, 112
state *see* government; public sector
Statue Square (Hong Kong) 90, 155

T

TfL (Transport for London) 76
theory
  about 182
  of governance of public space 182–3
Times Square (Hong Kong) 124, 125–6, *126*, 145–6
toll goods *see* club/toll goods
tragedy of the commons 17
trusts
  management of public space by 15, 46, 65, 68, 77–8, 85–6, 133, 135–40, 162–4
  not-for-profit 78
  ownership of public space 21, 63
Turkey 18

U

urban regeneration 61, 73–4, 76–8, 112, 132–3
  see also placemaking
users of public space
  attributes, valuing of 40, 45–6, 51, 64–5
  bottom-up input (*see* bottom-up)
  designing for 4
  engagement of 11, 81–2, 148–50, 160–2, 163–6
  interactions of 35
  management by 66, 85–6, 101, 106–7, 141–2, 169
  needs and preferences of 26, 38, 61, 66, 109, 146
  production of space by 26–7, 107

V

value
  governance of public space 183, 185, 186–7, 188–91
  of publicness 41
  of public space 5–6
  sense-making 188–91
  of users of public space 40, 45–6, 64–5
value-capture mechanisms 112
  see also investment in public space
Varna, G. 34, 37
Victoria Harbour (Hong Kong) 98, 117, 123
voice option (exit voice duality) 44, 46, 64–5, 69

W

Wallace, David Foster 25
waster pickers 101, *106*, 106–7, 176–7
Waterloo Millennium Green (London) 137–8, *138*, 162–3, 164
Watson, S. 34
Webster, C. 24, 30, 36, 44, 65
West Kowloon *see* WKCD (West Kowloon Cultural District); WKCDA (West Kowloon Cultural District Authority)
WGT (Waterloo Green Trust) 137
WKCD (West Kowloon Cultural District) 60, 90–1, 97, **99**
WKCDA (West Kowloon Cultural District Authority) 105
Worpole, K. 34

Y

Yu, Y. 113, 115

www.ingramcontent.com/pod-product-compliance
Lightning Source LLC
Chambersburg PA
CBHW051541020426
42333CB00016B/2046